BUSINESS STUDIES REVISION NOTES

FOR

JUNIOR CERTIFICATE

JOHN F. O'SULLIVAN

GILL & MACMILLAN

Preface

The aim of this book is to provide students with a comprehensive summary of the Junior Certificate Business Studies course, both Ordinary and Higher level.

It contains more than fifty fully worked solutions to past examination questions.

A glossary of clearly defined business terms is included at the end of many chapters.

Past examination papers are fully analysed with reference to specific questions outlined.

The end of the book contains advice on how to approach the examination; exam format with specific information on description of questions, marks per question and time allocation is included.

I hope that this book will be of major assistance when revising business studies in the months prior to the Junior Certificate examination.

John F. O'Sullivan BComm HDE
Business Studies Department
St Peter's Community School
Passage West
Co. Cork

This book is dedicated to Claire, Breffni, Shane, Cillian and Jennifer.

Gill & Macmillan Ltd
Goldenbridge
Dublin 8
with associated companies throughout the world

0 7171 2360 X

Print origination in Ireland by
Carrigboy Typesetting Services
Printed by ColourBooks Ltd, Dublin

Maeve Nea

Contents

Section One — The Business of Living

Section Two — Economic Awareness

Section Three — Enterprise

Section Four — Information Technology

*** Higher level only**

SECTION ONE — THE BUSINESS OF LIVING

BUDGETING

Chapter 1 — Income

A. Income
Income is money we receive.

B. Regular Income
Regular income is received each week or month, e.g. wages, salary, unemployment benefit.

C. Additional Income
Additional income is received occasionally, e.g. overtime, bonus, commission.

D. Benefit in Kind — Perks
Official payments for work in forms other than money, e.g. company car, lunch vouchers.

Unofficial — private telephone calls, paper, pens.

E. Main Sources of Income

Employed	Self-Employed	Unemployed
Wage Salary Overtime Commission Bonus	Profit from business	Unemployment benefit Family Income Supplement
Student	**Pensioner**	
Pocket money Wage — part-time work Grant	Old Age Pension Pension from work Wage — part-time work	

F. Gross Wage (Gross Pay)
Gross wage = basic pay + overtime + commission + bonus

G. Net Wage (Net Pay)
Net wage = gross pay – deductions

H. Deductions
There are two types of deduction, statutory deductions and non-statutory (voluntary) deductions.

I. Statutory Deductions

The two statutory deductions are PAYE and PRSI.

(1) **PAYE** (PAY AS YOU EARN)

This is income tax.

(a) Every employee is liable to pay income tax. Every employee is allowed to earn some money without paying any income tax on it. This is called a Tax-Free Allowance (TFA).

(b) The remainder of the income is called taxable income/pay.

(c) PAYE is calculated as a percentage of gross income after the person's Tax-Free Allowance has been deducted.

(2) **PRSI** (PAY-RELATED SOCIAL INSURANCE)

This is a contribution towards a social welfare benefit that may be claimed in the future, i.e. unemployment benefit (dole), sickness benefit and old age pension.

PRSI is charged as a percentage of gross pay.

What income tax is used for	What PRSI is used for
It helps to pay for state services: Gardaí Army Health services Public services	It provides the following benefits: Unemployment benefit Maternity benefit Sickness benefit Old age pension Disability benefit Deserted wife's benefit Widow's pension

J. Voluntary Deductions (NS Deductions)

These are deductions that the employee requests to be taken from his gross pay, e.g. union fees, Voluntary Health Insurance (VHI), pension (superannuation), car insurance, savings. The employer deducts these and passes them on to the relevant organisation.

K. Summary

Gross pay = Basic pay + Overtime + Bonus + Commission
Taxable pay = Gross pay – Tax-Free Allowance
Net pay = Gross pay – Total deductions

L. Business Terms

Basic Wage Payment for working a normal week.

Bonus Income in addition to basic pay.

Budget A plan of future income and expenditure.

Commission A payment based on each item sold to encourage salespeople to sell more goods.

Deductions Money taken from an employee's pay before he receives it.

Gross Pay Total earnings before deductions.

Income Tax Money paid to the government, i.e. PAYE.
Net Pay Take-home pay.
Overtime The payment for working extra hours.
Payslip The document that an employee gets on payday, giving details of pay and deductions.
Statutory Deductions Deductions compulsory by law paid to the government, i.e. PAYE, PRSI.
Superannuation Contributions paid towards a pension.
Taxable Income/Pay The amount of income that a person pays tax on.
Tax-Free Allowance Income earned on which tax is not payable.

Calculation of Net Pay and Preparation of Payslip — Sample Question and Solution

Question

Ann O'Dowd works in Euro Biscuits Ltd. The wages are IR£4 per hour for a basic forty-hour week, time and a half for the first ten hours of overtime and double time thereafter. On her first week she worked fifty-four hours. Tax-Free Allowance was IR£75 per week, rate of tax 40%, PRSI 10% of gross; other deductions were union fee IR£2, VHI IR£5, pension 5% of gross.

Calculate her net wage and complete payslip. **(15 marks)**

WAGE SLIP											
Name	Basic	O/T	Gross	Tax-Free Allowance	PAYE	PRSI	Union	VHI	Pension	Total Dedu.	Net Pay

Source: Department Sample Paper Higher Level.

Solution

(a) Calculation of Gross Wage

Gross Wage = Basic Wage + Overtime

Basic Wage:	40 hours @ IR£4 per hour	IR£160
Overtime:	10 hours @ IR£6 per hour	IR£60
	4 hours @ IR£8 per hour	IR£32
Gross Wage		IR£252

(b) Calculation of PAYE — **NB** PAYE is calculated on taxable income

Gross Wage	IR£252	
Less TFA	IR£75	
Taxable Income	IR£177	PAYE = 40% of IR£177 = IR£70.80

(c) Calculation of PRSI — **NB** PRSI is calculated on gross wage

PRSI = 10% IR£252 (Gross Wage) = IR£25.20

(d) Calculation of Pension

Pension = 5% of IR£252 (Gross Wage) = IR£12.60

(e) Find Total Deductions

	IR£
PAYE	70.80
PRSI	25.20
Union	2.00
VHI	5.00
Pension	12.60
Total Deductions	**115.60**

(f) Gross Wage – Deductions = Net Wage
IR£252 – IR£115.60 = IR£136.40

WAGE SLIP											
Name	Basic	O/T	Gross	Tax-Free Allowance	PAYE	PRSI	Union	VHI	Pension	Total Dedu.	Net Pay
Ann O'Dowd	160	92	252	75	70.80	25.20	2	5	12.60	115.60	136.40

PRACTICE QUESTIONS

(i) Question 1, Section A, Ordinary Level, 1994.
(ii) Question 19, Paper I, Section A, Higher Level, 1994.
(iii) Question 12, Paper I, Section A, Higher Level, 1993.

Chapter 2 — Expenditure

A. Types of Expenditure

(1) FIXED EXPENDITURE

A **fixed amount** must be paid out on a **fixed date**.

(2) IRREGULAR EXPENDITURE

Amount varies and/or the **payment date varies**.

(3) DISCRETIONARY EXPENDITURE

This is where the consumer has a **choice** after fixed and irregular expenditure has been paid.

B. Main Items of Household Expenditure

Fixed Expenditure	Irregular Expenditure	Discretionary
Mortgage	Telephone	Holidays
Rent	Electricity	Birthday presents
House insurance	Coal/Gas/Oil	Cinema/Theatre
Service charges	Groceries	Newspapers
TV licence	Clothes	Magazines
Car loan	School books	Meals out
Car tax	School uniforms	
Car insurance	Pocket money	
	Car service	
	Petrol/Diesel	

C. Filing Expenditure Records

Electricity bills, telephone bills and all other invoices, delivery notes and receipts should be carefully filed in a safe place so that they can be easily and quickly located when required.

D. Checking Bills — Invoices — Delivery Notes

All bills should be checked for accuracy before you pay them.

(1) ELECTRICITY BILL

This bill is made up of General Domestic (charge per unit used), Standing Charge (rental for service and meters) and Value Added Tax.

Example: Electricity Bill

Meter Reading		Units & Rate	Description	Amount
Present	Previous	(Pence)		
49,258	48,165	1,093 x 7.14	**General Domestic**	78.04
			Standing Charge	6.60
				84.64
			VAT @ 12.5% on 84.64	10.58
			Total Due IR£	**95.22**

(2) TELEPHONE BILL

This is made up of Line Rental, Equipment Rental, Calls and Value Added Tax.

Example: Telephone Bill

Line Rental			20.00
Equipment Rental			2.20
Calls	**Units**	**Rate**	
76 Local	76	0.0950	7.22
110 Inland	553	0.0950	52.53
1 International	77	0.0950	7.31
VAT on 89.26 @ 16%			14.28
		Total Due IR£	**103.54**

(3) INVOICE = BILL

Sent by seller to buyer when goods are bought on credit. Shows quantity, description, unit price, VAT, total cost.

(4) DELIVERY NOTE

Sent when goods are delivered. Signed by buyer. Proof of delivery.

(5) RECEIPT

List of items. Proof of payment.

E. Business Terms

False Economies Short-term saving ⇛ long-term cost, i.e. buying a cheap pair of shoes for IR£20 — last two months, a good pair of shoes for IR£60 — last two years.

Impulse Buying Buying things not planned or needed.

Opportunity Cost With limited income we must make choices. When we choose one item we must do without something else. This is called opportunity cost.

Priorities Spending on the most needed or most important items first.

PRACTICE QUESTIONS

(i) Question 6, Section A, Ordinary Level, Sample Paper.
(ii) Question 7, Section A, Ordinary Level, Sample Paper.
(iii) Question 9, Section A, Ordinary Level, 1994.
(iv) Question 10, Section A, Ordinary Level, 1994.
(v) Question 5, Paper I, Section A, Higher Level, 1992.
(vi) Question 11, Section A, Ordinary Level, 1994.

Chapter 3 — Household Budgeting

A. Budget

A budget is a financial plan which forecasts future income, expenditure and savings. We must estimate or guess what these figures will be.

B. Planning a Budget

(1) **Estimate future income** — include overtime, etc. and allow for expected pay increases.

(2) **Estimate future expenditure** — allow for increased costs, i.e. cost of living, and for possible future expenditure, e.g. holidays.

(3) **Compare estimated income with estimated expenditure.**

If estimated income > estimated expenditure → surplus (savings).
If estimated income < estimated expenditure → deficit (shortage).
If estimated income = estimated expenditure → breakeven.

(4) **Net cash = Total income – Total expenditure.**

(5) **Opening cash** is 'the amount of cash that the family have at the start of the month'.

(6) **Closing cash** is found by 'adding net cash to the opening cash' and is the amount of cash that the family **expect** to have at the end of the month.

(7) **Closing cash** of one month will be the opening cash of the next month.

C. Current Expenditure & Capital Expenditure, Accruals & Savings

(1) **Current expenditure** is spending on items necessary to run the house and family on a daily basis, e.g. food, entertainment, clothing, petrol.

(2) **Capital expenditure** is spending on items that will last a long period of time, e.g. house, car, television, video, cooker.

(3) **Accruals**

These are services that we do not pay for at the time of use, e.g. electricity, telephone. When we get the bill we pay the amount owed.

(4) **Savings**

This is putting money aside for the future, e.g. to buy a house or car, to finance children's education, holidays and emergencies.

D. Comparing Budget with Actual

Compare the actual income and expenditure with the budgeted income and expenditure. You will then see where the actual is different from the budgeted and be able to make whatever changes are necessary when drawing up the next budget.

E. Business Terms

Breakeven Income equals expenditure.

Budget A plan of future income and expenditure.

Closing Cash Opening Cash + Net Cash.

Consumer Durables Goods that will last for a long period of time.

Deficit Expenditure greater than income.

Estimate A guess at the size of the income and expenditure.

Net Cash Total income minus total expenditure.

Surplus Income greater than expenditure.

Examination-Style Questions and Solutions

Question 1.
Answer (a), (b) and (c). This is a Household Budget Question.

The following is a budget for the Lydon household for the first four months of 1994.

Opening Cash in Hand is IR£370.

Planned Income

- Richard Lydon earns IR£1,200 net, per month.
- Claire Lydon earns IR£1,350 net, per month.
- Child benefit is IR£60 per month.
- Richard expects to receive IR£250 interest on a building society investment in March.

Planned Expenditure

- House mortgage will be IR£450 per month.
- Repayments on Richard's car loan (to be fully paid by end of February) will cost IR£340 per month until then.
- Richard's annual car insurance IR£380 is due for payment in March.
- Claire's annual car insurance IR£520 is due for payment in April.
- House insurance premium, IR£240 per year, is payable monthly, starting in January.
- Household expenses are usually IR£630 per month.
- Car running costs are expected to be IR£90 per month for Richard and IR£50 per month for Claire.
- ESB bills for light and heat are expected to amount to IR£180 in January and IR£230 in March.
- A fill of heating oil, costing IR£360, will be needed in February.
- The telephone bill is expected to be IR£170 in February and IR£210 in April.
- Birthdays will cost IR£110 in January and IR£120 in April.
- Entertainment will cost IR£130 each month.
- The Lydon family have booked a holiday in February which will cost IR£1,500.

(a) Complete fully the blank household budget form (given at the end of the question) using all the above figures. **(50)**

(b) Work out the total cost of having two cars in the family for the four months and put this figure into the box at the end of the budget form. **(5)**

(c) Will the Lydon family have enough money to pay for their holiday in February? In the space provided at the end of the budget form, give **one** reason for your answer. **(5)**

(60 marks)

Source: Junior Certificate Ordinary Level 1994.

For use with Question 1. Household Budget

1. (a) LYDON FAMILY	JAN.	FEB.	MARCH	APRIL	TOTAL
Planned Income	IR£	IR£	IR£	IR£	IR£
Richard Lydon — Salary	1200	1200	1200	1200	4800
Claire Lydon — Salary	1350	1350	1350	1350	5400
Child Benefit	60	60	60	60	240
Interest from Building Society	—	—	250	—	250
TOTAL INCOME	2610	2610	2860	2610	10690
PLANNED EXPENDITURE					
Fixed					
Mortgage	450	450	450	450	1800
Car Loan	340	340	—	—	680
Car Insurance	—	—	—	520	520
House Insurance	240	240	240	240	960
Subtotal	810	810	850	990	3460
Irregular					
Household Expenses	630	630	630	630	2520
Car Running Costs	140	140	140	140	560
Light and Heat	180	360	230	—	770
Telephone	—	170	—	210	380
Subtotal	950	1300	1000	980	4230
Discretionary					
Birthdays	110	—	—	120	230
Entertainment	130	130	130	130	520
Holidays	—	1,500	—	—	1,500
Subtotal	240	1,630	130	250	2,250
TOTAL EXPENDITURE	2000	3740	1980	2220	9940
Net Cash	610	(1,130)	880	390	750
Opening Cash	370	980	(150)	730	370
Closing Cash	980	(150)	730	1120	1120

1. (b) Total cost of having two cars in the family:	
1. (c) Will they have enough money to pay for the holiday in February?	
Reason:	

Solution to Question 1.

For use with Question 1. Household Budget

1. (a) LYDON FAMILY	JAN.	FEB.	MARCH	APRIL	TOTAL
Planned Income	IR£	IR£	IR£	IR£	IR£
Richard Lydon — Salary	1,200	1,200	1,200	1,200	4,800
Claire Lydon — Salary	1,350	1,350	1,350	1,350	5,400
Child Benefit	60	60	60	60	240
Interest from Building Society			250		250
TOTAL INCOME	2,610	2,610	2,860	2,610	10,690
PLANNED EXPENDITURE					
Fixed					
Mortgage	450	450	450	450	1,800
Car Loan	340	340			680
Car Insurance			380	520	900
House Insurance	20	20	20	20	80
Subtotal	810	810	850	990	3,460
Irregular					
Household Expenses	630	630	630	630	2,520
Car Running Costs	140	140	140	140	560
Light and Heat	180	360	230		770
Telephone		170		210	380
Subtotal	950	1,300	1,000	980	4,230
Discretionary					
Birthdays	110			120	230
Entertainment	130	130	130	130	520
Holidays		1,500			1,500
Subtotal	240	1,630	130	250	2,250
TOTAL EXPENDITURE	2,000	3,740	1,980	2,220	9,940
Net Cash	610	–1,130	880	390	750
Opening Cash	370	980	–150	730	370
Closing Cash	980	–150	730	1,120	1,120

1. (b) Total cost of having two cars in the family:	IR£2,140
1. (c) Will they have enough money to pay for the holiday in February?	No.

Reason: *They will not have cash to pay for the holiday because total expenditure IR£3,740 exceeds total income IR£2,610. (They have a deficit of IR£1,130.)*

Question 2.
Answer all sections. This is a Household Budget Question.
2. (a) At the end of the question is a partially completed budget for the McCarthy family for a six-month period, January to June.

You are required to complete this form by filling in the figures in the 'Total' column and also the missing figures in the Section at the end dealing with '**Net Cash, Opening Cash and Closing Cash**'. **(13)**

For use with Question 2.

2. (a) McCarthy Family Budget: January–June							
	JAN. IR£	FEB. IR£	MAR. IR£	APRIL IR£	MAY IR£	JUNE IR£	TOTAL
Income							
Mr McCarthy — *Salary*	700	700	700	750	750	750	
Mrs McCarthy — *Salary*	700	700	700	700	700	700	
Child Benefit	40	40	40	40	40	40	
Other Income	—	—	—	60	—	—	
Total Income	1,440	1,440	1,440	1,550	1,490	1,490	
Expenditure							
Fixed							
Mortgage	400	400	400	400	400	400	
Personal Insurance	—	—	—	—	—	240	
Car Loan	350	350	350	350	350	350	
Car Tax	—	—	180	—	—	—	
Car Insurance	—	—	410	—	—	—	
House Insurance	—	—	180	—	—	—	
Irregular							
Housekeeping	370	370	370	380	380	380	
Car Service	—	60	—	—	80	—	
ESB	80	—	60	—	50	—	
Discretionary							
Birthdays	40	—	80	—	30	—	
Entertainment	60	60	60	60	60	60	
Total Expenditure	1,300	1,240	2,090	1,190	1,350	1,430	
Net Cash	140						
Opening Cash	20						
Closing Cash							

Answer the following questions in your Answerbook.

2. (b) What is the purpose of preparing a budget? **(3)**

2. (c) (i) How much income, in total, does the McCarthy family expect to receive in the six months?

(ii) What percentage of total expenditure will be spent, by the McCarthy family, on discretionary expenditure in this budget?

(iii) Give **one** example of **other income**. **(9)**

2. (d) (i) In what month is there a shortfall (deficit)?

(ii) Give a reason for the shortfall.

(iii) Suggest one way of overcoming this shortfall. **(9)**

2. (e) The McCarthys are considering saving for a family visit to America in five years time. Suggest a suitable place to invest their savings. Give a reason for your answer. **(6)**

Source: Junior Certificate Higher Level 1994. **(40 marks)**

Solution to Question 2.

2. (a) McCarthy Family Budget: January–June

	JAN. IR£	FEB. IR£	MARCH IR£	APRIL IR£	MAY IR£	JUNE IR£	TOTAL IR£
Income							
Mr McCarthy — *Salary*	700	700	700	750	750	750	*4,350*
Mrs McCarthy — *Salary*	700	700	700	700	700	700	*4,200*
Child Benefit	40	40	40	40	40	40	*240*
Other Income	—	—	—	60	—	—	*60*
Total Income	1,440	1,440	1,440	1,550	1,490	1,490	*8,850*
Expenditure							
Fixed							
Mortgage	400	400	400	400	400	400	*2,400*
Personal Insurance	—	—	—	—	—	240	*240*
Car Loan	350	350	350	350	350	350	*2,100*
Car Tax	—	—	180	—	—	—	*180*
Car Insurance	—	—	410	—	—	—	*410*
House Insurance	—	—	180	—	—	—	*180*
Irregular							
Housekeeping	370	370	370	380	380	380	*2,250*
Car Service	—	60	—	—	80	—	*140*
ESB	80	—	60	—	50	—	*190*
Discretionary							
Birthdays	40	—	80	—	30	—	*150*
Entertainment	60	60	60	60	60	60	*360*
Total Expenditure	1,300	1,240	2,090	1,190	1,350	1,430	*8,600*
Net Cash	140	*200*	*(650)*	*360*	*140*	*60*	*250*
Opening Cash	20	*160*	*360*	*(290)*	*70*	*210*	*20*
Closing Cash	*160*	*360*	*(290)*	*70*	*210*	*270*	*270*

2. (b) *To allocate limited income, avoid debt. To plan savings. To ensure that one lives within one's means.*

2. (c) *(i) IR£8,850.*

(ii) 5.9% (IR£510 x 100/IR£8,600).

(iii) Bank Interest (Deposit)/Tax Refund.

2. (d) *(i) March.*

(ii) Car tax and insurances in the same month.

(iii) Pay motor insurance by instalment.

2. (e) *National Instalment Savings/safe/guaranteed return/tax-free*

OR

Savings Certificates/safe/good return/tax-free.

Question 3.

Answer (a) and (b). This is a Household Budget Question.

3. (a) At the end of the question is a partially completed Personal Budget form for the Moran household for the second half of 1992.

You are required to complete this form for October, November, December, as well as all the 'Total' columns.

The following information should be taken into account.

- T. Moran expects to earn IR£150 a month in **extra** overtime in November and December.
- S. Moran will be getting a Christmas bonus of IR£100 in December.
- Child benefit is the same for each month.
- House mortgage is expected to increase by $2\frac{1}{2}$% beginning with the October payment.
- Car loan will be fully paid off by the end of November.
- Annual Car Insurance of IR£580 is due in full in December.
- Annual House Insurance premium of IR£260 is paid half-yearly in April and October.
- Household Costs (Groceries, etc.) are estimated as follows: October — IR£300; November — IR£330; December — IR£490.
- Car running costs are estimated at IR£50 per month, plus a car service in November costing a further IR£60.
- ESB is estimated at IR£50 per month for October and November and IR£65 for December.
- Telephone is estimated at IR£70 every two months.
- Entertainment expenses are estimated at IR£30 a month for October and November and IR£60 for December.
- Wallpapering of living room and hall will cost IR£280 in November and household decorating for Christmas will cost IR£100 in December.
- Christmas presents are expected to cost IR£150 in December. **(36)**

3. (b) Give two possible reasons why the ESB costs are expected to increase in December. **(4)**

Source: Junior Certificate Higher Level 1992. **(40 marks)**

For use with Question 3.

3. (a) Personal Budget for the Moran household for six months — July to December 1992

	July IR£	Aug. IR£	Sept. IR£	Oct. IR£	Nov. IR£	Dec. IR£	Total IR£
Expected Income							
T. Moran	600	600	600				
S. Moran	550	550	550				
Child Benefit	30	30	30				
TOTAL INCOME	1,180	1,180	1,180				
Planned Expenditure							
Fixed							
House Mortgage	360	360	360				
Car Loan	250	250	250				
Car Insurance	—	—	—				
House Insurance	—	—	—				
Subtotal	610	610	610				
Irregular							
Household Costs (incl. Groceries)	280	310	350				
Car Running Costs	50	50	50				
ESB	40	40	45				
Telephone	—	70	—				
Subtotal	370	470	445				
Discretionary							
Birthdays/Presents	—	60	—				
Entertainment	60	—	—				
Household Decoration	—	50	—				
Subtotal	60	110	—				
TOTAL EXPENDITURE	1,040	1,190	1,055				
Net Cash (Surplus/Deficit)	140	(–10)	125				
Opening Cash	80	220	210	335			
Closing Cash	220	210	335				

3. (b) (i)

(ii)

Solution to Question 3.

3. (a)

	JULY IR£	AUG. IR£	SEPT. IR£	OCT. IR£	NOV. IR£	DEC. IR£	TOTAL IR£
Income							
T. Moran	600	600	600	600	750	750	3,900
S. Moran	550	550	550	550	550	650	3,400
Child Benefit	30	30	30	30	30	30	180
TOTAL INCOME	1,180	1,180	1,180	1,180	1,330	1,430	7,480
Expenditure							
Fixed							
House Mortgage	360	360	360	369	369	369	2,187
Car Loan	250	250	250	250	250	—	1,250
Car Insurance	—	—	—	—	—	580	580
House Insurance	—	—	—	130	—	—	130
Subtotal	610	610	610	749	619	949	4,147
Irregular							
Household Costs (incl. Groceries)	280	310	350	300	330	490	2,060
Car Running Costs	50	50	50	50	110	50	360
ESB	40	40	45	50	50	65	290
Telephone	—	70	—	70	—	70	210
Subtotal	370	470	445	470	490	675	2,920
Discretionary							
Birthdays/Presents	—	60	—	—	—	150	210
Entertainment	60	—	—	30	30	60	180
Household Decoration	—	50	—	—	280	100	430
Subtotal	60	110	—	30	310	310	820
TOTAL EXPENDITURE	1,040	1,190	1,055	1,249	1,419	1,934	7,887
Net Cash (Surplus/Deficit)	140	(–10)	125	(69)	(89)	(504)	(407)
Opening Cash	80	220	210	335	266	177	80
Closing Cash	220	210	335	266	177	(327)	(327)

3. (b) (i) *Greater usage in winter.*
(ii) *Christmas cooking and holidays, etc.*

Question 4.
Answer (a) and (b).
This is a Household Budget Question.

4. (a) At the end of the question is a partially completed Personal Budget form for the Reidy family for 1993.

You are required to complete this form by filling in the figures for the 'Estimate April to December' column and the 'Total for Year' column. The following information should be taken into account.

- John Reidy is due a salary increase of 5% from 1 July 1993.
- Mary Reidy expects a special bonus of IR£320 in December 1993.
- Child benefit will continue each month as for the first three months of the year.
- House mortgage is expected to increase by IR£40 a month from 1 August 1993.
- House insurance, per month, will continue as for the first three months of the year.
- Household costs, per month, are expected to remain the same for each month until September and to increase by IR£30 a month beginning in October 1993.
- Car running costs are expected to remain at IR£80 a month with an additional car service cost of IR£90 in September 1993.
- ESB for the twelve months (January–December) is estimated at IR£1,150.
- Christmas presents are expected to cost IR£200 in December 1993.
- Entertainment is expected to cost IR£600 for the twelve months (January–December 1993).
- The family holiday in July 1993 is expected to cost IR£1,400. **(35)**

4. (b) Explain what is meant by the term 'Discretionary' expenditure. **(5)**
(Write your answer in the box at the end of the budget form.)

Source: Junior Certificate Higher Level 1993. **(40 marks)**

For use with Question 4.
Personal Budget for the Reidy household

4. (a)	JAN.	FEB.	MAR.	TOTAL JAN.–MAR.	ESTIMATE APR.–DEC.	TOTAL FOR YEAR JAN.–DEC.
Planned Income	IR£	IR£	IR£	IR£	IR£	IR£
Salaries						
John Reidy	660	660	660	1,980		
Mary Reidy	700	700	700	2,100		
Child Benefit	30	30	30	90		
TOTAL INCOME	1,390	1,390	1,390	4,170		
Planned Expenditure						
Fixed						
Mortgage	280	280	280	840		
Annual Car Tax	240	—	—	240		
Annual Car Insurance	—	—	650	650		
House Insurance	18	18	18	54		
Subtotal	538	298	948	1,784		
Irregular						
Household Costs	490	490	490	1,470		
Car Running Costs	80	80	80	240		
ESB	190	—	160	350		
Subtotal	760	570	730	2,060		
Discretionary						
Presents	—	40	—	40		
Entertainment	45	60	55	160		
Holidays	—	—	—	—		
Subtotal	45	100	55	200		
TOTAL EXPENDITURE	1,343	968	1,733	4,044		
Net Cash (Surplus/Deficit)	47	422	–343	126		
Opening Cash	75	122	544	75	201	75
Closing Cash	122	544	201	201		

WORKINGS

4. (b) Discretionary Expenditure ....
....
....
....

Solution to Question 4.
Personal Budget for the Reidy household

4. (a)	JAN.	FEB.	MAR.	TOTAL JAN.–MAR.	ESTIMATE APR.–DEC.	TOTAL FOR YEAR JAN.–DEC.
Planned Income	IR£	IR£	IR£	IR£	IR£	IR£
Salaries						
John Reidy	660	660	660	1,980	6,138	8,118
Mary Reidy	700	700	700	2,100	6,620	8,720
Child Benefit	30	30	30	90	270	360
TOTAL INCOME	1,390	1,390	1,390	4,170	13,028	17,198
Planned Expenditure						
Fixed						
Mortgage	280	280	280	840	2,720	3,560
Annual Car Tax	240	—	—	240	—	240
Annual Car Insurance	—	—	650	650	—	650
House Insurance	18	18	18	54	162	216
Subtotal	538	298	948	1,784	2,882	4,666
Irregular						
Household Costs	490	490	490	1,470	4,500	5,970
Car Running Costs	80	80	80	240	810	1,050
ESB	190	—	160	350	800	1,150
Subtotal	760	570	730	2,060	6,110	8,170
Discretionary						
Presents	—	40	—	40	200	240
Entertainment	45	60	55	160	440	600
Holidays	—	—	—	—	1,400	1,400
Subtotal	45	100	55	200	2,040	2,240
TOTAL EXPENDITURE	1,343	968	1,733	4,044	11,032	15,076
Net Cash (Surplus/Deficit)	47	422	–343	126	1,996	2,122
Opening Cash	75	122	544	75	201	75
Closing Cash	122	544	201	201	2,197	2,197

WORKINGS

4. (b) Discretionary Expenditure

Where the consumer has a choice after fixed and irregular expenditure have been paid.

PRACTICE QUESTIONS

(i) Question 1, Section B, Ordinary Level, Sample Paper.
(ii) Question 1, Section B, Ordinary Level, 1992.
(iii) Question 1, Section B, Ordinary Level, 1993.
(iv) Question 1, Paper 1, Section B, Higher Level, Sample Paper.

Chapter 4 — Household Accounts

A. Analysed Cash Book

Used to record actual income and expenditure of the household.

Most people keep some cash on them and make cash payments. Many people keep a bank account and pay for goods and services by cheque. In the Analysed Cash Book we have two columns on each side, one for Cash and one for Bank.

An Analysed Cash Book is laid out as follows:

Debit Receipts (Money in) ANALYSED CASH BOOK Credit Payments (Money out)

Date	Details	Cash	Bank	Date	Details	Cheque Nos.	Cash	Bank	Analysis Columns

Explanation

(1) The debit side (left side) records opening cash and money coming in/received.

(2) The credit side (right side) records money owed to the bank and money going out/paid out.

B.

Rule for Analysed Cash Book

DEBIT ALL MONEY RECEIVED
CREDIT ALL MONEY PAID OUT

C. Balancing Analysed Cash Book

- Balance only Cash and Bank columns.
- Add both columns.
- Find difference = balance.
- Put balance on smaller side.
- Total both sides.
- Bring down balance (B/d) on opposite side.
- Bank DR ⇛ asset – money in bank.
  CR ⇛ overdraft.
- Total analysis columns.

D. Contra Entry

Affects both sides of Cash Book.

TYPES

(1) Lodged Cash in Bank ⇛ Money into Bank ⇛ Debit
Money out of Cash ⇛ Credit

(2) Withdrew from Bank ⇛ Money out of Bank ⇛ Credit
Money into Cash ⇛ Debit

E. 'Did Household Budget Live Within Its Means?'

Every household should try to live within its means for the week/month. However, this isn't always possible. To answer this question you find total income for the period and compare it with total expenditure for the period. If income was greater than expenditure — the family lived within its means. If expenditure was greater than income — the family did not live within its means.

F. Business Terms

Balance The difference between the two sides of an account.
Contra Entry Where money is switched between the Cash A/C and Bank A/C.
Credit Right-hand side of Analysed Cash Book.
Debit Left-hand side of Analysed Cash Book.

Examination-Style Question and Solution

Question 1.
Answer (a), (b) and (c). This is a Household Analysed Cash Book Question.

Tom Roche, 14 Forest Drive, Galway, opened a current account in the local branch of Bank of Ireland on 1 May 1993. His account number is 57364217. He was given a cheque book, cheque card and a Pass card.

He made his first lodgment of IR£580 on the same date. It was made up as follows: Salary Cheque IR£500 and IR£80 in notes won in a local raffle.

During the first two weeks of May he had the following Bank transactions:

		IR£
May 2	Paid for groceries by cheque (no. 901)	60
May 3	Paid telephone by cheque (no. 902)	133
May 5	Withdrew cash by Pass card for entertainment	25
May 9	Paid ESB by cheque (no. 903)	64
May 10	Paid for groceries by cheque (no. 904)	59
May 11	Lodged cash from sale of old furniture	150
May 13	Paid for home heating by cheque (no. 905)	104
May 14	Paid monthly mortgage repayment by standing order	150

1. (a) Assuming you are Tom Roche, complete the lodgment form fully for 1 May 1993. (Use the blank document supplied at the end of the question.) **(10)**

1. (b) Write up the Analysed Cash Book, using the following money column headings.
Receipt side: Bank
Payments side: Bank; Groceries; Light & Heat; Entertainment; Other. **(22)**

1. (c) Based on the figures in Tom's Analysed Cash Book, do you think he was living within his means in May? Explain your answer briefly. **(8)**

Lodgment Record Subject to Verification | **LODGMENT** | **Bank of Ireland**

Name Tom Roche

Current Account Number

5	7	3	6	4	2	1	7

Please specify Account:
Current ☑ Savings ☐
Other ☐ ....

IR£ 150 -	

Name Tom Roche
Address 14 Forest Dr.
Galway Date May 1st.

Please specify Account:
Current ☑ Savings ☐ Other ☐ ....

Customer's Account Number

5	7	3	6	4	2	1	7

Notes	IR 150..
Coin	—
Total Cash	IR 150
Cheques	IR .....
Other	—
Total	IR 150

Source: Junior Certificate Higher Level 1993. **(40 marks)**

Solution to Question 1.
1. (a)

Lodgment Record Subject to Verification | **LODGMENT** | **Bank of Ireland**

Name *Tom Roche*

Current Account Number

5	7	3	6	4	2	1	7

Please specify Account:
Current ☑ Savings ☐
Other ☐ ....

IR£ 580	00

Name *Tom Roche*
Address *14 Forest Drive*
Galway Date *1-5-93*

Please specify Account:
Current ☑ Savings ☐ Other ☐ ....

Customer's Account Number

5	7	3	6	4	2	1	7

Notes	IR£80
Coin	—
Total Cash	IR£80
Cheques	IR£500
Other	—
Total	IR£580

1. (b) Household Account (Bank)

Date	Details	Bank	Date	Details	Cheque No.	Bank	Groceries	Light & Heat	Entertainment	Other
1/5/93	Lodgment	580	2/5/93	Groceries	901	60	60			
11/5/93	Lodgment	150	3/5/93	Telephone	902	133				133
			5/5/93	Cash withdrawal	ATM	25			25	
			9/5/93	ESB	903	64		64		
			10/5/93	Groceries	904	59	59			
			13/5/93	Oil	905	104		104		
			14/5/93	Mortgage	SO	150				150
						595	119	168	25	283
				Balance	C/d	135				
		730				730				
Balance B/d		135								

1. (c) *NO — Expenditure was IR£595 for the month while regular income is only IR£500 p.m. Additional once-off income in May was IR£80 raffle / IR£150 sale of furniture.*

OR

YES — He had IR£135 left over.

PRACTICE QUESTIONS

(i) Question 2, Section B, Ordinary Level, Sample Paper.
(ii) Question 2, Section B, Ordinary Level, 1992.
(iii) Question 2, Section B, Ordinary Level, 1994.

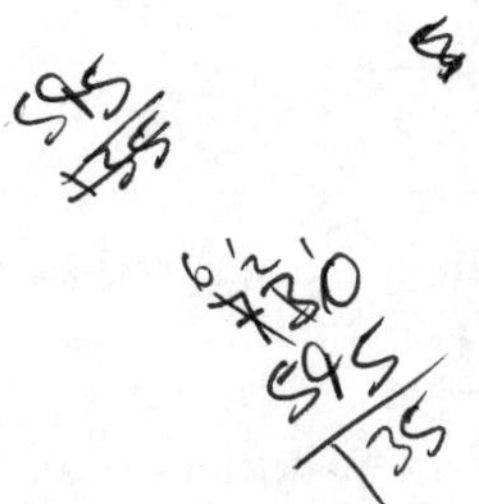

Chapter 5 — The Informed Consumer

A. Consumer

A consumer is a person who buys goods and services, e.g. food, clothes, cars, entertainment, newspapers, etc.

B. The Informed Consumer

- ☞ Is aware of legal rights.
- ☞ Is aware of organisations that protect him.
- ☞ Is able to make a complaint.
- ☞ Does not buy impulsively.
- ☞ Makes enquiries, etc.

C. Ordering Goods and Services

(1) **By letter** – keep a copy of the order-letter for future reference.
(2) **By telephone** – keep a written record and get the name of the person who took the order.
(3) **Personal call** – find out exact cost and view the goods.

D. Paying for Goods

When you order the goods you may be asked to pay a deposit — a small payment which is part of the purchase price made to ensure that the customer will return to collect the goods and pay the balance due.

E. Receipts

When you pay for the goods you should receive a receipt — this is written proof that payment was made and it may be required if there are any problems with the goods at a later date.

F. Symbols on Goods

Guaranteed Irish — symbol of quality — operated by Guaranteed Irish

Approved Quality Symbol — used on products that have reached a high standard

Pure New Wool

[***] will keep in freezer for three months

OR	Workings
Alternatively, students must pay only IR£3,600 – IR£20 (interest earned) = IR£3,580	$4{,}620 \times \frac{8}{100} \times \frac{1}{4} =$ *IR£92.40*

(ii)	*September balance*	*IR£1,020*
	Lodgment	*IR£3,600.00*
		IR£4,620.00
	3 months interest @8% =	*IR£92.40*
	Answer	*IR£4,712.40*

3. MONEY TRANSMISSION

Money transmission is transferring money from one person to another.
Methods of transferring money within Ireland:

A. Cash — Registered Mail

Notes may be sent through the post but the letter should be registered to ensure its safe transfer.

B. Cheque Payments

(1) CHEQUES
A person with a current account can make payments by cheque.

(2) BANK DRAFT
A bank draft is a cheque drawn by a bank on its own bank account. Very safe.

C. Direct Bank Payments

(1) STANDING ORDER
An order to a bank to make **regular fixed payments** from a bank account.

(2) DIRECT DEBIT
Permission given to a creditor to request payments **which may vary** from your bank account at regular intervals.

(3) CREDIT TRANSFER (BANK GIRO)
This is a way of transferring money directly into another person's or firm's bank account.

(4) PAY PATH
An employee's wages or salary can be paid directly into his bank account. Safe, convenient and cheaper for the employer than paying by cheque.

D. Card Payments

(1) AUTOMATED TELLER MACHINE (ATM) — CASH DISPENSERS
(a) Customer is given an ATM card and a personal identification number, PIN.
(b) Customer goes to ATM at any bank, inserts card in machine, keys in PIN.

(c) Customer can lodge, withdraw, check the balance, order a statement, order a cheque book, pay a bill.

(2) CREDIT CARD

(a) Customer is given a card and a credit limit.
(b) Goods and services can be purchased or bills paid up to this limit.
(c) Customer receives a monthly statement.
(d) Examples are Access and Visa.

(3) CHARGE CARD

(a) Similar to credit card.
(b) When statement is received customer must pay amount due.
(c) Examples are American Express and Diners.

(4) STORE CARD/FUEL CARD

(a) Department stores and oil companies give their customers store/fuel cards.
(b) Customers are given a credit limit.
(c) Examples include Clery's, Switzer's, Statoil, Shell.

E. An Post Payments

(1) POSTAL ORDER

(a) A postal order can be used to send amounts of money up to IR£50 through An Post.
(b) A fee called Poundage is charged.

(2) MONEY ORDER

(a) A money order is used if larger amounts — up to IR£500 — are to be sent through An Post.
(b) Poundage is also charged on money orders.

F. Transferring Money Abroad

(1) BANK DRAFT — STERLING DRAFT

A bank draft can also be purchased and made out in a foreign currency, e.g. £100 sterling.

(2) TRAVELLER'S CHEQUES

(a) If you are going abroad you can buy traveller's cheques in exchange for cash. They are available in different currencies.
(b) They have to be signed twice, once in the presence of the bank cashier issuing them and again in the presence of the person you are paying. The signatures must correspond.

(3) EUROCHEQUES AND EUROCHEQUE CARD

Similar to an ordinary cheque except that the cheque is written **in the currency** of the country you are visiting. The Eurocheque card is used to verify your identity and signature and covers cheques up to IR£140.

G. Single European Currency

The long-term aim of the European Union is to have a single currency by 1999. Euro bosses are saying it should be called the **Euro** and will be used by all EU countries.

Examination-Style Question and Solution

Question 1.
Answer (a) and (b). This is a Banking Question.

1. (a) State a method of payment provided by Banks, which you would recommend, in **each** case below.

(i) A tenant wishes to pay rent of IR£80 monthly, directly from her own bank current account to the landlord's bank account.

Answer: *Standing Order.*

(ii) A student, who does not have a bank account, wishes to pay exam fees directly into the bank account of the Department of Education.

Answer: *Credit Transfer.*

(iii) A student wishes to send £26.78 sterling to a London publisher for a book.

Answer: *Sterling Bank Draft.*

(iv) Mrs O'Connell wants to have her telephone bill paid in future directly by her bank from her current account.

Answer: *Direct Debit.* **(24)**

1. (b) Eithne Dunne, Ahamore, Castlecomer, Co. Kilkenny, has a current account No. 42367898 at the Castlecomer branch of the Bank of Ireland.

On 20 May 1994 Eithne visited her bank with IR£40 notes and IR£10 coins to send, by credit transfer, to her niece, Maura O'Gorman.

Maura O'Gorman keeps her account, No. 10864219, with the Allied Irish Banks Ltd, Rathmines branch, Dublin.

Assuming you are Eithne Dunne, complete fully the Credit Transfer form, using the blank document supplied at the end of the question, from the information supplied. **(16)**

Credit Transfer SUBJECT TO VERIFICATION — Destination Branch Code 90 – 04 – 07 — BANK GIRO CREDIT TRANSFER

To Bank	TO BANK Date	Notes		
Branch	Branch	Coin		
A/c	CREDIT ACCOUNT	Total Cash		
Account Number	Account Number	Cheques (See over)		
	Ref. No.	Tx	TOTAL £		

£

Brand/Initials

CASH. LODG.		99
NO. REMS.		98
CASH WITHDR.		97

Paid in by

Address

A/C/N

Brand Initials

Credit Transfer SUBJECT TO VERIFICATION — Destination Branch Code: 90 – 04 – 07 — BANK GIRO CREDIT TRANSFER

To Bank *A/B*
Branch *Rathmines*
A/c *Maura O'Gorman*
Account Number

1	0	8	6	4	2	1	9

£ 50	—

Brand Initials

TO BANK *Allied Irish Banks* Date
Branch *Rathmines*
CREDIT ACCOUNT *Maura O'Gorman*
Account Number

Ref. No.	1	0	8	6	4	2	1	9	Tx

Brand/Initials

CASH. LODG.		99	
NO. REMS.		98	A/C/N
CASH WITHDR.		97	

Notes	40	—
Coin	10	—
Total Cash	50	—
Cheques (See over)	—	
TOTAL £	50	—

Paid in by *Eithne Dunne*
Address *Ahamore*
Castlecomer
Co. Kilkenny

Source: Junior Certificate Higher Level 1994. **(40 marks)**

4. BANK ACCOUNTS

A. Deposit Account — Savings Account

A Deposit Account is a savings account. Money invested earns interest and can be withdrawn on demand at any bank.

B. Cashsave Account

This is similar to a Deposit Account except that you can lodge or withdraw using an ATM.

C. How to Open Deposit/Cashsave Account

- Application form — name, address, occupation.
- Given Deposit Book and ATM card.

D. Lodging Money to a Deposit Account

- Complete lodgment slip.
- Present slip, cash and deposit book to cashier — balance will be updated and account credited.

E. Withdrawing Money from Deposit Account

- Complete withdrawal slip.

  OR
- Use your ATM card if Cashsave Account.

F. Current Account

If you want to use a cheque book to make payments you must open a Current Account. Money in a Current Account does not earn interest.

G. How to Open a Current Account

- Application form — name, address, occupation.
- Submit reference if not known to bank.
- Give specimen signature.
- Lodge money.
- You are given A/C number, cheque book, cheque card, ATM card and PIN.

H. Lodging Money to a Current Account

- Lodgment slip

OR

- ATM lodgment

OR

- Credit Transfer.

LODGMENT RECORD
Subject to verification

LODGMENT

Bank of Ireland

Name(s)
John Ryan

Account Number
8 7 7 6 5 2 3 8

£ 710 —

Please specify Account:
Current ☑ **Savings** ☐
Other ☐

Note: Cheques, etc. are accepted subject to examination and verification and are transmitted for collection at customer's risk. Though credited to account when paid in they should not be drawn against until cleared. Customers should keep details of cheques lodged.
Thank you for banking with us.

Please specify Account: **Current** ☑ **Savings** ☐ **Other** ☐
Name(s) *John Ryan*
Address *24 Main Street Cork*
Date *24/9/96*
Paid in by *John Ryan*

Brand/Initials

FOR BANK USE
SERIAL NUMBER 9 0 4 8 3 2

Customer's Account Number
8 7 7 6 5 2 3 8

Tx

Notes	200	—
Coin	50	—
Total Cash	250	—
Cheque Total	460	—
Total	710	—

I. Withdrawing Money from a Current Account

- Withdrawal slip

OR

- Write a cheque

OR

- ATM withdrawal

OR

- Standing order or direct debit.

WITHDRAWAL RECORD | WITHDRAWAL | Bank of Ireland

Name(s) John Ryan
24 Main St, Cork
Account Number
8 7 1 6 5 2 3 8
£ 200 —
Please specify Account:
Current ☑ Savings ☐
Other ☐ . . . .
. . . .
Thank you for banking with us.

Please specify Account: **Current** ☑ **Savings** ☐ **Other** ☐
Received the sum of (words) Two hundred pounds
Date 15/10/96
Name of Account Holder(s) John Ryan
Signature(s) John Ryan

JOINT SAVINGS ACCOUNT
I certify that all parties in the Account are alive at this date.
Signed:

Brand/Initials
SERIAL NUMBER
9 0 4 8 3 2
Customer's Account Number
8 7 1 6 5 2 3 8
Address 24 Main St
Cork
Tx
£ 200 —

J. Bank Overdraft

(1) Bank overdraft is where a person writes cheques or withdraws more money than the amount held in the account.
(2) An agreed limit is set by bank.
(3) Interest on overdrawn amounts on reducing balance.

K. Preparation of Bank Account

All Current Account customers should keep their own personal bank accounts to record:

(1) **Opening Balance.**
(2) **Lodgments** to the account.
(3) **Withdrawals** or **payments** made from the account.
(4) **Closing Balance.**

BANK ACCOUNT — FORMAT

The bank account can be laid out using a **T Account Ledger** format or in the **continuous balancing ledger format.**

NB Ordinary level students can use either format. Higher level students must be able to use **both** formats.

L. Bank Statement

Current account holders receive regular bank statements. It is a copy of the customer's account from the **bank's point of view**. It shows transactions known to the bank.

A bank statement shows:
(1) Opening balance — Balance column.
(2) Lodgments into the account — Credit column.
(3) Payments from the account — Debit column.
(4) Closing balance in the account on a particular date.

M. Comparing Bank Account and Bank Statements

When you receive a bank statement the final figure shows what the bank says you have in your account. This figure may be different from the figure in your own personal bank account.

REASONS FOR DIFFERENCE

(1) Cheques written — not yet cashed.
(2) Lodgments made — but not shown on statement.
(3) Certain items will appear in the **bank statement** that the **account holder will not know about until the statement arrives**, e.g. standing orders, direct debits, current account fees, interest charged, government duty on cheque books, credit transfers into the account.

When the balance shown in the bank statement does not agree with the balance in the customer's own bank account **a bank reconciliation statement** must be prepared.

HOW TO RECONCILE THE TWO BALANCES

(1) CORRECT OR UPDATE THE BANK ACCOUNT

Look at bank statement and at bank account. **Identify items known to bank.**

Credit bank account with items that were taken out of the account, e.g. bank interest, standing orders, direct debits, current account fees, government duty on cheque books.

Debit the bank account with items that went into the account, e.g. credit transfers, salary paid direct to account.

The bank account is now correct.

(2) PREPARE A BANK RECONCILIATION STATEMENT

Start with balance as per bank statement.

Add lodgments not credited.

Subtract cheques not presented for payment.

Your answer will be balance as per corrected bank account.

Example: Bank A/C — Bank Statement — Bank Reconciliation Statement
(a) Bank Account is prepared by the customer

DR + Bank A/C CR –

						Ch. No.	
1/1/96	Balance	B/d	500✓	1/1/96	Giggs	Ch. 1	400✓
1/1/96	Cantona		500✓	1/1/96	Wages		100✗
1/1/96	Cole		10✗	1/1/96	Sharp	Ch. 2	400✓
				1/1/96	Balance C/d		110
			1,010				1,010
1/1/96	Balance	B/d	110				
					(Customer has IR£110 in bank)		

(b) Bank Statement is prepared by Bank

Bank Statement – +

Date	Details	Debit	Credit	Balance
1/1/96	Balance			500 ✓
1/1/96	Cheque No. 1	400 ✓		100
1/1/96	Lodgment		500 ✓	600
1/1/96	Bank Charges	20 ✗		580
1/1/96	Cheque No. 2	400 ✓		180

According to the bank the customer has IR£180 in bank.

(c) Corrected Bank Account

Items that are in the Bank Statement but not in Bank A/C

Corrected Bank A/C

1/1/96	Balance	B/d	110	1/1/96	Bank Charges		20
				1/1/96	Balance	C/d	90
			110				110
1/1/96	Balance	B/d	90				

(d) Bank Reconciliation Statement (To reconcile the difference)

Balance as per Bank Statement	**180**
Add Lodgment not Credited — Cole (DR in bank not in bank statement)	**10**
	190
Less Cheque not Presented — Wages (CR in bank not in bank statement)	**100**
Balance as per Bank Account	**90**

N. Business Terms

Bank Overdraft Money owed to bank — current account with a minus balance.
Bank Reconciliation Statement Prepared to reconcile bank account and bank statement.
Bank Statement Contains details of all transactions in a customer's current account.
Current Account Customer receives cheque book — no interest paid on account.
Deposit Account Savings account where interest is earned on money invested.
Government Duty on Cheques Tax collected by the government on cheques.

Examination-Style Question and Solution

Question 1.
Answer all sections. This is a Banking Question.

Michael Lynch has a current account with Bank of Ireland.
He received this bank statement on 30 March 1992.

Bank of Ireland

CURRENT ACCOUNT

Post to

Michael Lynch
13 Woodlands Park,
Palmerstown,
Dublin 20

90–07–72
Branch Code

70
Statement Number

30 March 1992
Date of Statement

74107628
Account Number

Date	Details		Debit	Credit	Balance
28 FEB	BALANCE FORWARD			1,081	
8 MAR	CHEQUE	393	126		955
10 MAR	CHEQUE	392	54		901
11 MAR	CREDIT TRANSFER			100	1,001
13 MAR	ATM		150		851
20 MAR	FIRST NBS	SO	160		691
22 MAR	IRISH LIFE	DD	68		623
27 MAR	CHEQUE	395	120		503
29 MAR	CURRENT ACC.	Fees	6		497

Study this bank statement and answer the following questions:

1. (a) On what date was the statement issued? **(3)**

1. (b) On 28 February did M. Lynch have an overdraft or have money in the bank? **(3)**

1. (c) Why are the cheque numbers not in sequence (order)? Explain your answer. **(4)**

1. (d) List two possible items which could be included in the heading 'Current Account Fees' on 29 March. **(4)**

1. (e) Explain the main difference between a direct debit (DD) and a standing order (SO) as a means of making payments. **(6)**

1. (f) The following is Michael Lynch's own account of his bank transactions. Compare this Account with the Bank Statement he received from the bank. Make whatever adjustments that are necessary to Michael's own records in your answer-book and then prepare a Bank Reconciliation Statement at 31 March 1992. **(20)**

(M. Lynch's own records)

BANK ACCOUNT

		F	£			F	Cheq. No.	£
Feb. 28	Balance	B/d	1,081	Mar. 1	ESB		392	54
Mar. 30	Lodgment		355	6	ELF Garage		393	126
				13	Cash ATM		—	150
				20	First Nat. Bld. Soc.		SO	160
				22	Irish Life Assur.		DD	68
				27	Shopwell Ltd		394	75
				28	Mulligans Hardware		395	120
				30	Balance	C/d		683
			1,436					1,436
Mar. 31	Balance	B/d	683					

(40 marks)

Source: Junior Certificate Higher Level 1992.

Solution to Question 1.

1. (a) *30 March 1992.*

1. (b) *Money in the bank.*

1. (c) *The cheques may have been presented for payment in a random fashion.*

1. (d) *Withdrawal charges, standing order charges, direct debit charges, credit transfer fees, charges for ordering cheque books.*

1. (e) *Direct debit — for regular payments of varying amounts, e.g. ESB, telephone.*
Standing order — for regular payments of fixed amounts, e.g. fixed mortgage, insurance premiums, hire purchase payments.

1. (f) *Adjustments to Michael's own records.*

Bank Account — T Account Presentation

Mar. 31	Balance	B/d	683	Current Account	Fees	6
	Credit Transfer		100	Balance	C/d	777
			783			783
	Balance	B/d	777			

OR

Bank Account Continuous Balancing Format				
Date	**Details**	**Debit**	**Credit**	**Balance**
Mar. 31	Balance		683	
	Credit Transfer	100		783
	Current Account Fees		6	777

Bank Reconciliation Statement

Balance as per Bank Statement	497
ADD Lodgment Not Credited	355
	852
DEDUCT Cheque 394 not presented for payment	75
Balance as per corrected bank account	777

PRACTICE QUESTIONS

(i) Question 7, Section B, Ordinary Level, 1993.
(ii) Question 2, Paper I, Section B, Higher Level, Sample Paper.

5. CHEQUES

A. Definition of Cheque

A cheque is a written instruction from the holder of a current account to his bank to pay a stated sum of money out of the holder's account to the person named in the cheque or to the bearer.

B. Parties to a Cheque

(1) Drawer — Person who writes the cheque.
(2) Drawee — Bank where drawer holds his account.
(3) Payee — Person to whom the cheque is payable.

C. Cheque

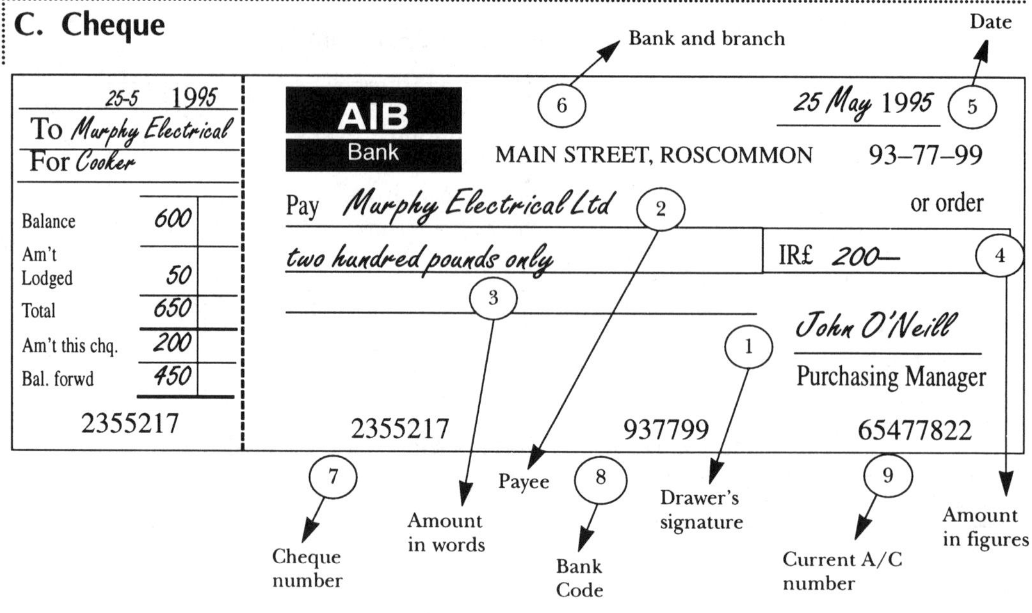

D. Counterfoil of Cheque (Stub)

The purpose of the counterfoil is to record the amount of the cheque, the name of the person paid and the date that the cheque was written. The amount left in the account after the cheque is also recorded. The account holder uses completed counterfoils to write up his own bank records.

E. Rules for Completing a Cheque

- Keep words close together.
- Keep figures close to £ sign.
- Complete stub.
- Initial corrections.
- Cross cheque.

F. Cheque Card/Banker's Card

(1) An identity card given to creditworthy current account holders.
(2) Guarantees cheque up to IR£100.
(3) Many banks now have a combined ATM/cheque card and photograph.
(4) Cheques can be cashed at outlets where you are not personally known.
(5) Cheque must be signed in the presence of seller.

G. Crossing a Cheque

Drawing two parallel lines across the face of the cheque. This makes the cheque safe as it must be paid into the bank account of the payee.

Types of Crossing

(1) General Crossing

(2) Special Crossing

Cheque can be paid only into payee account.

H. Endorsing/Negotiating a Cheque

The payee signs the back of the cheque and passes it on to a third party.

I. Different Types of Cheque

(1) **Or Order Cheques** — have 'or order' printed on them. The cheque may be endorsed and passed on.
(2) **Stale cheque** — more than six months old.
(3) **Postdated cheque** — date in the future.
(4) **Antedated Cheque** — has a date before the date of issue.
(5) **Blank cheque** — vital information is missing.
(6) **Open cheque** — not crossed.
(7) **Receipt cheque** — a cheque that must be signed by the payee before cashing.
(8) **Dishonoured cheques/Bounced cheques** — cheques which the bank refuses to pay. The cheques will be returned to the payee marked R/D — Refer to Drawer.

J. Why Banks Refuse to Cash a Cheque

(1) If the cheque is stale.
(2) If drawer dies or becomes bankrupt.
(3) If drawer has not enough money in the account.
(4) If amount in words does not match figures.
(5) If forgery is suspected.
(6) If signature does not match specimen signature.
(7) If cheque is not signed.

K. Cashing a Cheque

When you receive a cheque you can:
(1) Lodge it in your bank account.
(2) Endorse it and give it to someone else.
(3) Cash it in a shop where you are known.

6. OTHER BANKING SERVICES

A. Term Loan

(1) Given for a fixed term, usually from two to seven years.
(2) Given for a specific purpose.
(3) Repaid in fixed monthly instalments.
(4) Must be negotiated with the bank manager.

B. Mortgages — House Loans

Banks give house loans. The deeds of the premises will be given as collateral — security.

C. Strongroom Facilities

For storage of valuables and jewellery, or deeds of premises.

D. Purchase and Sale of Shares

Banks provide the facility for purchasing and selling shares in companies quoted on the stock exchange.

E. Financial Advice

To individuals, the farming community and business community.

F. Phonelink

Customers check their accounts over the telephone.

G. Trustee or Executor

Banks act as trustee or executor for their customers in relation to wills.

H. Income Tax and Life Assurance

Banks provide advice in relation to income tax and life assurance.

I. Night Safe

A facility where money can be lodged in the bank after bank closing time through a chute located in the bank wall; a leather wallet and key are provided.

J. Foreign Exchange

All banks provide a foreign exchange service. This is the exchanging of one currency for another.

K. Business Terms

Executor A person appointed by another person to ensure that his estate is distributed according to his will.

Life Assurance Policy providing money for family after death of main earner in family.

Mortgage House loan, deeds of house are given as security.

Share Part-ownership of a company.

Stock Exchange A market where shares are bought and sold.

Strongroom A safe for storage of valuables and important documents.

Trustee A person appointed by another person to manage funds.

7. MAIN FINANCIAL INSTITUTIONS AND THEIR SERVICES

	Names	Main Services
COMMERCIAL BANKS	Allied Irish Banks ATM Card = Banklink Bank of Ireland ATM Card = Pass Ulster Bank National Irish Bank ATM Card = Autobank	Savings, Lending Money Transmission Foreign Exchange Specialised Financial Services Specialised Advice
BUILDING SOCIETIES	Irish Permanent Educational Building Society First National Irish Nationwide ICS Building Society	Savings, Lending Money Transmission Foreign Exchange Specialised Financial Services Specialised Advice
TRUSTEE SAVINGS BANK	From 1 January 1992 all Trustee Savings Banks are known as TSB ATM Card = Cash Card	Savings, Lending Money Transmission Foreign Exchange Specialised Financial Services Specialised Advice
CREDIT UNION	There are about 500 Credit Unions in Ireland, e.g. ASTI, TUI, Credit Unions	Savings, Lending at low interest rates
AN POST	There are about 400 Post Offices nationwide	Savings, Lending — Post Loan Money Transmission Foreign Exchange
STATE BANKS	ICC Bank ACC Bank	Loans to Industry, Loans to Agricultural Sector, Savings

Chapter 9 — Credit and Borrowing

1. CREDIT

A. How We Can Buy Goods and Services

Goods and services can be bought by:
(1) Cash
(2) Credit
(3) Borrowing.

B. Credit

(1) When we buy goods on credit we get the goods immediately and pay later.
(2) Before a person is given credit a business will make sure that he is creditworthy, i.e. check to see if he will repay the money.
(3) Ways of Checking Creditworthiness/Credit Status:
- ➢ Bank can be asked for information on your financial position.
- ➢ Reference from other firms that you deal with.
- ➢ Credit Status Enquiry Agency.
- ➢ Sales representatives.

REASONS FOR SELLING GOODS ON CREDIT
(1) To attract new customers.
(2) To increase sales and profit.
(3) To help genuine customers short of cash temporarily.
(4) To compete with other firms offering credit.

HOW A BUSINESS CAN REDUCE ITS LOSSES CAUSED BY BAD DEBTS
(1) Offer discounts for prompt payment.
(2) Have a good credit control system and good accounting system.
(3) Retain ownership of goods until payment is received.
(4) Sell for cash only.

C. Types of Credit

(1) CONSUMER CREDIT
This is where consumers buy goods and use services and pay the seller/supplier at a later date, e.g. milk, electricity, telephone, local shop.

(2) CREDIT CARD
When a consumer buys goods and services using a credit card the bill is paid by the credit card company and the consumer then pays the credit card company within the agreed credit period. Examples include Visa, Access.

(3) HIRE PURCHASE

➢ Hire purchase is a system of buying goods on credit by paying an initial deposit and paying the balance owed by regular instalments over an agreed period of time.

The buyer obtains **the immediate use of the goods** but does not become the legal owner until the **last instalment is paid**.

PARTIES INVOLVED IN HIRE PURCHASE

(a) Consumer/Buyer
(b) Retailer/Seller
(c) HP Company.

EXAMPLE OF A HIRE PURCHASE TRANSACTION

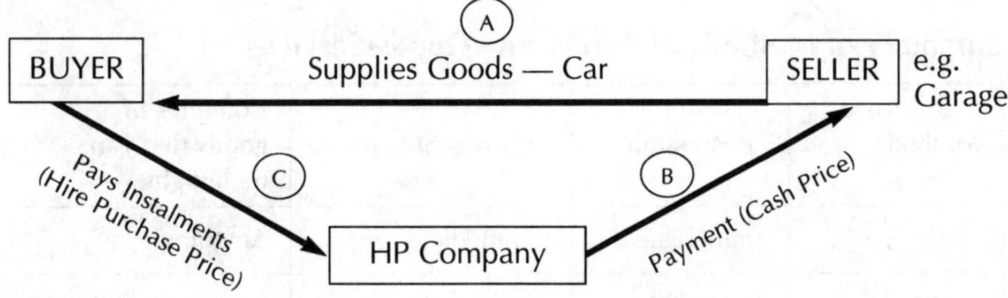

CONSUMER PROTECTION IN RELATION TO HIRE PURCHASE

Consumers are protected by the Hire Purchase Acts 1946 and 1960, which state the following:

(a) A hire purchase **agreement** must be prepared and signed by both parties.
(b) This agreement must show:

➢ Cash price of goods.
➢ Hire purchase price.
➢ APR — Annual Percentage Rate.
➢ Number of instalments.
➢ Amount of each instalment.
➢ Description of the goods.

(c) The agreement must also **contain the right of the hirer to terminate** the agreement.

➢ If at least **half of the hire purchase** is paid the goods are then returned to the hire purchase company.

(d) The agreement also contains the following restrictions on the hire purchase company's right to recover the goods:

➢ Without hirer's consent the hire purchase company has no authority to enter the hirer's premises to take back the goods.
➢ If one-third or more of the hire purchase price is paid the hire purchase company cannot take back the goods without a court order.

(e) A copy of the agreement must be sent to the hirer within fourteen days.

(4) LEASING/RENTING

(a) When you lease/rent something you have the **use** of the item, e.g. television, car, video, but you will never **own** it.

(b) A regular payment is made for the use of the item.

(c) Leasing/Renting makes financial sense only if you need the item for just a short period of time or have no ambition to own it, e.g. video cassette.

(5) DEFERRED PAYMENT/BUDGET ACCOUNT

This is where an item is purchased, e.g. suite of furniture, with a deposit being paid and the balance paid in instalments. **Ownership of the goods passes to the buyer when the deposit is paid.** If the buyer defaults in payment the goods cannot be repossessed but the seller can sue the buyer for the balance outstanding.

D. Summary of Methods of Purchasing Goods/Services

	Method	Possession	Ownership	Examples of goods that can be bought
1.	Cash	Immediate	Immediate	Anything
2.	Consumer Credit	Immediate	Immediate	Groceries, ESB, telephone, gas, milk, etc.
3.	Credit Card	Immediate	Immediate	Most items, e.g. petrol, groceries, holidays, etc.
4.	Hire Purchase	Immediate	On payment of last instalment	Cars, TVs, electrical equipment, computers, etc.
5.	Leasing/ Renting	Immediate	Never own goods	Cars, TVs, houses, videos, dress suits, etc.
6.	Deferred Payment	Immediate	Immediate	Furniture, carpets, electrical goods, TVs, etc.

Examination-Style Question and Solution

Question 1.

Answer all sections. This is a Hire Purchase Question.

Eoin and Úna Murphy purchased a video after seeing the following advertisement in a shop.

Hire Purchase Credit available

'EASY PAYMENTS'

IR£60 Deposit Plus IR£15 monthly for 2 years

All the repayments were made on time until Eoin lost his job $1^1/_2$ years later. As a result they failed to make one of the repayments. A week later a hire purchase company representative entered their house, without permission, and took the video away.

1. (a) The above advertisement is illegal, as it does not include certain information required by law. Identify **two** additional items of information that a legal advertisement for hire purchase credit should include. **(12)**
1. (b) What was illegal about the behaviour of the hire purchase company representative? **(4)**
1. (c) Who was the lawful owner of the video at the time it was repossessed by the hire purchase company? **(4)**
1. (d) What is the main disadvantage of buying on hire purchase? **(4)**
1. (e) If Eoin and Úna had made all their repayments, what would be the total cost of the video? **(4)**
1. (f) Name **two** other ways they could have financed the purchase of the video other than by hire purchase credit. **(12)**

Source: Junior Certificate Higher Level 1994. **(40 marks)**

Solution to Question 1.

1. (a) *Cash Price, APR, Total Credit Price.*
1. (b) *The hire purchase representative should have a court order to*
(i) enter the dwelling house;
(ii) repossess the goods when more than one-third has been paid. He didn't have the court order and permission.
1. (c) *Hire purchase company.*
1. (d) *(i) It is expensive. Hire purchase companies charge a flat rate of interest which results in a very high APR.*
(ii) Consumers may spend more than they can afford.
(iii) A lot of future earnings may be spent on hire purchase.
1. (e) *IR£15 per month* x *24 months* + *IR£60 deposit*
= *IR£360* + *IR£60* = *IR£420*
1. (f) *(i) Bank loan, credit union loan, or loan from TSB or building society.*
(ii) Buy it out of personal savings.
(iii) Deferred payment.

PRACTICE QUESTIONS

(i) Question 20, Section A, Paper I, Higher Level, 1993.
(ii) Question 12, Section A, Paper I, Higher Level, Sample Paper.
(iii) Question 3, Section B, Ordinary Level, 1993.

2. BORROWING

A. Borrowing

Borrow the money and repay the lending agency in the future with interest (cost).

B. Factors to be Considered Before Borrowing

Before borrowing we must ask ourselves a number of questions:
(1) Do we need the goods or services?
(2) Can we meet the repayments?
(3) What security/collateral can we offer the lender?

C. Collateral/Security

Lender will require collateral or security. This means that you hand over/sign over some valuable asset. The lender will hold this asset until the loan is repaid.

ACCEPTABLE FORMS OF SECURITY/COLLATERAL

- ➢ Deeds of premises or property.
- ➢ Life Assurance Policy.
- ➢ Share Certificates.
- ➢ Guarantor.

D. Advantages of Borrowing

(1) Enables people to buy goods without saving for a long time.
(2) Increases standard of living.
(3) Helps people in difficult financial situations.

E. Disadvantages of Borrowing

(1) Carries a high cost — rate of interest.
(2) Commits borrower to repayments in the future.
(3) High borrowings cause many social problems.

F. Applying for a Loan

- ➢ Fill out loan application form.
- ➢ Meet lender.
- ➢ Agree terms of repayment.

G. Information Required by Lender on Application Form

- ➢ Name, address, age, occupation, employment, income.
- ➢ Amount of loan.
- ➢ Purpose of loan.
- ➢ Length of time required to repay.
- ➢ Security available.
- ➢ Track record.
- ➢ Other commitments.

H. Factors Taken into Consideration by Bank Before Lending

(1) Financial position of borrower.
(2) Creditworthiness of borrower.
(3) Collateral/security available.
(4) Purpose of loan.
(5) Duration of loan.

I. Cost of Borrowing

The cost of borrowing is the rate of interest charged by the lender.

(1) FLAT RATE OF INTEREST

Interest is charged on the original loan amount over the full duration of the loan. No credit is given for repayments made.

(2) TRUE RATE OF INTEREST/APR

Interest is charged on the **reducing balance of the loan**, i.e. it is calculated on the amount outstanding after each instalment is paid. Another name for true rate is APR, **Annual Percentage Rate**, and it includes other costs in taking out a loan, e.g. administration fees, stamp duty and insurance. Since 1 January 1991 a lending institution must by law show the annual percentage rate on any advertisement for a loan. This allows consumers to make comparisons between lending agencies.

J. Advertising Credit Facilities to Consumers

All borrowers have a right to know:
➢ Cash price.
➢ Credit price.
➢ APR.
➢ Amount of instalments.
➢ Number of instalments.

K. Rights of Borrower

The rights of the borrower are protected by legislation including:
(1) Hire Purchase Acts 1946 and 1960.
(2) Sale of Goods and Supply of Services Act 1980.

L. Responsibilities of Borrower

(1) To provide true and accurate information to the lender.
(2) To pay the monthly instalments on time.
(3) To repay the loan in full.

M. Bankruptcy

If a person borrows and is unwilling or unable to repay his debts he can be declared bankrupt by the High Court. His name may be printed in *Stubbs Gazette.*

N. Duration of Loans

Loans can be for the short term, up to one year; medium term, one to five years; or long term, five to twenty years. Here are some of the most **common reasons** for borrowing matched with the **sources available** and the **duration of the borrowing**.

	REASONS	SOURCES AVAILABLE	DURATION
1.	Christmas expenses	Bank overdraft, credit card, credit union, moneylender	Short-term
2.	Temporary shortage of cash	Bank overdraft	Short-term
3.	Furniture	Short-term bank loan, credit union	Short-term
4.	Holidays	Bank overdraft, credit card, credit union	Short-term
5.	Telephone bill/ESB bill	Moneylender, credit card, bank overdraft	Short-term
6.	Communion, Confirmation expenses	Credit card, credit union, bank overdraft	Short-term
7.	College expenses	Credit union/Short-term loan	Short-term
8.	Car	Bank term loan, credit union, hire purchase	Medium-term
9.	Computer	Bank term loan, credit union, hire purchase	Medium-term
10.	House improvements	Bank term loan, credit union	Medium-term
11.	Conservatory	Bank term loan, credit union	Medium-term
12.	House purchase	Building society mortgage, bank mortgage	Long-term
13.	House extension	Building society loan, bank loan	Long-term

O. Lending Agencies

(1) COMMERCIAL BANK

Commercial banks operate lending in a number of ways.

(a) Term loan: a loan given for a stated reason, for a specified period of time.

(b) Bank overdraft: where the bank manager gives permission to a current account holder to overdraw up to a certain limit.

(c) Mortgage: a home loan given by the bank for the purchase of a house.

(d) Bridging loan: short-term finance given to people who have a mortgage approved but are awaiting receipt of building society loan.

(2) BUILDING SOCIETIES

Building societies provide home loans.

(3) AN POST

An Post offers loans through Bowmaker Bank for the purchase of cars, home improvements, furniture, etc. Up to IR£15,000 can be borrowed for up to five years.

(4) TRUSTEE SAVINGS BANK

TSB provides house mortgages, bridging loans and loans for house improvements. It also provides personal loans for cars, holidays, furniture, etc.

(5) CREDIT UNION

You must be a member of a credit union with a savings record to qualify for a loan. The credit union will lend a multiple of the amount saved (two or three times). Loans are given for many purposes, including cars, furniture, holidays and electrical goods, and are usually for small amounts.

(6) HIRE PURCHASE

This was dealt with earlier in the chapter (see p. 57).

(7) MONEYLENDERS

People will borrow from moneylenders if they have difficulty in borrowing from other financial institutions. They charge extremely high rates of interest. Licensed moneylenders have a licence from the Revenue Commissioners to operate. APR must be quoted on all loans. An unlicensed moneylender lends without a licence.

(8) PAWNBROKERS

A pawnbroker will lend money on the security of something valuable, e.g. jewellery. If the loan is not repaid the security can be sold to repay the loan.

P. Business Terms

Bankruptcy A person can be declared bankrupt if he cannot pay what he owes.
Bridging Loan Short-term loan given to person awaiting receipt of building society loan.
Collateral Security given against a loan.
Creditor Person who is owed money.
Flat Rate of Interest Interest calculated on the full amount borrowed for the full period of the loan.
Guarantor A person who undertakes to repay the loan if the borrower cannot.
Moneylender A person who lends money at very high rates of interest.
Mortgage A home loan where the deeds of the house are given as security.
Overdraft Writing cheques for or withdrawing more than the amount in a current account.
Pawnbroker A person who lends on the security of valuables.
Share Certificate A certificate stating that you own part of a company.

Examination-Style Question and Solution

Question 1.

Answer all sections. This is a Cost of Borrowing Question.

On 1 January 1991 T. McKenna obtained the following information in respect of a Solara 20" colour television set (list price IR£499). An investigation into the position reveals her options to be:

Rental Only: IR£4.25 per week (one month's rental payable in advance). A minimum of a one-year contract must be taken out and it can thereafter be ended by one month's notice in writing by either side.

Rental Purchase: A IR£50 deposit plus IR£15 per month for four years. At the end of that period the set could be purchased outright on payment of a further IR£10.

Cash Purchase: 20" Solara IR£449.

McKenna has saved IR£50 but has been told by the bank manager that she can borrow up to IR£400 on term loan. The term loan would be at the rate of IR£3.50 per month (including interest) for each IR£100 borrowed.

You are asked to:

1. (a) Calculate the cost of each of the three methods above for the period to 31 December 1994. **(18)**

1. (b) Recommend with reasons a particular method to T. McKenna. **(16)**

1. (c) Give three possible additional costs of T. McKenna having a TV set. **(6)**

Source: Junior Certificate Higher Level Sample Paper. **(40 marks)**

Solution to Question 1.

1. (a) *Cost of each of the three methods*

Rental Only	*52 weeks @ IR£4.25 = IR£221 x 4 yrs =*	*IR£884*
Rental Purchase	*Deposit IR£50*	
	IR£15 x 12 months = 180 x 4 yrs = IR£720	*IR£770*
Cash Purchase	*Cash price IR£449 Saved IR£50 Borrowing IR£400*	
	Cost of Borrowing IR£400 for 4 years @ IR£3.50 per IR£100	
	48 months x IR£3.50 = IR£168 x 4 = IR£672 + Deposit IR£50	
		IR£722

1. (b) *I would recommend that T. McKenna borrow the IR£400 and use the cash purchase method because:*

(i) It is the cheapest method.

(ii) It will give T. McKenna immediate ownership of the TV.

1. (c) *Three possible additional costs of having a TV set:*

(i) Increased insurance cover.

(ii) Television licence.

(iii) Service contract.

(iv) Increased ESB charges.

(v) Cost of cable and aerial.

PRACTICE QUESTION

(i) Question 17, Section A, Paper I, Higher Level, 1994.

Chapter 10 — Insurance

A. What Is Insurance?

Insurance is protection against a possible loss which we hope will not happen, e.g. a house going on fire or a car accident. A fee called a premium is paid to the insurance company for this cover.

B. How Insurance Works

It is based on the idea of many people paying premiums into an insurance company fund and any person who suffers a loss being able to claim compensation.

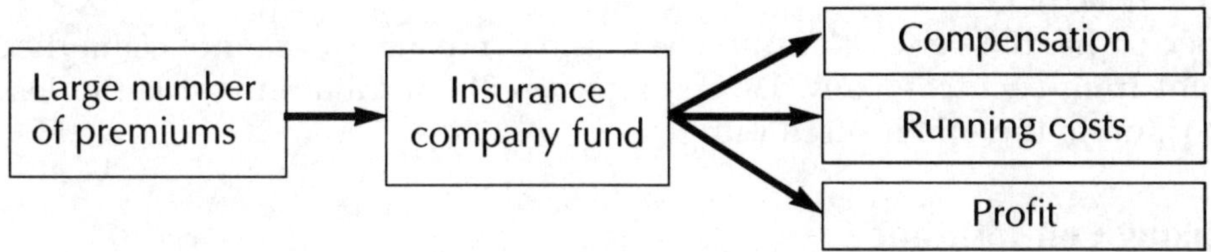

C. Risks

INSURABLE RISKS AND NON-INSURABLE RISKS

(1) Insurable risks are risks that can be insured against, e.g. house against fire and theft.

(2) Uninsurable risks are risks that cannot be insured against, e.g. damage caused by war or earthquakes, losses due to bad management.

D. Need for Adequate Insurance

Any insurance taken out by an individual or household should be adequate, it should cover **all risks** and be large enough to cover any loss that might occur.

E. Basic Principles of Insurance

Insurance operates under a set of basic rules called the basic principles of insurance. They are:

(1) Insurable interest
(2) Utmost good faith
(3) Indemnity
(4) Subrogation
(5) Contribution.

(1) INSURABLE INTEREST

In order to insure something you must have an **insurable interest** in the item. You must benefit by its existence and suffer financially by its loss, e.g. you can insure your house but not your neighbour's house.

(2) UTMOST GOOD FAITH

When completing a proposal form for insurance, you must answer all the questions truthfully and disclose all material facts/relevant information.

(3) INDEMNITY

You cannot make a profit out of insurance. The aim of insurance is to place the insured in the same position financially as before the loss and not in a better position.

(4) SUBROGATION

When an insurance company compensates the insured for the loss, it can proceed to claim compensation from the person who caused the loss; once compensation has been paid the damaged item becomes the property of the insurance company.

(5) CONTRIBUTION

If a person has the same risk insured with two companies he cannot claim the full amount from each company. Each company will contribute towards the loss in proportion to the sum insured with it.

F. Taking Out Insurance

Insurance is costly so it is in a person's interest to get the best possible quotation. You can do this by

(i) contacting insurance companies directly, or by
(ii) contacting an insurance broker who will get quotations from many companies.

(1) PROPOSAL FORM

This is an application form for insurance. All questions must be truthfully and accurately answered giving all relevant details — the principle of utmost good faith.

(2) ACTUARY

An actuary will assess the risk and calculate the premium.

(3) PREMIUM

This is the fee charged for insurance cover.

(4) POLICY

This is written evidence of the contract of insurance. It contains details of what risks are covered.

(5) COVER NOTE

Sometimes there may be a delay in the preparation of the policy. In the meantime the insurance company will issue a cover note. This provides evidence that insurance cover exists.

(6) CERTIFICATE OF INSURANCE

In motor insurance a certificate of insurance is issued. This is proof of the existence of insurance. A portion of this document called the insurance disc is detached and displayed on the windscreen of the car to show that the car is insured.

(7) RENEWAL NOTICE

This is notice to remind you that the next premium is due.

(8) DAYS OF GRACE

These are additional days given by the insurance company to pay the renewal premium from the due date. There are no days of grace in motor insurance.

G. Making a Claim

When a loss occurs and you want to claim compensation:

(1) Notify your insurance company and give them your policy number.

(2) The insurance company will send you a **claim form** to return giving details of the loss suffered.

(3) Obtain estimates and quotations for repairing the damage or replacing the loss.

(4) The insurance company will check your policy to make sure that the loss suffered was as a direct result of the insured risk. This is known as **proximate cause**.

(5) An **assessor** is then sent to examine the damage or loss and assess how much compensation should be paid.

(6) Claim may be settled by

- Cash.
- Replacement of item insured.
- Repair.
- Reinstatement.

H. Overinsured/Underinsured/Average Clause

(1) OVERINSURED

If you have overinsured you will receive only compensation amounting to market value of the item.

(2) UNDERINSURED

If you are underinsured and the item is completely destroyed you will receive only compensation amounting to the value for which the item is insured.

(3) AVERAGE CLAUSE — PARTIAL LOSS

Average clause applies in the case of a **partial** loss where the insurance cover is for less than the market value of the item lost, i.e. you are underinsured.

Example — Average Clause

House valued at IR£100,000 insured for IR£80,000.
Fire causes IR£10,000 worth of damage.

Q. How much compensation will be paid?

A. House is only eight-tenths, i.e. four-fifths, insured so the amount of compensation will be four-fifths of IR£10,000, which is IR£8,000.

NB If you are only partly insured you will receive only partial compensation.

I. Types of Insurance

There are four main categories of insurance for the household and the individual. They are:

Personal	Property	Motor	Life
Salary protection insurance Voluntary Health Insurance Personal accident insurance Sports injuries insurance Pay-Related Social Insurance Travel/Holiday insurance Wedding insurance	Fire insurance Burglary insurance All risks policy	Third party insurance Third party fire and theft Comprehensive insurance	Whole life assurance Endowment assurance Term assurance Mortgage protection plan

PERSONAL INSURANCE

(1) Salary Protection

Provides a payment of three-quarters of salary if you have to give up work because of accident or illness.

(2) Voluntary Health Insurance (VHI)

Covers the cost of consultants and hospital bills.

(3) Personal Accident Insurance

Insures you against accidents.

(4) Sports Injuries Insurance

Covers loss of income and the cost of medical bills if you are injured while involved in sport.

(5) Pay-Related Social Insurance (PRSI)

Covers loss of income due to illness or unemployment.

(6) Travel/Holiday Insurance

Covers goods and luggage stolen while travelling on holidays and medical bills.

(7) Wedding Insurance

Covers the risk of the hotel being overbooked, or the wedding being cancelled, or the photographs or video not developing for some reason.

PROPERTY INSURANCE

(1) Fire Insurance

Covers building and contents against fire, or flooding or storm damage.

(2) Burglary Insurance

Covers theft or damage to contents as a result of a break-in.

(3) All Risks Policy

Householders can also take out an all risks policy which covers fire, burglary, public liability, as well as other risks such as storm damage, flooding, etc.

MOTOR INSURANCE

Car insurance is compulsory under the Road Traffic Act 1934.

(1) Third Party Insurance

This policy covers damage to others, their medical bills and damage to their property (car) that may arise as a result of an accident for which you are responsible. It does not cover damage to insured's own vehicle nor insured's medical bills.

(2) Third Party, Fire and Theft Insurance

This covers third party claims and also damage to your vehicle as a result of a fire or loss of your vehicle as a result of theft.

(3) Comprehensive Insurance

This policy is more expensive as it covers more risks. As well as third parties and their property (car), fire and theft, it covers damage to the policy holder's own vehicle and also the policy holder's medical expenses which may arise as a result of an accident he himself has caused.

LIFE ASSURANCE

Life assurance is there to help families who lose the income earner through death. Life assurance covers risks that definitely happen — death.

(1) Whole life assurance

The assured pays premiums for the rest of his life. When the assured dies a lump sum is paid to his dependants.

(2) Endowment policy

The assured pays premiums up to a certain age, e.g. sixty years. The lump sum is paid on the assured reaching this age or on death of assured, whichever comes first.

(3) Term assurance

This is where a policy is taken out for a specified period of time, e.g. ten years. If the assured dies within the ten years his dependants will receive the lump sum. If the assured lives past the ten years no payment is made. This type of policy is often used as security for a term loan.

(4) Mortgage protection policy

This policy is taken out by all mortgage holders. If the mortgage holder dies before the mortgage is paid the policy will clear the mortgage and the house will become the property of the mortgage holder's dependants.

SURRENDER VALUE

This arises where a policy holder decides to stop paying the premiums on a life assurance policy. The policy can be cancelled, usually after about two years, and a sum of money known as surrender value will be paid to the policy holder. However, it will be much less than the value of the premiums paid.

J. Calculating Insurance Premiums

The premium to be paid for insurance cover will be calculated by an actuary. The amount of the premium will depend on many things.

(i) Value of item.
(ii) The risk involved.

(iii) Age of insured.
(iv) The loadings on the policy.
(v) The amount of no claims bonus (car insurance).

(1) MOTOR INSURANCE PREMIUMS

The **basic premium** is based on type of cover required, value and age of car, cubic capacity of engine.

Loadings are added for: provisional licence, first insurance, being under twenty-five, urban address, use of car for business, accident record.

Deductions of the basic premium plus loading may be made for: non-drinker, no claims bonus, full licence.

Premium = basic + loadings – deductions.

Question — Calculation of Motor Insurance Premium

The Allied United Insurance Company quotes the following for car insurance: third party IR£30 per IR£1,000 car value; fire and theft IR£5 per IR£1,000; comprehensive IR£70 per IR£1,000.

Loadings: Provisional licence 20%; first insurance 30%; urban address 20%; being under twenty-five 25%; use of car for business 25%.

Deductions: Non-drinker 10%; no claims bonus 20%; full licence 10%.

John Kelly is seeking his first insurance. He is a travelling salesman living in Galway. He is twenty-four years old. He drives a car valued at IR£10,000. He has a full licence and an accident-free record. He is a non-drinker and has a full no claims bonus. He requires comprehensive insurance. Calculate his motor insurance premium.

Solution	Basic premium IR£70 x 10			**IR£700**
	Loadings:	Use of car for business 700 x 25%	IR£175	
		Urban address 700 x 20%	IR£140	
		Under twenty-five years 700 x 25%	IR£175	
		First insurance 700 x 30%	IR£210	IR£700
				IR£1,400
	Less Deductions:	Non-drinker 1,400 x 10%	IR£140	
		No claims bonus 1,400 x 20%	IR£280	
		Full licence 1,400 x 10%	IR£140	IR£560
	TOTAL PREMIUM DUE			**IR£840**

Loading: An amount added on to the premium because of an additional risk, e.g. being under twenty-five years of age.

No Claims Bonus: If the insured has an accident-free record and does not make a claim during the year, the next premium will be reduced by a certain percentage.

(2) HOUSE INSURANCE PREMIUMS

Basic premium is based on the value of the house and its contents.

Loadings may be added for residing in an urban area.

Deductions may be made for having a burglar alarm, for having a smoke detector, and for being part of a community alert scheme.

Question — Calculation of House Insurance Premium

The Western Insurance Company quotes the following for house insurance:
Buildings IR£4 per IR£1,000
Contents IR£6 per IR£1,000

Loadings: Urban area 20%.

Deductions: Approved alarm 10%; smoke detector 5%; residing in community alert area 5%.

Joe and Maria Kelleher wish to insure their house for IR£70,000 and contents for IR£30,000. They live in Cork city. They have an approved alarm fitted and a smoke detector. Calculate their insurance premium.

Solution	Buildings 70,000 x IR£4 per IR£1,000	IR£280	
	Contents 30,000 x IR£6 per IR£1,000	IR£180	IR£460
	Loadings: Urban area 460 x 20%		IR£92
			IR£552
	Deductions: Alarm system 552 x 10% =	IR£55.20	
	Smoke detector 552 x 5% =	IR£27.60	IR£82.80
	TOTAL PREMIUM DUE		IR£469.20

HOW TO REDUCE COST OF HOUSEHOLD INSURANCE

(1) Fit a burglar alarm/fire alarm.
(2) Install a smoke detector.
(3) Become part of a community alert scheme.

(3) LIFE ASSURANCE PREMIUMS

Basic premium is calculated by referring to a ready reckoner which will give a figure per IR£1,000 lump sum payable on death.

The figure will depend on age, gender, whether you are a smoker/non-smoker.

Loadings: Premium may be loaded for medical history, dangerous occupation, dangerous hobbies and sporting interests.

Question — Calculation of Life Assurance Premium

Irish Assurance Company quotes the following: male aged thirty-five years, non-smoker — IR£9.72 per IR£1,000, lump sum payable in twenty years time.

Loadings: Medical condition 10%, dangerous occupation 10%, dangerous hobbies 5%.

Denis is a bomb disposal expert. He is aged thirty-five and a non-smoker. He wants to take out an endowment life assurance policy for IR£200,000 payable in twenty years time. He had a bypass heart operation two years ago. In his spare time he likes parachuting. Calculate his life assurance premium.

Solution	Basic premium IR£9.72 x 200		=	IR£1,944
	Loadings: Medical condition 10%	IR£194.40		
	Dangerous occupation 10%	IR£194.40		
	Dangerous hobby 5%	IR£97.20		IR£486
	TOTAL PREMIUMS DUE		=	IR£2,430 p.a.

K. Benefits of Insurance

(1) Life assurance provides a lump sum payment to the assured's dependants on death of assured.
(2) Life assurance is a form of saving.
(3) A life assurance policy can be used as security for a loan.
(4) Insurance gives everyone protection against loss or damage.

L. Insurance Companies Operating in Ireland

(1) Irish Life Assurance
(2) New PMPA Insurance Company
(3) New Ireland Assurance Company
(4) Hibernian Insurance Company
(5) Church & General Insurance Company

Examination-Style Questions and Solutions

Question 1.
Answer all sections. This is an Insurance Question.

The Noonan family purchased their first house recently with the help of a building society mortgage. They paid IR£45,000 for their home and they have spent IR£15,000 on furniture and fittings.

Tom and Mary are now wondering about insurance and ask for your advice. They want to know the following.

1. (a) Are they required by law to insure the family property? (Give an explanation for your answer.) **(4)**

1. (b) Tom and Mary want you to calculate the total premium they would have to pay using the following information. It costs 20p for each IR£100 of buildings insured and 90p for each IR£100 of contents insured. (Show your workings.) **(10)**

1. (c) The Noonans think that the premium is very high, especially for the contents. They are now thinking of insuring the contents for just IR£10,000. They do not see the point of insuring the contents for the full value.

Show what compensation they would get if they had the contents insured for just IR£10,000 and if, as a result of a small fire, IR£3,000 worth of contents were destroyed. **(16)**

1. (d) Tom and Mary are also considering taking out life assurance but they know very little about it. Explain briefly for them the following:

(i) The difference between insurance and assurance;

(ii) The difference between a Whole Life Assurance policy and an Endowment Policy. **(10)**

Source: Junior Certificate Higher Level 1992. **(40 marks)**

Solution to Question 1.

1. (a) *No. The only insurance that is compulsory by law is motor vehicle insurance. Property insurance is optional.*

1. (b) *Building valued at IR£45,000*

45,000 ÷ 100 = 450 x 20p = IR£90

Furniture and fittings valued at IR£15,000

15,000 ÷ 100 = 150 x 90p = IR£135

Total premium = IR£225

1. (c) *Contents are insured for only two-thirds of their value*

$$\left(\frac{10,000}{15,000} = 2/3\right)$$

2/3 of 3,000 = IR£2,000

Compensation paid will be IR£2,000.

1. (d) *(i) Insurance — is protection against events which might happen, e.g. fire.*

Assurance — is protection against something that will happen, e.g. death.

(ii) Whole Life Assurance — pay premiums for rest of life, lump sum is payable on death only.

Endowment policy — sum of money is paid after agreed number of years or on death, whichever comes first.

Question 2.

Answer all sections. This is an Insurance Question.

2. (a) Explain the difference between insurable and non-insurable risks. (Give **one** example of each.) **(10)**

2. (b) Before taking out insurance, a person must complete a proposal form. State **three** pieces of information that must be answered in the proposal form for house insurance. **(12)**

2. (c) What do insurance companies mean by the term '**insurable interest**'? Explain briefly. **(6)**

2. (d) John and Mary O'Brien live in their own house, have a family car and are both employed in full-time jobs.

(i) What insurance cover, if any, are they required to have by law? **(6)**

(ii) State two other insurance/assurance policies which you would recommend to them. **(6)**

Source: Junior Certificate Higher Level 1993. **(40 marks)**

Solution to Question 2.

2. (a) *Insurable risk — a risk that you can get insurance cover for, e.g. fire, burglary, accident.*

Non-insurable risk — a risk that you cannot get insurance cover for. The insurance companies will not take on the risk proposed, e.g. losses due to bad management.

2. (b) *Proposal Form*

(i) Personal details (name, address, etc.)
(ii) Details of risk required to be covered.
(iii) Sum insured.
(iv) Any previous claims.
(v) Signature of applicant.

2. (c) *Insurable Interest*

You must have a financial interest in the item that is to be insured. You must gain by its existence and suffer by its loss.

2. (d) *(i) Third party car insurance and PRSI.*

(ii) House buildings insurance, house contents insurance, life assurance, VHI, personal accident insurance, salary protection insurance, serious illness insurance.

PRACTICE QUESTION

(i) Question 6, Section B, Ordinary Level, 1993.

SECTION TWO — ECONOMIC AWARENESS

NATIONAL BUSINESS

Chapter 11 — Economic Framework

A. Needs and Wants
An individual or family has three **basic needs** to survive: food, shelter and clothing. Once these needs are satisfied, people **want** other things, like cars, TVs, videos, big houses.

B. Scarcity and Choice
To produce the goods that people need and want four things are required: **land**, **money**, **workers** and someone with the **idea**. It is not possible to produce everything we need and want because resources are scarce. Thus choices must be made about which goods and services are to be produced.

C. Economics
Economics is the study of how scarce resources are used to produce the goods and services that people need and want.

D. Ireland's Economic Resources/Factors of Production
There are four main resources in the country used to produce goods and services. These resources are called factors of production and are **land**, **labour**, **capital** and **enterprise**.

FACTORS OF PRODUCTION

Factors of Production	Explanation of Factors of Production	Payment for Use of Factor/Reward
1. Land	All things supplied by nature for producing goods, i.e. land, sea, rivers, mines, gas fields, forests. From these we get raw materials which are made into finished goods.	Anyone with land is paid **rent** for the use of the land.
2. Labour	People employed to produce the goods or provide the service.	People are paid **wages** for the work they do.
3. Capital	Money invested to run a business. This money is used to buy or build factories, equipment, machinery needed to convert raw materials into finished goods.	People who provide money are paid **interest** for the use of their money.
4. Enterprise	Someone who has a business idea and is willing to take the risk of setting up a business is called an entrepreneur.	If the business is successful the person gets a **profit** as payment for taking the risk of running a business.

E. Opportunity Cost/Making a Choice

Because resources are scarce, choices have to be made when producing goods. When it is decided to produce one product the opportunity cost is the other products that cannot be produced.

F. Economic Systems

Each country wants to make best use of its scarce resources so choices must be made:

(i) What goods and services are to be produced.
(ii) Who will produce the goods and services.

The amount of choice that individuals or businesspeople have depends on the economic system that the country has.

There are three main economic systems:

(1) FREE ENTERPRISE ECONOMY

Consumers decide what they want to buy. Producers will supply the goods that people demand. Most choices are made by individuals and entrepreneurs and there is little government involvement, e.g. USA.

(2) CENTRALLY PLANNED ECONOMY

Government decides what goods are to be produced and individuals are given no say, e.g. China.

(3) MIXED ECONOMY

Mixed economy countries have a large amount of government intervention and a large amount of private enterprise. Many decisions are made by the government and individuals are free to choose the goods and services they require, e.g. Ireland.

G. Economic Growth

The total amount of goods and services produced in a country in a year is called Gross National Product (GNP).

If this total amount of goods and services produced (GNP) increases from that of the previous year, the country has economic growth.

FORMULA FOR CALCULATING ECONOMIC GROWTH

$$\text{Economic growth} = \frac{\text{Increase in production (GNP)} \times 100\%}{\text{Last year's production (GNP)}}$$

Example

Total production of goods and services 1994 = IR£600 million
Total production of goods and services 1995 = IR£620 million

$$\text{Economic growth} = \frac{20\text{m} \times 100\%}{600\text{m}} = 3.3\%$$

Economic growth can sometimes be negative. When this happens, the country is said to be in a **recession**.

Ireland's rate of economic growth is about 3%.

HOW CAN A COUNTRY ACHIEVE ECONOMIC GROWTH?

(1) Keep inflation down.
(2) Keep interest rates down.
(3) Keep government borrowing down.
(4) Increase exports.

ADVANTAGES OF ECONOMIC GROWTH

(1) Higher standard of living for people.
(2) More employment will be created and workers will earn more.

H. Inflation

Inflation means rising prices. Rising prices means that the cost of living is increasing, i.e. cost of food, clothes, fuel is increasing.

Consumer Price Index (CPI) is used to measure inflation. This is a list of goods and their prices which is compared from one period to the next.

FORMULA FOR CALCULATING RATE OF INFLATION

$$\text{Rate of inflation} = \frac{\text{Increase in price x 100}}{\text{Previous price}}$$

Example Cost of living 1994 IR£9,000
Cost of living 1995 IR£9,275

$$\text{Rate of inflation} = \frac{\text{IR£275 x 100}}{\text{IR£9,000}} = 3\%$$

Ireland's rate of inflation was around 3% in the mid-1990s.

CAUSES OF INFLATION

(1) **Demand Pull Inflation** = Demand > Supply ⇛ Prices rise.
(2) **Cost Push Inflation** = Cost of production increases ⇛ Prices rise.
(3) Cost of imported raw materials rising, e.g. oil.

ADVANTAGES OF LOW INFLATION TO A COUNTRY

(1) Economic growth is aided.
(2) Cost of living is kept down.
(3) Goods can be produced much more cheaply so it will be easier to sell them abroad.

I. Business Terms

Basic Needs Things necessary for survival: food, clothes, shelter.
Centrally Planned Economy Government decides what goods are produced.

Cost Push Inflation Increased costs push up price.
CPI Consumer Price Index. Shows changes in the cost of living.
Deflation Falling prices.
Demand Pull Inflation Excess demand pulls up price.
Economic Goods Products that people want and are prepared to pay money for.
Economic Growth An increase in Gross National Product from one year to the next.
Economist A person who studies economics.
Entrepreneur A person with a business idea who is willing to take a risk.
Factors of Production Land, labour, capital, enterprise.
Free Enterprise Choices made by individuals and entrepreneurs — little government involvement.
GNP — Gross National Product Total goods and services produced by a country in a year.
Inflation Rising prices.
Mixed Economy Some private enterprise and some government intervention.
National Economy Whole country.
Opportunity Cost When one product is chosen another product must be sacrificed.
Profit The reward for enterprise.
Recession Where GNP declines from one period to the next.
Resources Things used to produce goods and services.
Third World Countries Poor/underdeveloped countries, e.g. India.
Wants Things that people would like to buy.
Wealth Stock of goods owned by an individual or country.

Examination-Style Question and Solution

Question 1.
Answer all sections. This is a Question on Inflation.

The Bar Graph below refers to the inflation rate of a country called SOMBIA.

Bar Graph of Inflation Rates (1989–1993)

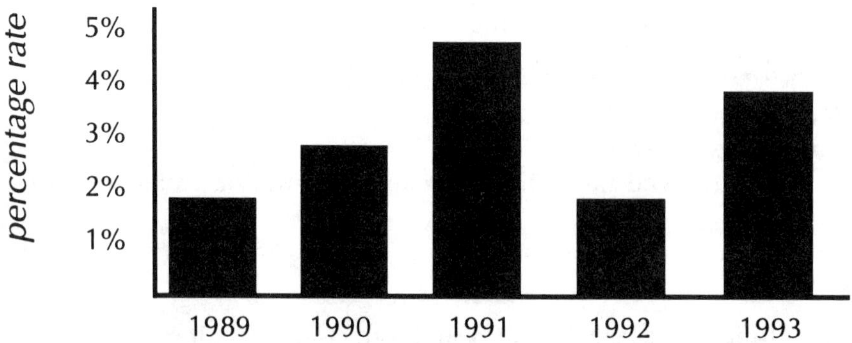

1. (a) Explain what is meant by the term **inflation.** (4)
1. (b) Calculate the average rate of inflation for the five years shown in the graph above. (4)
1. (c) What change occurred in the rate of inflation in 1992 compared to 1991? (4)
1. (d) Give **one** economic benefit to Ireland of having its inflation rate lower than that of its main trading competitors. (4)

Source: Junior Certificate Higher Level 1994.

Solution to Question 1.

1. (a) *An increase in the general level of prices from one period to the next.*

OR

An increase in the cost of living from one year to the next.

1. (b) *3.2%.*

1. (c) *Fell by 3%.*

1. (d) *(i) Irish goods will be more competitive on the Irish market and on foreign markets.*
(ii) Stronger Punt.
(iii) More employment.
(iv) More foreign investment.
(v) Better balance of payments.

PRACTICE QUESTIONS

(i) Question 3, Section A, Ordinary Level, 1994.
(ii) Question 7, Section B, Sample Paper.
(iii) Question 14, Section A, Paper I, Higher Level, 1994.

Chapter 12 — National Budgeting

A. National Budget

(1) A national budget is a **plan** of government **income** and **expenditure** for the country.
(2) The government plans where the income will come from and how the money will be spent (expenditure).
(3) Each government department **estimates** how much money it will need to run the department for the year.
(4) The **Department of Finance** decides how much each department can spend for the year ahead.
(5) The Department of Finance also decides how it is going to find this money.
(6) The **Minister for Finance** makes the budget speech in the Dáil on the last Wednesday of January each year telling the nation about the budget.

B. Government Budgets

The government must prepare two budgets:
(1) **Current Budget:** This outlines the expenditure needed to run the country on a day-to-day basis and where income to finance this will come from.
(2) **Capital Budget:** This outlines the expenditure on capital projects (long-term projects) and where the income to finance these projects will come from.

C. Current Budget

(1) CURRENT EXPENDITURE

This is expenditure on the day-to-day running of the country.
(a) **Wages and salaries** of civil servants, teachers, gardaí, army, prison officers.
(b) **Social welfare benefits**, e.g. unemployment benefit, old age pensions, children's allowances, etc.
(c) **Running costs of government departments**, e.g. telephone, stationery, heating and lighting.
(d) **Interest on borrowings**, i.e. national debt. Interest must be paid on money borrowed by the government over the years.

(2) CURRENT INCOME

This is income received by the government on a regular basis (monthly/annually) and it is used to cover current expenditure. The main sources of current income are set out below, the principal one being taxation.

TAXATION REVENUE

(a) **Income Tax:** Tax paid by all workers through the PAYE system.
(b) **Value Added Tax (VAT):** Tax on goods and services.
(c) **Customs Duties:** Tax on goods coming into the country.

(d) Excise Duties: Tax on certain goods produced in the country, e.g. whiskey, petrol, cigarettes, beer.
(e) Corporation Tax: Tax on company profit.
(f) Deposit Interest Retention Tax (DIRT): Tax on interest earned in a deposit account.

NON-TAX REVENUE

(a) Profit from state firms, e.g. Telecom Éireann.
(b) EC grants.
(c) Lottery funds.

D. Balancing Current Budget

(1) BALANCED BUDGET

Current expenditure = Current income
e.g. IR£10,600m IR£10,600m.

(2) BUDGET SURPLUS

Current expenditure < Current income
e.g. IR£10,200m IR£10,600m

Budget surplus = IR£400m.

WHAT CAN THE GOVERNMENT DO WITH A BUDGET SURPLUS?

(a) Reduce taxation.
(b) Increase social welfare.
(c) Pay off some of the national debt.
(d) Put some of the surplus towards capital expenditure, thus reducing borrowing.
(e) Increase spending in some departments to give a better service, e.g. health and education.

(3) BUDGET DEFICIT

Current expenditure > Current income
e.g. IR£10,200m IR£10,000m

Budget deficit IR£200m.

HOW CAN THE GOVERNMENT ELIMINATE A BUDGET DEFICIT?

(a) Increase taxation.
(b) Reduce expenditure by cutting back on some services.
(c) Borrow the amount of the shortfall.

E. Capital Budget

(1) CAPITAL EXPENDITURE

This is money spent on long-term projects, e.g. new roads, new schools, new hospitals, airports, railway stations. These items are called the **infrastructure** of the state.

PUBLIC UTILITIES

Much of the government spending is on services that are essential for the efficient running of the state, e.g. roads, railways, airports, harbours, ports, telephone, electricity, gas, water, sewerage, postal service, schools, hospitals.

(2) CAPITAL INCOME

This is income received 'once only' and is used for capital expenditure. Borrowing is the main source of capital income. Capital income has also been received by the government from the **sale of state companies** to private shareholders, called **privatisation**.

F. Balancing Capital Budget

The capital budget will always balance because the amount of capital expenditure will be matched by capital income and borrowing.

G. National Debt

National debt is the **total amount of money that has been borrowed** by the government over the years. Interest has to be paid on this debt and it is very high.

H. Local Authorities

County councils and corporations provide many services in the local area, e.g. water supply, sewerage schemes, refuse collection. They get most of their income from central government but they also charge for their services. These charges are known as service charges, e.g. service charges for water supply and refuse collection.

I. Business Terms

Balanced Budget Government income is equal to government expenditure.

Book of Estimates Book published by government showing how much each government department needs to spend for the year.

Budget Deficit Government expenditure is greater than government income.

Budget Surplus Government income is greater than government expenditure.

Capital Expenditure Government expenditure on long-term projects, i.e. roads, schools, etc.

Capital Income Income received by the government on a once-off basis.

Corporation Tax Tax on company profits.

Current Expenditure Expenditure on day-to-day running of the country.

Current Income Income received by the government on a regular basis.

Debt Servicing Paying interest on the national debt.

Department of Finance The department in charge of government money.

Excise Duty Tax on certain home-produced goods, e.g. whiskey.

Local Authorities The bodies that provide essential services in local areas.

Minister for Finance The person in charge of Department of Finance.

National Debt Total amount of money borrowed by government.

Public Utilities Essential services provided by the government, e.g. roads, harbours, water supply.
Rates Tax on business property paid to local authority.
VAT Tax on goods and services.

Examination-Style Questions and Solutions

Question 1.

1. (a) Prepare the National Budget for 1991 from the following details:

Income: Income Tax IR£3,200m; EC and Other Receipts IR£2,100m; VAT IR£2,100m; Customs and Excise IR£1,900m; Corporation Tax IR£500m; Capital Tax IR£100m; Other Receipts IR£1,000m.

Expenditure: Security IR£800m; Social Welfare IR£3,000m; Education IR£1,368m; Health IR£1,400m; Agriculture IR£400m; Debt Service IR£2,432m; Miscellaneous IR£2,000m. **(8)**

1. (b) Was this budget a surplus or a deficit budget? **(3)**
1. (c) (i) What was the main source of government income?
(ii) What percentage of total expenditure was spent on education?
(iii) Give two examples of expenditure on security. **(6)**
1. (d) If you were Minister for Finance suggest two changes you might make to the above budget. Give your reasons. **(6)**
1. (e) If inflation increased total expenditure by 5% and VAT was down by 10%, what effect would these have on the budget outcome? (Show your workings.) **(8)**
1. (f) Explain two effects of the increasing level of unemployment on the national budget. **(9)**

Source: Junior Certificate Sample Paper Higher Level. **(40 marks)**

Solution to Question 1.

1. (a) **National Budget for 1991**

Income	IR£m	Expenditure	IR£m
Income Tax	3,200	Security	800
EC and Other Receipts	2,100	Social Welfare	3,000
VAT	2,100	Education	1,368
Customs and Excise	1,900	Health	1,400
Corporation Tax	500	Agriculture	400
Capital Tax	100	Debt Service	2,432
Other Receipts	1,000	Miscellaneous	2,000
Total Income	10,900	Total Expenditure	11,400

INCOME – EXPENDITURE
10,900 – 11,400 = (IR£500m)

1. (b) *This was a deficit budget.*

1. (c) *(i) Main source of income was income tax.*

(ii) Percentage spent on education:

$$\text{Formula} = \frac{\text{Education spending} \times 100}{\text{Total expenditure}}$$

$$\frac{1{,}368 \times 100}{11{,}400} = 12\%$$

(iii) Security spending: gardaí, army, navy.

1. (d)

ACTION	REASON
(i) Reduce income tax.	*(i) Employees paying too much tax.*
(ii) Increase corporation and capital gains tax.	*(ii) Business not paying fair share of tax.*
(iii) Spend more on education.	*(iii) Provide youth with good education.*

1. (e) *Inflation increased total expenditure by 5%.*

Inflation 5% of IR£11,400m	*IR£570m.*
Expenditure increased by	*IR£570m.*
New expenditure figure would be	*IR£11,970.*
VAT reduction by 10%.	
10% of IR£2,100m	*IR£210m.*
Income reduced by	*IR£210m.*
New income total	*IR£10,690m.*

New budget deficit would be IR£1,280m (IR£10,690m – IR£11,970m).

1. (f) *Two effects of increasing level of unemployment:*

(i) Income from income tax will decrease.

(ii) Expenditure on social welfare will increase.

Question 2.

Answer all sections. This is a Government Income and Expenditure Question.

The estimated government current budget for 1993 is as follows:

Government current income IR£9,796
Government current expenditure IR£10,366

Answer the following questions:

2. (a) What is the amount of the difference in the two figures given, and what is the economic term used to describe this difference? **(8)**

2. (b) Which government department prepares the National Budget? **(4)**

2. (c) Give **two** examples of government **current income** and **two** examples of government **current expenditure.** (8)

2. (d) State **three ways** in which a government could use a current budget surplus. (12)

2. (e) Give **one** example of government **capital expenditure** and **one** example of government **capital income.** (8)

Source: Junior Certificate Higher Level 1993. **(40 marks)**

Solution to Question 2.

2. (a) *IR£570 million — budget deficit.*

2. (b) *Department of Finance.*

2. (c)

CURRENT INCOME	CURRENT EXPENDITURE
(i) Income tax. *(ii) VAT, DIRT.* *(iii) EC grant.* *(iv) Profit from state companies.* *(v) Lottery surplus.* *(vi) Other indirect taxes.*	*(i) Salaries of teachers, nurses, gardaí, etc.* *(ii) Social welfare payments.* *(iii) Interest on government borrowings.* *(iv) Heating and maintenance of government buildings.*

2. (d) *Ways in which a government could use a current budget surplus:*
(i) Reduce taxation.
(ii) Increase current expenditure.
(iii) Finance capital expenditure.
(iv) A mixture of all three above.

2. (e)

CAPITAL EXPENDITURE	CAPITAL INCOME
(i) New roads. *(ii) New hospitals.* *(iii) New schools.* *(iv) New equipment.*	*(i) Sale of state companies.* *(ii) Borrowing.*

PRACTICE QUESTIONS

(i) Question 7, Section B, Ordinary Level, 1994.
(ii) Question 10, Section A, Paper I, Higher Level, 1993.
(iii) Question 12, Section A, Paper I, Higher Level, 1994.

Chapter 13 — Foreign Trade

A. Foreign Trade

Foreign trade occurs when Ireland buys goods and services from other countries or sells goods and services to other countries.

B. Importing

(1) VISIBLE IMPORTS

These are **goods** that Ireland buys from other countries, e.g. cars, oil, fruit, coffee, wine, clothes.

(2) INVISIBLE IMPORTS

These are **services** that Ireland buys from other countries, e.g. Irish students going abroad on a school tour. Irish money goes to a foreign country.

(3) WHY DOES IRELAND IMPORT GOODS AND SERVICES?

(a) Unsuitable climate, e.g. oranges, bananas, tea.
(b) Raw materials required for production, e.g. oil, coal, steel.
(c) Irish consumers want **variety.**
(d) Certain countries have **natural skills**, e.g. French wines.

(4) SOURCES AND TYPES OF IMPORTS

SOURCES OF IMPORTS	VISIBLE IMPORTS (GOODS)	INVISIBLE IMPORTS (SERVICES)
1992 — IR£13,195m	Food	Foreign entertainers on tour in Ireland
UK 38.9% = IR£5,132m	Oil, petrol, coal	Irish students on foreign school tours
USA 14.27% = IR£1,873m	Chemicals	Irish people holidaying abroad
Germany 8.4% = IR£1,108m	Clothes and footwear	Irish people travelling on foreign ships or airlines
Japan 5.0% = IR£659m	Electrical goods	Irish people borrowing from a foreign bank
France 4.5% = IR£593m	Timber	Irish people getting insurance from a foreign insurance company
Netherlands 4.4% = IR£580m	Computers/Transport equipment	
Italy 2.4% = IR£316m	Machinery, communication equipment	
Belgium and Luxembourg 2% = IR£277m		
Other EU states 5.9% 778m		
All other areas 14.3% 1,886m		

NB Irish money goes to a foreign country.

C. Exporting

(1) VISIBLE EXPORTS

These are **goods** that Ireland sells to other countries, e.g. meat, dairy products, live animals, chemicals.

(2) INVISIBLE EXPORTS

These are **services** that Ireland sells to other countries, e.g. Spanish students coming to Ireland to learn English during the summer. Foreign money comes into Ireland.

(3) WHY DOES IRELAND EXPORT GOODS AND SERVICES?

(a) To **earn foreign money** to pay for imports.
(b) The Irish market is too small.
(c) Surplus production, e.g. beef.
(d) Demand for Irish products by consumers abroad, e.g. Kerrygold butter.

(4) DESTINATIONS AND TYPES OF EXPORTS

DESTINATIONS OF EXPORTS	VISIBLE EXPORTS (GOODS)	INVISIBLE EXPORTS (SERVICES)
1992 — IR£16,629m UK 26.5% = IR£4,406m USA 8.2% = IR£1,363m Germany 12.7% = IR£2,111m Japan 2.9% = IR£482m France 9.6% = IR£1,596m Netherlands 7.0% = IR£1,164m Italy 4.1% = IR£681m Belgium and Luxembourg 4.9% = IR£814m Other EU states 9.3% = IR£1,546m All other areas 14.7% = IR£2,444m	Live animals Meat Dairy products Food products Chemical and pharmaceuticals Engineering products Computer equipment Scientific equipment	Irish entertainers giving concerts abroad A foreigner taking out insurance with an Irish company Foreigners borrowing money from an Irish bank Irish people working abroad and sending money to Ireland Foreign travellers using Irish airlines or Irish ferries

NB Foreign money comes into Ireland.

(5) STATE INVOLVEMENT IN EXPORTING

The state organisation An Bord Tráchtála — the Irish Trade Board — assists Irish exports in the following ways:

(a) Provides information on foreign markets, shipping and transport.
(b) Arranges meetings with foreign buyers.
(c) Provides information on trade regulations, packaging and language.
(d) Organises trade fairs and exhibitions abroad.
(e) Arranges training courses for salespeople.

D. European Union

The EEC was established in 1957 with the aim of eliminating **trade barriers between member states**. This means there is **'free trade'** between the members. Ireland joined in 1973. The EU is now a group of fifteen members. The European Union came into force on 1 November 1993 following the ratification of the Maastricht Treaty by all twelve members. The aim is to promote democracy, peace, prosperity and a fairer distribution of wealth. In March 1994 accession talks with Austria,

Finland and Sweden were successfully concluded and they joined the EU on 1 January 1995.

E. Aims of EU

(1) **Free trade** between member countries.
(2) **Free movement of people** between member countries.
(3) **Free movement of money** between member states.
(4) **Common currency.**
(5) To provide **financial assistance** to the less prosperous regions of the EU.

F. Single European Act

The Single European Act came into effect on 1 January 1993 and all trade barriers were removed.

The effect of this is:
(1) Irish people can look for work in any EU country.
(2) Less delay at border checkpoints, and customs documents will not be required.
(3) Irish people will be able to save/borrow money from any bank in any EU state.
(4) Irish people will be able to take out insurance in any member state.
(5) Taxes throughout the EU will be the same.
(6) Businesses can set up wherever they wish within the EU.

G. Benefits of EU Membership to Ireland

(1) Access to a European market — 350 million.
(2) EU finance — farmers and industry.
(3) EU finance — infrastructure, i.e. roads, communications, etc.

H. European Union, Countries, Currency, Language

COUNTRY	DATE JOINED	CURRENCY	LANGUAGE
France	1957	Franc (FF)	French
Germany	1957	Deutschmark (DM)	German
Italy	1957	Lira	Italian
Belgium	1957	Belgian Franc	French/Flemish
Netherlands	1957	Guilder	Dutch
Luxembourg	1957	Franc	French/German
United Kingdom	1973	Pound Sterling (£)	English
Ireland	1973	Punt (IR£)	English/Irish
Denmark	1973	Krone	Danish
Greece	1981	Drachma	Greek
Spain	1986	Peseta	Spanish
Portugal	1986	Escudo	Portuguese
Austria	1995	Schilling	German
Finland	1995	Markka	Finnish/Swedish
Sweden	1995	Krona	Swedish

I. Rate of Exchange

Every country has its own currency. If you want to buy goods or services from another country or travel to another country you must convert your IR£ (Punts) into that currency. Foreign currency can be bought at banks, building societies and Bureaux de Change. The cost of this currency is the rate of exchange.

BUYING FOREIGN CURRENCY
Use 'Sell at' rate.

Example

John touring Germany wishes to convert IR£200 into Deutschmarks.
'Sell at' rate: 2.60, 'Buy at' rate: 2.74.
This means that for every IR£1 John will get 2.60 DM.

Formula: Converting IR£ to foreign currency
Multiply IR£ x bank sell rate

Answer: IR£200 x 2.60 DM = 520 DM.

SELLING FOREIGN CURRENCY
Use 'Buy at' rate.

Example

John has 25 DM left on returning from Germany. He wishes to convert it back to Punts.
'Sell at' rate: 2.60, 'Buy at' rate: 2.74.
This means that for 2.74 DM John will get IR£1.

Formula: Converting currency into IR£
Divide foreign currency by bank buy rate

Answer: 25 DM ÷ 2.74 DM = IR£9.12.

J. Balance of Trade — Higher Level

Balance of Trade = Visible Exports – Visible Imports.
If visible exports > visible imports we have a surplus.
If visible exports < visible imports we have a deficit.

K. Balance of Payments — Higher Level

Balance of payments is the difference between all money coming into a country (total exports) and all money going out of a country (total imports).

Balance of payments = total exports – total imports.
If total exports > total imports — surplus on balance of payments.
If total exports < total imports — deficit on balance of payments.

Example — Higher Level
Visible exports IR£16,629m. Invisible exports IR£900m.
Visible imports IR£13,195m. Invisible imports IR£970m.

BALANCE OF PAYMENTS:			IR£
Balance of Trade	Visible exports		16,629m
	Visible imports		13,195m
	Balance of trade surplus		3,434m
Invisible Trade	Invisible imports	970m	
	Invisible exports	900m	
	Deficit on invisible trade		–70m
	Balance of payments surplus		3,364m

NB Balance of payments includes visible and invisible trade.

L. Business Terms

Balance of Payments Total exports – total imports.
Balance of Trade Visible exports – visible imports.
Bord Tráchtála Irish Export Board.
CAP Common Agricultural Policy.
Currency Money of a country.
Deficit Imports greater than exports.
Embargo Ban on certain imports.
EMU Economic and Monetary Union.
ERM Exchange Rate Mechanism.
EU European Union.
Exporting Selling goods and services to other countries.
Free Trade No duties to be paid on imports.
Import Substitution Producing goods in Ireland to replace imported goods.
Importing Buying goods and services from other countries.
Invisible Export Services sold abroad.
Invisible Import Services purchased from abroad.
Invisible Trade Services imported and exported.
Maastricht Treaty Treaty signed by twelve member states setting up the European Union.
Quota Limit on amount of goods imported.
Rate of Exchange Value of one currency in terms of another currency.
SEA — Single European Act Laid down framework for internal market.
Surplus Exports greater than imports.
Visible Export Physical goods sold abroad.
Visible Import Physical goods purchased from abroad.
Visible Trade Physical goods imported and exported.

G. Bar Code

- ➢ Series of parallel lines, thirteen digits.
- ➢ Shows country of origin, product number, company number, check digit.
- ➢ Records price — receipt is produced.
- ➢ Stock record reduced by one.

H. Business Terms

Loss Leader A product sold at a very low price to attract customers.

Price War Where shops selling similar products undercut each other to attract customers.

PRACTICE QUESTION

(i) Question 7, Paper I, Section A, Higher Level, 1994.

Chapter 6 — Consumer Rights and Protection

A. Why Do Consumers Need Protection?

To ensure that the standards of goods and services available to the public are reasonable and acceptable.

B. How Is the Consumer Protected?

- The government protects the consumer by passing **laws.**
- **Agencies** have been set up to inform and protect individual consumers.

C. Laws

WHAT ARE MY RIGHTS WHEN BUYING GOODS?

When you buy goods or services you enter into a contract with the seller. You pay your money and in return the seller is obliged to provide goods and services that meet certain conditions.

SALE OF GOODS AND SUPPLY OF SERVICES ACT 1980

This sets out the conditions with which goods and services must comply, which are as follows:

(1) Goods should be of **merchantable quality**.
(2) Goods should be **fit for their purpose**.
(3) Goods should be **as described.**
(4) If goods are bought by **sample** they should correspond with sample.
(5) Suppliers of services should:

(a) Have the **necessary skill** to provide the service, e.g. car mechanic.
(b) Provide the service with **proper care and diligence**.
(c) Ensure that **materials and parts** used in the service will be of **merchantable quality**.

(6) It is the **seller** who is responsible for putting things right.
(7) A **guarantee** is a bonus in addition to your normal legal rights. If you have a valid complaint it may be easier to claim under the guarantee. A guarantee is where the manufacturer/supplier undertakes to repair or replace any defective part without charge during the period of the guarantee, which is usually one year.
(8) If you buy goods in a **sale** they should be of merchantable quality fit for purpose and as described.
(9) It does not matter whether you pay **cash**, buy on **credit**, **rent**, or buy on **hire purchase**, the goods must be of merchantable quality, fit for purpose and as described.
(10) If you buy a **motor car** it should be of merchantable quality, fit for purpose and as described. You have a right to expect that the car is safe — free from any fault that would make it a danger to the public or to anyone in the car.

(11) Illegal Shop Notices:

NO MONEY REFUNDED

CREDIT NOTES ONLY

NO LIABILITY ACCEPTED FOR FAULTY GOODS

GOODS WILL NOT BE EXCHANGED

These notices are illegal and should not be displayed. You are not bound to accept a credit note. If your complaint is valid you can refuse all offers of a credit note and insist on a cash refund.

CONSUMER INFORMATION ACT 1978

The purpose of this Act is to protect consumers against false or misleading claims about goods, services and prices. It makes the following stipulations:

(1) It is an offence for a supplier to give a false or misleading **description of goods**.
(2) It is an offence for a **supplier of services** to make false or misleading claims about the services it offers.
(3) It is an offence to publish an **advertisement** that will mislead the public.
(4) All statements about **prices** must be accurate. The following are offences:

(a) Charging extra for items that appear to be included in the price.
(b) Giving a false price reduction, e.g. goods advertised in a sale reduced from IR£79 to IR£49 should have been on sale for IR£79 for at least twenty-eight consecutive days in the previous three months.
(c) Displaying a price excluding VAT.

(5) The Consumer Information Act also established the **Office of Director of Consumer Affairs and Fair Trade**, which is responsible for enforcing the provisions of the Act.

EC LEGISLATION ON LABELLING AND PRICE

FOOD LABELS — WHAT THE LABELS SHOULD SHOW

(1) Name of food.
(2) List of ingredients in descending order of weight.
(3) Quantity.
(4) 'Best before date' for almost all food.
(5) Storage conditions or conditions of use.
(6) Name and address of manufacturer or seller.
(7) Particulars of place of origin.
(8) Instructions for use where necessary.

PRICING OF FOOD

(1) All foodstuffs must display a selling price.
(2) Food sold in bulk or loose must display a unit price.

D. Agencies that Protect the Consumer

CONSUMER ASSOCIATION OF IRELAND

(1) Protects the interests of consumers in Ireland.
(2) Provides information to members through its monthly magazine, *Consumer Choice.*
(3) Helps consumers to solve complaints.

OFFICE OF DIRECTOR OF CONSUMER AFFAIRS

(1) Enforces the Consumer Information Act.
(2) Promotes better standards of advertising.
(3) Informs consumers about their rights.

OFFICE OF OMBUDSMAN

(1) **Ombudsman for Public Bodies** — Investigates complaints from the public about government agencies, e.g. Telecom, An Post.
(2) **Ombudsman for Credit Institutions** — Investigates complaints from the public against financial institutions, e.g. banks or building societies.
(3) **Ombudsman for the Insurance Industry** — Investigates complaints from the public against the insurance industry.

TRADE ASSOCIATIONS

Deal with complaints by the public against their members and try to settle disputes, e.g. Irish Travel Agents Association, Society of Irish Motor Industry.

EOLAS

Sets standards for goods and services. Tests products to see whether they reach the required standard.

ADVERTISING STANDARDS AUTHORITY

Promotes better standards of advertising.

SMALL CLAIMS COURT

For a fee of IR£5 a consumer can make a claim of up to IR£500 — no solicitors are involved.

MEDIA

Television, radio and the newspapers, e.g. *The Gay Byrne Show, The Gerry Ryan Show, Liveline* with Marian Finucane.

PRACTICE QUESTION

(i) Question 5, Paper I, Section A, Higher Level, 1992.

Chapter 7 — Consumer Complaints
Caveat Emptor — Let the Buyer Beware

A. Genuine Complaints

If goods are not of merchantable quality, or not as described, or not fit for their purpose, you then have a valid complaint and are entitled to some remedy, such as **cash refund**, **replacement** or **repair**.

B. Non-Valid Complaint

A complaint is not valid and the consumer has no rights if

(1) You change your mind about the goods after buying them.
(2) A fault arises due to misuse.
(3) A fault was pointed out at the time of purchase.

C. Where to Complain

(1) Complain firstly to the **supplier**.
(2) If negotiations fail there may be a third party such as a **trade association**.
(3) **Consumer Association of Ireland**.
(4) **Office of Director of Consumer Affairs**.
(5) **Media** — make your complaint public.
(6) If all the above fail you may have to consider taking **legal action**.

D. How to Complain

(1) Inform shop in writing or in person as soon as possible.
(2) Bring back the product and show evidence of purchase, i.e. receipt or credit card receipt.
(3) State your complaint clearly.
(4) State clearly what you want: refund/replacement/repair.
(5) If no agreement consult a third party.

E. Written Complaints

(1) Write clearly.
(2) Give details and **evidence** of purchase. Enclose copy of receipt.
(3) State complaint clearly.
(4) State clearly what you want done about it: refund/replacement/repair.
(5) Give details of when and where you may be contacted.
(6) Keep a copy of letter for future reference.

F. Compensation

A consumer who has a valid complaint may be entitled to:

(1) Full **cash refund**.
(2) **Replacement** of the goods.
(3) **Repair** — where problem is of a minor nature.

WHAT ABOUT A CREDIT NOTE?

A consumer may be offered a credit note instead of a cash refund. This allows him to buy something else in the same shop to the value of the credit note. You are not bound to accept a credit note.

WHAT ABOUT A REPAIR?

A repair may be an acceptable solution if the problem is of a minor nature.

G. Business Terms

Caveat Emptor 'Let the buyer beware' — goods should be carefully examined before purchase.

Redress Some form of compensation (remedy).

H. Examples of Consumer Complaints

COMPLAINT	PROBLEM	CONSUMER RIGHTS
New car battery will not start car	Battery not of **merchantable quality**	Replacement or refund
Stain remover does not remove stain	Stain remover **not fit for purpose**	Replacement or refund
Shoe polish described as black on box but navy when applied	Polish **not as described**	Replacement
Lawnmower breaks down after service	**Service not provided by person with necessary skill**	Proper service and compensation for inconvenience
Car described as never crashed but it was	**False description of goods**	Refund
Photographs developed in one hour — but takes one day	**False description of services**	No rights, but consumer should inform Director of Consumer Affairs

Examination-Style Questions and Solutions

Question 1.

Answer (a) and (b). This is a Consumer Question and a Letter of Complaint.

Mary Noonan bought a new jacket in Angels Boutique on a recent holiday. She paid IR£45 for it. On her return home she noticed that the stitching on one sleeve was ripped and also that one shoulder was larger than the other. She was very disappointed. As the boutique is over seventy miles from where she lives, she has decided to write to them about it and return the jacket. She is not sure whether or not she should return the receipt. She is looking for a full cash refund.

1. (a) Using your knowledge of consumer legislation, answer the following questions:

(i) What is the legal basis for Mary's complaint? Explain it briefly. **(7)**

(ii) Do you think Mary is entitled to a full refund? Give a reason for your answer. **(7)**

(iii) If the boutique owner offered Mary a credit note for the full amount should she accept it? Explain your answer. **(7)**

(iv) What advice would you give Mary on whether or not she should include the receipt with her letter? **(4)**

1. (b) Assuming you are Mary Noonan, write the letter of complaint to the Manager of Angels Boutique. (You may choose any addresses, date, etc. that are required yourself.) **(15)**

Source: Junior Certificate Higher Level 1993. **(40 marks)**

Solution to Question 1.

1. (a) *(i) Goods sold should be of merchantable quality — Sale of Goods and Supply of Services Act 1980.*

(ii) YES as the faults were significant — one shoulder larger than the other.

(iii) NO.

➢ She is entitled to a full refund and should not be restricted to buying an alternative in that shop only.

➢ She lives seventy miles away from the boutique — she may never go back again.

OR

YES if she is satisfied that she will use it in the same shop within a reasonable time.

(iv) Send a copy or its reference number with the letter, hold the original receipt as evidence of purchase.

1. (b) Letter of Complaint to Angels Boutique

76 North Main Street
Macroom
Co. Cork

10 August 1993

For the attention of Mary Doherty

The Manager
Angels Boutique Patrick Street
Limerick

Re: Faulty Jacket

Dear Ms Doherty,

On Saturday 5 August 1993, I bought a new jacket in your shop for IR£45 (copy of receipt enclosed). On bringing it home I noticed that the stitching on one sleeve was ripped and also that one shoulder was larger than the other.

I am very disappointed and wish to return the jacket. I would be very grateful if you would give me a full cash refund of IR£45.

I await your reply.

Yours sincerely

Mary Noonan

Mary Noonan

Enc (2)

Question 2.

Answer (a), (b) and (c). This is a Consumer Question.

Using your knowledge of consumer law you are asked to read the following consumer problems and to answer the questions that follow.

2. (a) A two-week-old vacuum cleaner keeps breaking down — sometimes the suction power picks up all the dirt and other times it is very poor and hardly picks up anything.

The shop where it was bought refuses to help, saying that it is the manufacturer's fault, and tells the customer to write directly to the manufacturer.

Answer the following questions (give one reason in each case in support of your opinion).

(i) Is the shop liable?
(ii) Is the manufacturer liable?
(iii) What remedy do you think the customer is entitled to?
(iv) What advice would you give the shopkeeper in dealing with complaints of this kind? **(20)**

2. (b) A friend of yours recently bought an expensive coat which the shop assistant clearly said was 100% 'pure new wool'.

A week later your friend discovered a small label on the inside of the sleeve which said 80% nylon. Your friend is very disappointed.

Answer the following questions (give one reason in each case in support of your opinion).

(i) What principle of consumer law has been broken in this situation?
(ii) In your opinion is your friend entitled to either a full refund or a credit note? **(12)**

2. (c) The following sign was recently seen hanging at the check-out of a large department store:

SORRY
IT IS COMPANY POLICY
NOT TO GIVE CASH REFUNDS

You are asked to comment briefly on what this sign says. **(8)**

Source: Junior Certificate Higher Level 1992. **(40 marks)**

Solution to Question 2.

2. (a) *(i) YES. Contract is with the shop — shop is liable to the consumer — shop will have recourse to manufacturer for faulty product.*

(ii) YES. Goods not of merchantable quality, not fit for purpose. Manufacturer directly liable to shopkeeper and indirectly liable to consumer.

(iii) Three possible answers here:

Replacement — It is very new and it is a basic fault, not a minor one.

OR

Repair — Maybe a minor adjustment will get it working properly. Repair may be acceptable.

OR

Refund — Probably best remedy.
Vacuum cleaner not fit for purpose — it is a basic fault and customer perhaps has no confidence in it and is entitled to a full cash refund.

(iv) ➢ *Listen with courtesy to complaint.*
➢ *Investigate complaint — examine product.*
➢ *Advise customer what he proposes as a solution.*
➢ *Get customer agreement if possible.*

2. (b) *(i) Misleading claim about coat/false description — Consumer Information Act 1978.*
(ii) Full refund — the product was not as it was represented to be.

2. (c) *This sign is illegal — retailers may not take away a consumer's rights by displaying such a sign. It cuts across a consumer's basic right where a refund is the appropriate and correct solution.*

PRACTICE QUESTIONS

(i) Question 3, Section B, Ordinary Level, Sample Paper.
(ii) Question 3, Section B, Ordinary Level, 1992.

FINANCIAL SERVICES FOR THE CONSUMER

Chapter 8 — Money and Banking

1. FORMS OF MONEY

A. Barter

Before money was introduced people had a system of barter or exchanging one product for another.

B. Money

The problems with barter led to the introduction of money which had a standard value. Gold and silver were chosen and minted into coins.

C. Paper Money

People gave their gold and silver to a goldsmith for safe keeping. The goldsmith gave the person a receipt. These receipts were then used to buy goods and services. The person in possession of these receipts returned to the goldsmith and collected the gold.

D. Characteristics of Money

Money has to be:
(1) **Portable** — easy to carry.
(2) **Valuable** — acceptable in exchange for goods and services.
(3) **Scarce** — be in short supply.
(4) **Divisible** — can be broken down into small denominations.
(5) **Durable** — last a long time.

E. Functions of Money

(1) **Medium of exchange**
(2) **Measure of value**
(3) **Store of value**
(4) **Standard of deferred payment.**

F. Legal Tender

Legal money of a country is issued by the Central Bank and must be accepted.

All paper money is legal tender. All coins are legal tender. Every country has its own legal tender called **currency**. This money can be used within the country but not outside it, e.g. Ireland — Punt (IR£), Britain — Sterling (£Stg.).

G. Forms of Money Today

(1) Notes and coins
(2) Cheques
(3) Credit cards.

H. Business Terms

Cheque Written instruction by a current account holder to his bank to pay a stated amount of money to a named person.
Credit Card Plastic money, buy now — pay later with interest.
Currency A country's legal tender, notes and coins.
Legal Tender Legal money of a country. Must be accepted in payment of a debt.
Punt Official Irish currency.
Sterling Official British currency.
Token Money Coins which do not contain their actual value in metal.

---

2. SAVING

A. Saving

SAVING MEANS NOT SPENDING

REASONS FOR SAVING
(1) Future purchases, e.g. house, car.
(2) Unforeseen events, illness, accident.
(3) Children's education.
(4) Income for the future.
(5) Holidays.

B. Investing

Investing means making your savings work so that they will earn interest.

WHY INVEST YOUR SAVINGS?
(1) To earn interest.
(2) For safety reasons.

C. Factors to be Considered Before Deciding Where to Invest

The wise investor will consider the following:

(1) **Safety**
(2) **Interest**
(3) **Liquidity**
(4) **Tax**
(5) **Future benefits**
(6) **Convenience.**

D. Financial Institutions for Investing Your Savings

(1) COMMERCIAL BANK

(a) Deposit account or savings account
- **Interest** is paid and is subject to **Deposit Interest Retention Tax** (DIRT).
- Money is **safe** and can be **withdrawn on demand**.

(b) Cash save account

- Similar to deposit account with the advantage of being able to withdraw money at any Automated Teller Machine (ATM).

(2) TRUSTEE SAVINGS BANK (TSB)

(a) Deposit account and cash save account

(b) Investment account

- **Large sums** can be deposited.
- **Interest rates are higher.**
- **Month's notice** required to withdraw.
- Interest is subject to **DIRT.**

(3) BUILDING SOCIETY

(a) Deposit account

- Interest is subject to **DIRT.**
- **Limit on amount** that can be withdrawn on demand.
- **Savings record** — you can apply for a mortgage (House Loan).

(4) CREDIT UNION

(a) Savings account

- Interest is **not subject** to DIRT.
- Members can obtain **low interest rate loans** (1% per month).

(5) AN POST

All savings invested with An Post are very safe, they are state-guaranteed.

(a) Saving stamps

- Cost 50p each.

(b) Deposit account

- **Interest** is paid on deposits.
- Interest is subject to **DIRT**.
- Up to **IR£100** can be withdrawn on demand daily.

(c) National instalment saving

- Save a **fixed amount** between IR£10 and IR£200 every month for twelve months.
- The money is then **left on deposit** for a period of one to five years.
- At present the rate of interest guaranteed is **50% after five years**.
- Interest is **tax-free.**

(d) Savings certificates

- Sold in units of IR£10.
- Guaranteed return is 40% after five years.
- Interest is **tax-free**.

(e) Savings bonds

- Sold in units of IR£50.
- Guaranteed return of 20.4% after three years.
- Interest is tax-free.

(f) Prize bonds
- Cost IR£5.
- No interest but all numbers are entered in a weekly draw.

(6) STATE BANKS

The Agricultural Credit Corporation, now ACCBank, and Industrial Credit Corporation, now ICC Bank, **encourage saving** by offering attractive rates of interest.

(7) STOCKS AND SHARES

People could invest their savings in **shares in companies**. The investor would
- Get a **dividend**.
- Make a **capital gain** if share price increases.

(8) INSURANCE COMPANIES
- A person could save by taking out an **endowment policy**.

E. Calculating Interest on a Deposit Account

Interest on a deposit account is calculated on a simple interest or compound interest basis.

(1) SIMPLE INTEREST

The interest is calculated on a fixed principal over a period of time.
Formula:

$$\text{Interest} = \frac{\text{Principal x Rate x Time}}{100}$$

(2) COMPOUND INTEREST

CAR	(Compound Annual Rate) is used to compare interest in one financial institution with another.

The interest earned in one year is added on to the principal and the next year interest is calculated on this new principal.

F. Deposit Interest Retention Tax

(1) A **tax on interest** earned in a Deposit Account.
(2) It is **deducted at 27%** rate by the financial institution and sent to the Revenue Commissioners.

Example

Gross Interest Earned	IR£400
Less DIRT 27%	IR£108
Net Interest	IR£292

G. Summary of Investment Institutions

	Safety	Interest	Liquidity	Tax	Future Benefits	Convenience
Commercial Bank	Safe	Yes	On Demand	DIRT	Mortgages Other Loans & Services	Extended Opening Hours ATM — All Time
Trustee Savings Bank	Safe	Yes	On Demand	DIRT	Mortgages Other Loans & Services	Extended Opening Hours ATM — All Time
Building Society	Safe	Yes	Limit — Societies Differ	DIRT	Mortgages Other Loans & Services	Extended Opening Hours ATM — All Time
Credit Union	Safe	Yes	On Demand	None	Small Loans	Normal Day
An Post Deposit A/C	Safe	Yes	On Demand	DIRT	Post Loan	Normal Day
NIS	Safe	Yes	On Demand	None	Post Loan	Normal Day
Saving Certs	Safe	Yes	Notice	None	Post Loan	Normal Day
Saving Bonds	Safe	Yes	Notice	None	Post Loan	Normal Day
Prize Bonds	Safe	No	On Demand	None		Normal Day
State Banks	Safe	Yes	On Demand	DIRT	Loans & Services	Normal Day
Stocks and Shares	Risky	Dividend	May sell at any time	Income Tax		
Insurance Companies	Safe	No	Difficult	Lump Sum Tax-Free		

Examination-Style Question and Solution

Question 1.
Answer all sections. This question deals with a Treasurer — investing money, interest calculations and foreign exchange.

You have been appointed treasurer of the organising committee for next year's school tour to France. There are thirty students travelling and the total cost per student is IR£170. Students have been saving IR£10 each per week for the five weeks up to 31 May. This money was kept in the school safe until 31 May. As treasurer, you are responsible for collecting this money and investing it wisely.

1. (a) Suggest **three** possible places where this money could be invested, giving one advantage for **each** place mentioned. **(9)**

1. (b) Calculate how much money has been saved by 31 May. **(4)**

1. (c) A deposit of IR£500 is sent to the tour company on 31 May. The balance is invested on 1 June. Assuming a rate of interest of 8% per annum, how much money would be in the investment account on 1 September? (Ignore tax.) Show your workings. **(8)**

1. (d) All the students pay the balance due on their return to school on 1 September.

(i) Calculate how much money the students pay on 1 September. **(4)**

(ii) If this money is added to the same investment account on 1 September, calculate how much money would be in this account, in total, on 1 December. (Rate of interest 8% per annum; ignore tax.) Show your workings. **(10)**

(35 marks)

Source: Junior Certificate Higher Level 1993.

Solution to Question 1.

1. (a) *(i) Commercial Bank/Trustee Savings Bank*

- *Withdrawal on demand.*
- *Money is safe.*
- *Money earns interest.*

(ii) Building Society

- *Competitive interest rates.*
- *Can get mortgage in future.*
- *Money earns interest.*

(iii) Credit Union

- *Local and convenient.*
- *Can avail of low interest rate loans in future.*

(iv) An Post

- *Money state-guaranteed.*
- *Convenient/good opening hours.*
- *Competitive rates of interest.*

1. (b) *30 students x IR£10 ea. = IR£300 x 5 weeks = IR£1,500*

1. (c)

31 May amount saved	*IR£1,500*
Deposit sent to tour company	*IR£500*
Balance to invest	*IR£1,000*

Money invested @8% for 3 months (1/4 of yr) — June, July, August.
Calculations IR£1,000 @8% 1 yr = IR£80
1/4 of year = IR£20
Answer = Principal IR£1,000 + Interest IR£20 = IR£1,020

1. (d) *(i) Students have already paid IR£10 ea. x 5 weeks = IR£50*

Cost of tour	*IR£170*	
Saved already	*IR£50*	
Balance to pay 1 Sept.	*IR£120*	*ea. x 30 students = IR£3,600*

Examination-Style Question and Solution

Question 1.
This is a Question on Balance of Payments.
1. (a) The following figures refer to SOMBIA international trade.

	£
Export of visible goods	950 million
Export of invisible items	280 million
Import of visible goods	640 million
Import of invisible items	360 million

From the above figures, calculate:
(i) the Balance of Trade, and
(ii) the Balance of Payments on Current Account. (Show your workings.) **(12)**

1. (b) (i) Which country buys the largest percentage of Ireland's exports? **(4)**
(ii) Suggest **one** thing which **each** of the following groups could do to help the Irish Balance of Payments?
- Irish Consumers (Shoppers)
- Irish Producers (Manufacturers). **(8)**

Source: Junior Certificate Higher Level 1994.

Solution to Question 1.
1. (a) *Balance of Trade and Balance of Payments*

	£	£
Export of visible goods	*950m*	
– Import of visible goods	*640m*	
Balance of trade surplus		*310m*
Export of invisible items	*280m*	
– Import of invisible items	*360m*	
Deficit on invisible trade		*–80m*
Surplus on Balance of Payment Current Account		*230m*

1. (b) *(i) The UK*
(ii) Irish consumers could buy Irish goods and services.
Irish producers could:
- *Use Irish raw materials*
- *Become more competitive and efficient.*

PRACTICE QUESTIONS

(i) Question 9, Section A, Paper I, Sample Paper, Higher Level.
(ii) Question 14, Section A, Paper I, Higher Level, 1992.
(iii) Question 16, Section A, Paper I, Higher Level, 1992.
(iv) Question 16, Section A, Paper I, Higher Level, 1993.
(v) Question 5D, Section B, Paper I, Higher Level, 1993.

Chapter 14 — Forms of Business

In Ireland businesses are owned by one person, two or more people, or by the state.

MAIN FORMS OF BUSINESS UNIT

- Sole Trader — owned by one person.
- Co-operatives — owned by eight or more people, called members.
- State Companies — owned by state.
- Private Limited Company — owned by at least two people, called shareholders.

A. Sole Trader

A sole trader is a person who owns and manages his own business.

CHARACTERISTICS	TYPES	ADVANTAGES	DISADVANTAGES
(1) Owned by **one person**. (2) Owner makes **all decisions**. (3) Owner keeps all **profit** — suffers all losses. (4) Owner has **unlimited liability**.	(1) Retailers. (2) Services. (3) Professional Services.	(1) Easy to set up. (2) Personal attention to customers. (3) Owner makes all decisions. (4) Owner can keep all profit. (5) May give credit. (6) May offer a delivery service.	(1) Unlimited liability. (2) Lack of capital hinders expansion. (3) Prices may be higher than in supermarkets. (4) Extra work outside trading hours. (5) Owner bears all losses. (6) No continuity of business.

B. Co-operatives

A co-operative is a business owned and run by its members.

The first co-operative was in Rochdale in England. The first Irish co-operative was established in Drumcollogher in Limerick in 1889.

CHARACTERISTICS	FORMATION	ADVANTAGES	DISADVANTAGES
(1) To become a member a person must buy one share costing IR£1. (2) Each member has one vote. (3) Profit is distributed among members. (4) Members have limited liability. (5) Managed by a committee.	(1) Eight people are required. (2) Apply to Registrar of Friendly Societies. (3) Certificate of Incorporation is issued. (4) Report annually to Registrar of Friendly Societies.	(1) Shareholders have limited liability. (2) One vote per member. (3) Members own co-operative — a big incentive to do their business with co-operative. (4) Profits are returned to members.	(1) Lack of finance. (2) No incentive to buy more shares. (3) Management committee may not have the business expertise to run a modern business.

TYPES OF CO-OPERATIVE

(1) Producer Co-operatives

Producer co-operatives are mainly agricultural co-operatives. They collect the raw material from the farmers, e.g. milk, process it and sell the finished product, e.g. cheese.

(2) Consumer Co-operatives

These co-operatives buy directly from the manufacturer and sell to members and non-members.

(3) Worker Co-operatives

These are set up where businesses close down and the workers decide to put in money and set up a worker co-operative, e.g. Carrigdhoun Pottery in Co. Cork.

(4) Financial Co-operatives, e.g. credit unions

These are set up by people sharing a common interest, e.g. same town, same job (ASTI Credit Union for teachers). They encourage savings and provide loans at a low rate of interest (1% per month).

CO-OPERATIVES BECOMING PUBLIC LIMITED COMPANIES — PLCs

One of the major problems co-operatives have had in the past is the **lack of capital for expansion**. To overcome this problem some of the major co-operatives have converted their status from co-operatives to PLCs (Public Limited Companies). We now have four PLC co-operatives: Kerry Group PLC, Waterford Foods PLC, Golden Vale PLC and Avonmore Foods PLC.

ADVANTAGES OF CONVERTING TO PLCs

(a) Finance is available by selling shares to the public.
(b) Shareholders can sell their shares at the Stock Exchange.

C. State Ownership

State companies are owned and controlled by the state.

REASONS FOR STATE INVOLVEMENT	FORMATION	CHARACTERISTICS	ADVANTAGES	DISADVANTAGES
(1) To provide **essential services.** (2) To develop the country's **natural resources.** (3) To rescue firms in **danger of closing down.** (4) To promote **Irish businesses at home and abroad.** (5) To provide **training for unemployed**, e.g. FÁS.	Most state companies were set up by passing an Act of the Oireachtas.	(1) Owned, financed and controlled by the government. (2) Each state company is responsible to a government minister. (3) The minister appoints a board of directors to run the company. (4) Profit is reinvested in the company or given to the government.	(1) Provide essential services. (2) Provide a lot of employment.	(1) Some are in a monopoly situation with no competition, which may lead to inefficiency. (2) No profit motive, which also leads to inefficiency. (3) Some state firms suffer **large losses** borne by taxpayer.

NAMES, INITIALS AND MAIN ACTIVITY OF STATE COMPANIES

NAME	INITIALS	MAIN ACTIVITY
(1) Production		
Electricity Supply Board	ESB	Provision of electricity throughout Ireland.
Bord na Móna		Development of peat resources. Production of turf, briquettes and peat moss.
Irish Fertiliser Industries	IFI	Production of fertiliser.
Coillte		Planting of forests and sale of timber.
Irish Steel		Production of steel and galvanised sheeting.
(2) Transport		
Coras Iompair Éireann	CIE	Provision of transport by roads and rail throughout Ireland.
Three Companies:		
(a) Dublin Bus		Dublin city bus service.
(b) Bus Éireann		Bus service for rest of Ireland.
(c) Iarnród Éireann (Irish Rail)		Rail service for passengers and goods throughout the country.
Aer Lingus		Air transport service.
(3) Marketing/Export		
Bord Fáilte		Promotion of Irish tourist industry.
Bord Tráchtála	BTT	Promotion of Irish goods at home and abroad.
Bord Iascaigh Mhara	BIM	Promotion of Irish-Sea fishing industry.
(4) Training		
Foras Aiseanna Saothair	FÁS	Training workers and the unemployed.
(5) Research		
Eolas		Promotion of research and technology in industry.
Teagasc		Research in agriculture and horticulture.
(6) Finance		
Industrial Credit Corporation	ICC	Finance for Irish industry.
Agricultural Credit Company	ACCBank	Finance for Irish farmers.
(7) Services		
Radio Telefís Éireann	RTE	Radio and television services.
An Post		National postal service.
Telecom Éireann		National telephone and information service.
Bord Gáis Éireann	BGE	Distribution of natural gas.
Voluntary Health Insurance	VHI	Provision of hospital insurance cover.
(8) Promotion		
Industrial Development Authority	IDA	Development of industry in Ireland.

NATIONALISATION
State takes over a firm previously owned by shareholders.

PRIVATISATION
State sells off a state company to the public.

REASONS FOR PRIVATISATION

(1) Raises finance for government.
(2) State no longer responsible for these state companies.

HOW STATE COMPANIES ARE FINANCED

(1) Borrowing.
(2) Grants.
(3) Issuing government stock to public.
(4) Charging for services.

D. Private Limited Company (Ltd)

A private limited company is where a group of people numbering between two and fifty come together and form a business. The owners are called shareholders. They invest money in the company. The profit is divided up among the shareholders and distributed in the form of **dividends**.

CHARACTERISTICS	ADVANTAGES	DISADVANTAGES
(1) Between two and fifty shareholders. (2) Shareholders have limited liability. (3) 'Ltd' written after the name. (4) Shares cannot be sold to the public. (5) The annual accounts are sent to the Registrar of Companies. They are not published.	(1) Shareholders have limited liability. (2) Extra capital available. (3) Continuity of existence.	(1) Costly to set up. (2) A lot of legal requirements when forming a company. (3) Shares cannot be transferred to the general public.

FORMATION OF A PRIVATE LIMITED COMPANY

(1) To form a private limited company you must have at least two shareholders and a maximum of fifty. The company is **owned** by these shareholders.
(2) The people involved in the formation of a company are called the **Promoters**. They employ:
(a) An accountant — to advise on financial affairs.
(b) A solicitor — to prepare the legal documents which must be sent to the Registrar of Companies:

- Memorandum of Association
- Articles of Association
- Declaration of Compliance with Companies Acts 1963–1990
- Statement of Capital of the Company.

DOCUMENTS INVOLVED IN THE FORMATION OF A COMPANY

(1) Memorandum of Association

This sets out the relationship of the company to the general public, i.e. rules and regulations governing company's dealing with public.

CONTENTS		SAMPLE MEMORANDUM OF ASSOCIATION	
(a) Name of company with 'Ltd' after last word.	⇛	(a) Name of company is *Lakeside Fruit Farm Ltd.*	
(b) Objectives of company (i.e. type of business).	⇛	(b) Objects for which company is established are *fruit-growing.*	
(c) Statement of limited liability.	⇛	(c) The liability of the company is limited.	
(d) Share capital of company. How much money can be raised from selling shares.	⇛	(d) The share capital of the company is *IR£50,000* divided into *50,000 shares @ IR£1 each.*	
		We the several persons whose names, addresses and descriptions are subscribed wish to be formed into a company in pursuance of the Memorandum of Association and we agree to take the number of shares in the capital of the Company set opposite our respective names.	
(e) Names of those forming the company and number of shares taken.	⇛	(e) Name, address and description of each subscriber.	Number of shares taken by each subscriber.
	⇛	*John O'Mahony* **Director** *Cork*	*15,000*
	⇛	*Claire O'Mahony* **Director** *Cork*	*15,000*
(f) Date and signatures	⇛	(f) Date *01.1.95*	Signatures: *John O'Mahony/ Claire O'Mahony.*

(2) Articles of Association

This document sets out the internal rules and regulations of the company.

CONTENTS		SAMPLE ARTICLES OF ASSOCIATION	
Name of Company	⇛	Articles of Association of *Lakeside Fruit Farm Ltd.*	
(a) Details of share capital.	⇛	(a) Share capital of company is *IR£50,000 divided into 50,000 shares @ IR£1 each.*	
(b) Shareholders' voting rights.	⇛	(b) Shareholders' voting rights *One vote per share.*	
(c) Regulation regarding General Meetings.	⇛	(c) General Meetings *AGM will be held on first Tuesday in January.*	
(d) How directors are to be elected.	⇛	(d) Election of directors *At AGM and will hold office for one year.*	
(e) Powers and duties of directors.	⇛	(e) Powers and duties of directors *Responsible for day-to-day running of company.*	
(f) Borrowing powers of company.	⇛	(f) Borrowing powers of company *Up to IR£1,000,000.*	
(g) Procedure for winding up company.	⇛	(g) How company can be wound up *Company can be wound up if it becomes insolvent.*	
(h) Directors' names and addresses.	⇛	(h) DIRECTORS' NAMES	AND ADDRESSES
		John O'Mahony	*Cork*
		Claire O'Mahony	*Cork*
(i) Date and signature	⇛	(i) Date *01.1.95*	Signatures *John O'Mahony Claire O'Mahony.*

(3) Declaration of Compliance with Companies Acts 1963–1990

This document states that the company will comply with the Companies Acts 1963–1990.

(4) Statement of Capital of the Company

This document states the **Authorised Share Capital** of the company, i.e. the maximum amount of capital that the company can raise.

REGISTRAR OF COMPANIES

The documents are sent to the Registrar of Companies. The Registrar will check all the documents carefully to see if they are in order. If everything is in order a **Certificate of Incorporation** is issued.

CERTIFICATE OF INCORPORATION

(1) This is the birth certificate of a company.
(2) It has a separate legal existence from its owners.
(3) The shareholders have limited liability.
(4) Company can sue and be sued in its own name.

BOARD OF DIRECTORS

When the company is incorporated it will hold a meeting of shareholders, who elect a board of directors to run the company on a day-to-day basis. They report to the shareholders annually on the performance of the company at the Annual General Meeting (AGM).

RECORDING SHARE CAPITAL IN THE BOOKS OF A PRIVATE LIMITED COMPANY

From the memorandum and articles we see that on 1 January 1995 John and Claire O'Mahony formed a private limited company called Lakeside Fruit Farm Ltd. They each purchased 15,000 shares @ IR£1 each in the company. The money received by the company was lodged in a company bank account. On 10 January they purchased equipment for IR£20,000.

(1) Record the issue of the shares in the ordinary Share Capital A/C and Bank A/C.
(2) Record the purchase of the equipment in the appropriate accounts.
(3) Make out the trial balance of Lakeside Fruit Farm Ltd on 11 January 1995.

EXPLANATION
Basic Rule of Double Entry Book-Keeping
Debit — Receiving Account
Credit — Giving Account

(1) Lakeside Fruit Farm Ltd has received IR£30,000, which was lodged in the bank. **Debit bank account** (receiving account). Company now owes IR£30,000 to its shareholders, John and Claire O'Mahony, who purchased the shares. **Credit share capital account** (giving account).

Bank Account

01.1.95	Ordinary Share Capital A/C	30,000	10.1.95	Equipment A/C	20,000
			11.1.95	Balance C/d	10,000
		30,000			30,000
11.1.95	Balance C/d	10,000			

Ordinary Share Capital Account

			01.1.95	Bank	30,000

(2) On 10 January 1995 Lakeside Fruit Farm Ltd purchased equipment for IR£20,000. **Debit equipment account** (receiving account). **Credit bank account** (giving account).

Equipment Account

10.1.95	**Bank**	**20,000**	

(3) Trial Balance of Lakeside Fruit Farm Ltd on 11.1.95

The trial balance brings together the balance from the accounts and lists them in two separate columns, **Debit** and **Credit**.

Bank 10,000 Debit.
Ordinary Share Capital 30,000 Credit.
Equipment 20,000 Debit.

The trial balance must balance.

Trial Balance of Lakeside Fruit Farm Ltd on 11.1.95

		Debit	**Credit**
	Bank	**10,000**	
	Ordinary Share Capital		**30,000**
	Equipment	**20,000**	
		30,000	**30,000**

E. Business Terms

AGM — Annual General Meeting Annual meeting of shareholders.
Articles of Association Sets out internal rules and regulations of the company.
Auditor Checks accounts of a business.
Authorised Share Capital Maximum amount of capital that can be raised through selling of shares.
Board of Directors Appointed by shareholders to run the company.
Certificate of Incorporation Birth certificate of a company.
Co-operative A business owned and run by members.
Credit Union An institution which encourages savings and provides loans at low interest rates.
Dividend Part of profit that each shareholder receives from a company.
Double Entry Book-Keeping In book-keeping there are two sides to every transaction. The receiving (Debit) and giving (Credit).
Issued Share Capital Actual amount of shares that the company has sold.
Limited Liability Investor can lose only capital invested in a business.
Memorandum of Association Outlines company's dealing with public.
Nationalisation State taking over a private enterprise company.
Private Limited Company A company that is owned by between two and fifty shareholders. It has limited liability.

Privatisation State sells a state company to the public.
Producer Co-operative A co-operative which produces a product.
Promoters People involved in the formation of a company.
Registrar of Companies Office for keeping information on all companies formed in Ireland.
Shareholder A person who buys shares in a company.
Sole Trader A person who owns and runs his own business.
State-Owned Company A business owned and controlled by the state.
Trial Balance A list of balances from all accounts in the ledger.
Unlimited Liability An investor can lose money invested in a business and his own personal assets if business fails.

Examination-Style Question and Solution

Question 1.

Answer all sections. This is an Integrated Company Formation Question.

On 1 January 1993 Ann Smyth of 2 Top St, Carlow, and Patrick Daly of 15 Cork Rd, Carlow, formed a private Limited Company called WOOD FUN LTD. They prepared a Memorandum of Association and sent it and all the other necessary documents to the Registrar of Companies. A Certificate of Incorporation was then issued.

The objects of the company are to manufacture and sell wooden toys.

The authorised share capital of WOOD FUN LTD is 40,000 IR£1 ordinary shares.

On 11 January 1993 Ann Smyth purchased 15,000 shares and Patrick Daly purchased 16,000 shares. The money received from the issue of these shares was lodged to the company bank account.

On 12 January the company purchased by cheque equipment costing IR£15,000.

You are required to:

1. **(a)** Complete the Memorandum of Association on the blank document supplied with this paper. **(15)**

1. **(b)** Name one other document which should be sent to the Registrar of Companies when forming a company. **(5)**

1. **(c)** Record the issue of the shares on 11 January 1993 in the Ordinary Share Capital Account and the Bank Account of Wood Fun Ltd. **(5)**

1. **(d)** Record the transaction that took place on 12 January 1993 in the appropriate accounts. **(10)**

1. **(e)** Prepare a Trial Balance for Wood Fun Ltd on 13 January 1993. **(5)**

MEMORANDUM OF ASSOCIATION

1. **The Name of the Company is** __________________________

2. **The Objects for which the Company is established are:**

____

____

3. **The Liability of the members is limited.**

4. **The Share Capital of the Company is** ________________ **divided into** ____

____

WE, the several persons whose names, addresses and descriptions are subscribed wish to be formed into a Company in pursuance of the Memorandum of Association and we agree to take the number of shares in the Capital of the Company set opposite our respective names.

Name, Address and Description of each Subscriber	Number of Shares taken by each Subscriber

Dated ____________________

Source: Junior Certificate Higher Level 1993. **(40 marks)**

Solution to Question 1.

For use with Question 1 (a)

MEMORANDUM OF ASSOCIATION

1. **The Name of the Company is** *Wood Fun Ltd*

2. **The Objects for which the Company is established are:**
The manufacture and sale of wooden toys

3. **The Liability of the members is limited.**

4. **The Share Capital of the Company is** *IR£40,000* **divided into** *40,000 IR£1 ordinary shares*

WE, the several persons whose names, addresses and descriptions are subscribed, wish to be formed into a Company in pursuance of the Memorandum of Association and we agree to take the number of shares in the Capital of the Company set opposite our respective names.

Name, Address and Description of each Subscriber	Number of Shares taken by each Subscriber
Ann Smyth, 2 Top Street, Carlow	*15,000*
Patrick Daly, 15 Cork Road, Carlow	*16,000*

Dated *1 January 1993*

1. (b) *Any document from the following: Articles of Association, List of Directors, Statement of Capital, Declaration of Compliance with the Companies Act.*

1. (c) & (d)

Ordinary Share Capital Account

			11/1/93	Bank	31,000

Equipment Account

12/1/93	Bank	15,000			

Bank Account

11/1/93	Ordinary Share Capital	31,000	12/1/93	Equipment	15,000
			13/1/93	Balance C/d	16,000
		31,000			31,000
14/1/93	Balance B/d	16,000			

1. (e)

Trial Balance as on 13 January 1993

Date	Details	Debit	Credit
	Ordinary Share Capital		31,000
	Equipment	15,000	
	Bank	16,000	
		31,000	31,000

PRACTICE QUESTIONS

(i) Question 5, Paper II, Higher Level, 1992.
(ii) Question 4, Paper II, Higher Level, 1994.

Chapter 15 — Finance for Business

Why companies need finance	Length of time money is needed	Match use with source	Collateral required on loans
(1) Purchase assets (2) Pay expenses	Short-term (0–1 yr) Medium-term (1–5 yrs) Long-term (over 5 yrs)	Purchase premises ⇒ Long-term source Purchase stock ⇒ Short-term source	(1) Title deeds (2) Personal guarantor (3) Life policies (4) Stocks and shares

SOURCES OF FINANCE

Short-Term Sources (0–1 year)		
Purpose	**Sources**	**Explanation**
Purchase of stock Payment of wages	Taxation	VAT, PAYE, PRSI, paid every two months, used as a free loan until collection.
Insurance	Trade credit	Buy goods on credit, usually thirty days = free loan.
Telephone, rent	Bank overdraft	Overdraw current account up to a certain limit.
	Expenses accrued	Delayed payment of bills — use of free money.
	Factoring	Selling debtors for cash.

Medium-Term Sources (1–5 yrs)		
Purpose	**Sources**	**Explanation**
Vehicles Furniture and fittings Computers	Hire purchase	Pay by instalments. The firm will not own goods purchased until last instalment is paid.
	Term loan	Loan for a period up to five years, given for specific reason and repaid by instalments.
	Leasing	Similar to renting, pay rentals but the firm will never own asset.

Long-Term Sources (5 yrs upwards)		
Purpose	**Sources**	**Explanation**
Land Premises Extensions Equipment Machinery	Capital	Invested by owner — sole trader/partnership. Companies sell shares to public — shareholders.
	Retained earnings	Profit made retained in business.
	BES	Business Expansion Scheme. A person who invests in a company in BES scheme can write off amount invested against income tax.
	Sale and leaseback	Sell an asset for cash and arrange to lease it back.
	Mortgage	Long-term loan — title deeds of premises are given as collateral.
	Government grants and EC grants	Government agencies provide grants to business, e.g. Bord Fáilte, BIM, IDA, FÁS, Bord Tráchtála — non-repayable.

Examination-Style Question and Solution

Question 1.

Tick the most suitable source of finance for each of the following items required by Ideal Motors Ltd:

Items	Sources		
	Short-Term	Medium-Term	Long-Term
Buildings			✓
Computer		✓	
Cars for resale	✓		
Advertising	✓		

Source: Junior Certificate Sample Paper Higher Level. **(4)**

PRACTICE QUESTIONS

(i) Question 2, Section A, Paper I, Higher Level, 1993.
(ii) Question 4, Section A, Paper I, Higher Level, 1994.

Chapter 16 — Financial Planning for Business

John and Claire O'Mahony, owners of Lakeside Fruit Farm Ltd, wish to purchase ten acres of land at a cost of IR£20,000 to extend their soft-fruit-growing business. They also wish to purchase a delivery van at a cost of IR£10,000. They are seeking a bank loan of IR£30,000 repayable over ten years.

A. Applying for a Loan

Borrower must be clear on:

(1) Purpose of loan.
(2) Size of loan.
(3) Repayment period.
(4) Security available.
(5) Rates of interest.
(6) Monthly payment.

B. What Information Must Be Presented to Bank When Seeking a Loan?

(1) Letter of application.
(2) Loan application form.
(3) Business plan.
(4) Cash flow forecast.
(5) Final accounts over two or three years.
(6) Projected accounts.
(7) Details of collateral.
(8) Proof of ability to repay.

(1) LETTER OF APPLICATION FOR LOAN

See p. 107.

(2) LOAN APPLICATION FORM: ALLIED IRISH BANKS

Name of Business	*Lakeside Fruit Farm Ltd.*
Address of Business	*Long Lane Cork.*
Name(s) of Owners	*John O'Mahony/Claire O'Mahony.*
Address of Owners	*Long Lane Cork.*
History of Business	*Our fruit business has been in existence for two years. It has made a profit every year.*
Qualifications of Management	*John has a degree in horticulture, Claire has a diploma in fruit-growing.*
Bank Accounts	*Deposit and current account in AIB Cork.*
Purpose of Loan	*Purchase land and a delivery van.*
Amount of Loan	*IR£30,000.*
Repayment Period	*Ten years.*
Ability to Repay	*See accounts and projected profit/loss account.*
Security Available	*Deeds of land.*
Marketing Details	*Wholesale/Retail market in Cork.*
Signed	*John O'Mahony/Claire O'Mahony* **Date** *10 March 1997.*

LAKESIDE FRUIT FARM LTD
Long Lane — Cork

VAT No. 2684168

Tel (021) 892145
Telex (021) 364185
Fax (021) 892146

10 March 1997

To Mr G. Murphy
Manager
AIB
Cork

Dear Mr Murphy

We want to apply for a bank loan of IR£30,000 to purchase ten acres of land and a delivery van.

We have been involved in growing fruit for two years and throughout this time we have been renting land. We have now decided to purchase land of our own costing IR£20,000. We also need a delivery van costing IR£10,000.

We plan to repay this loan over a ten-year period making an annual payment out of profit.

We enclose a completed loan application form, details of our business are contained in our business plan. We also enclose a Cash Flow Forecast and our Projected Trading and Profit and Loss Account indicates that the business will be successful and profitable.

We also enclose a copy of our accounts over the last two years. We have decided that the deeds of the land will be put forward to the bank as security for the loan.

We await a favourable response.

Yours sincerely

John and Claire O'Mahony.

Encl. 5

(3) BUSINESS PLAN

When applying for a loan it will be necessary to make out a Business Plan which will show how the owners see their business developing in the future. A business that fails to plan, plans to fail. A good business plan should cover the following areas: management, marketing, finance and production.

CONTENTS OF A BUSINESS PLAN

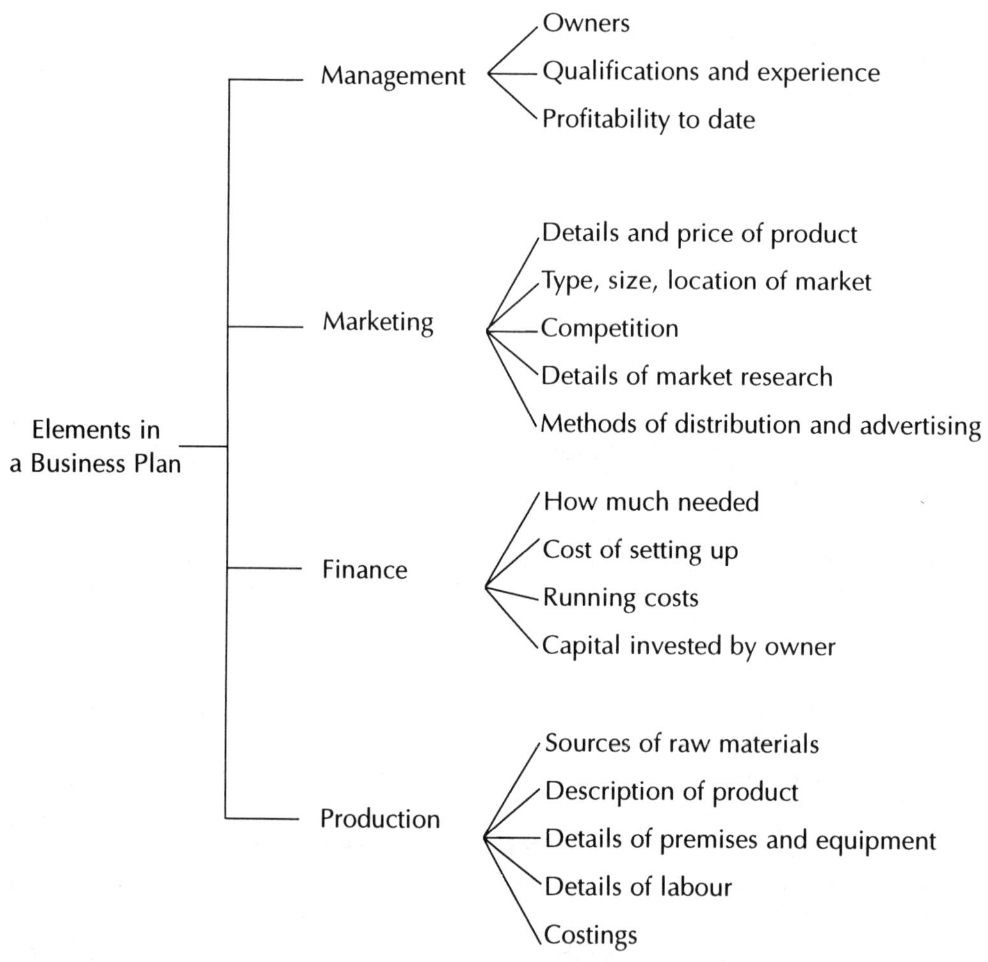

COSTINGS

There are two costs involved in producing a product:

(1) **Fixed costs** — Must be paid irrespective of how much is produced.

(2) **Variable Costs** — Increase as production increases.

Fixed costs + variable costs = Total costs.

$$\textbf{Cost per unit} = \frac{\textbf{Total Cost}}{\textbf{Unit Produced}} + \textbf{Mark-Up} = \textbf{Selling Price}$$

WHY ARE BUSINESS PLANS NECESSARY?

(1) Required when applying for a loan.
(2) Help management making decisions.
(3) To compare actual with planned performance.

LAKESIDE FRUIT FARM LTD BUSINESS PLAN

1. MANAGEMENT

Lakeside Fruit Farm Ltd is a private limited company set up in January 1995. **Owners:** John and Claire O'Mahony. **Qualifications:** John has a degree in horticulture and Claire has a diploma in fruit-farming.

2. MARKETING

Products: Raspberries, strawberries, loganberries, blackcurrants.
Market: Wholesale/retail market in Cork, shop on the farm, local jam factory.
Distribution: The fruit is distributed daily to the market.
Advertising: Weekends in the local papers.

3. FINANCE

Capital invested: The owners have each invested IR£5,000 in the business. **Purpose of finance:** To purchase ten acres of land for IR£20,000 and a delivery van for IR£10,000. **Repayment:** Over a ten-year period, by annual payment out of profit. **Enclosed:** (i) Financial accounts over the last two years; (ii) a projected set of accounts; (iii) a cash flow forecast.

4. PRODUCTION

Fruit production: April until October. **Employment:** Owners work full-time on the farm and twenty part-time students are employed fruit-picking during season. **Packaging:** Fruit is prepared and packed in a large store on the farm. All packing materials are purchased from a local supplier. **Enclosed:** Production costings.
Signed: John O'Mahony, Claire O'Mahony.

(4) CASH FLOW FORECAST

A Cash Flow Forecast shows **expected receipts** and **expected payments**: Net Cash, Opening Cash and Closing Cash (similar to a household budget).

RECEIPTS OF A BUSINESS

Sales, owners' capital, sale of assets, receipts from debtors, bank interest received, loans received, government grants.

PAYMENTS OF A BUSINESS

Purchases of stock, purchase of premises, machinery, equipment, computers, wages, rent, rates, insurance, heat and light, repayment of loans, telephone, advertising.

REASON FOR PREPARING CASH FLOW FORECAST

(1) To show whether repayments can be met.
(2) To highlight any cash shortages.

CASH FLOW FORECAST 1997 LAKESIDE FRUIT FARM LTD													
	Jan.	Feb.	Mar.	Apr.	May	June	July	Aug.	Sept.	Oct.	Nov.	Dec.	Total
Receipts													
Sales	900	700	200	1,000	1,700	2,600	2,500	2,000	1,600	1,100	600	900	15,800
Government Grant	—	—	—	—	—	—	—	—	—	—	—	—	
Loan	—	—	—	—	30,000	—	—	—	—	—	—	—	30,000
A Total Receipts	900	700	200	1,000	31,700	2,600	2,500	2,000	1,600	1,100	600	900	45,800
Payments													
Purchases	200	180	600	300	400	600	400	500	200	400	450	460	4,690
Wages	—	—	—	250	380	450	420	350	300	500	200	—	2,850
Rent of Land	30	30	30	30	30	30	30	30	30	30	30	30	360
Telephone	80	—	150	—	180	—	160	—	130	—	180	—	880
Advertising	40	30	60	80	100	250	200	160	150	200	250	200	1,720
Purchase of Land	—	—	—	—	20,000	—	—	—	—	—	—	—	20,000
Purchase of Van	—	—	—	—	10,000	—	—	—	—	—	—	—	10,000
B Total Payments	350	240	840	660	31,090	1,330	1,210	1,040	810	1,130	1,110	690	40,500
C Net Cash (A – B)	550	460	–640	340	610	1,270	1,290	960	790	–30	–510	210	5,300
D Opening Cash	200	750	1,210	570	910	1,520	2,790	4,080	5,040	5,830	5,800	5,290	200
Closing Cash (C + D)	750	1,210	570	910	1,520	2,790	4,080	5,040	5,830	5,800	5,290	5,500	5,500

(5) TRADING AND PROFIT AND LOSS ACCOUNT

Trading and Profit and Loss Account of Lakeside Fruit Farm Ltd for Years Ending 31 December 1995 and 31 December 1996

Trading and Profit and Loss Account for Year Ending 31/12/95			Trading and Profit and Loss Account for Year Ending 31/12/96		
Sales		12,700	Sales		13,600
Purchases		4,820	Purchases		4,710
Gross Profit		7,880	Gross Profit		8,890
Less Expenses			**Less Expenses**		
Wages	1,620		Wages	1,910	
Rent	360		Rent	360	
Telephone	700		Telephone	750	
Advertising	1,200	3,880	Advertising	1,530	4,550
Net Profit		4,000	**Net Profit**		4,340

(6) PROJECTED PROFIT FOR 1997

From the cash flow forecast we can prepare a projected trading and profit and loss account for 1997.

Lakeside Fruit Farm Ltd Projected Trading and Profit and Loss Account for Year Ending 31 December 1997

Sales		15,800
Purchases		4,690
Gross Profit		11,110
Less Expenses		
Wages	2,850	
Rent	360	
Telephone	880	
Advertising	1,720	
Total Expenses		5,810
Projected Net Profit		**5,300**

(7) DETAILS OF COLLATERAL/SECURITY

A bank will look for collateral from a business that is borrowing money. Lakeside Fruit Farm Ltd is offering the deeds of the land as collateral. Other types of collateral offered on business loans are:

(a) Deeds of premises.

(b) Personal written guarantee by the owners.

(8) PROOF OF ABILITY TO REPAY

The net profit shown by the accounts for 1995, 1996 and projected for 1997 is as follows:

Accounts	1995	1996	Projected 1997
Net Profit	4,000	4,340	5,300

The trend is towards increasing profit.

C. Recording the Loan in the Books of the Company

When the business receives the loan it must be recorded in the books as follows:

➢ Debit bank account of business.
➢ Credit loan account AIB bank (Lender).
➢ Assume the loan was received on 20 March 1997.

Bank Account — Lakeside Fruit Farm

20 Mar 1997	Loan AIB	30,000			

Loan Account AIB Bank

			20 Mar 1997	Bank	30,000

Examination-Style Question and Solution

Question 1.

Answer (a), (b) and (c). This is a Cash Flow Statement Question.

1. (a) On a separate sheet supplied with this paper is a partially completed Cash Flow Statement. You are required to complete this form for the months of March, April, May and June, as well as all the Total columns.

The following information should be taken into account.

➢ Monthly sales are expected to increase by 30% beginning in April.
➢ A European Union (EU) grant of IR£40,000 for equipment is expected in May.
➢ The shareholders are to invest an additional IR£50,000 in the business in June.
➢ Light and heat is expected to decrease by 15% in the months of March and May.
➢ Rent and wages are expected to remain the same every month.
➢ A new advertising campaign during May will cost IR£10,000.
➢ A second motor vehicle will be purchased in April at a cost of IR£30,000.
➢ New equipment costing IR£170,000 will be purchased in April.
➢ Purchases will increase each month by 12% beginning in March. **(28)**

1. (b) State **two** important pieces of information which NAMBOOG LTD can obtain from this Cash Flow Statement. **(6)**

1. (c) NAMBOOG LTD forgot to allow for overtime payments of IR£5,000 for the period. State how this omission will affect the net cash position at the end of June. **(6)**

Source: Junior Certificate Higher Level 1994. **(40 marks)**

Cash Flow Statement of Namboog Ltd for Period Jan.–June 1994

	JAN. IR£	FEB. IR£	MARCH IR£	APRIL IR£	MAY IR£	JUNE IR£	TOTAL FOR JAN.–JUNE IR£
RECEIPTS							
Sales	40,000	40,000					
EU Grant	—	—					
Share Capital	—	—					
A Total Receipts	40,000	40,000					
Payments							
Light and Heat	1,600	—					
Rent	500	500					
Wages	2,500	2,500					
Advertising	—	—					
Motor Vehicles	—	25,000					
New Equipment	—	—					
Purchases	16,000	16,000					
B Total Payments	20,600	44,000					
C Net Cash (A – B)	19,400	–4,000					
D Opening Cash	3,000	22,400	18,400				
Closing Cash (C + D)	22,400	18,400					

Solution to Question 1.

1. (a) Cash Flow Statement of Namboog Ltd for Period Jan.–June 1994

	JAN. IR£	FEB. IR£	MARCH IR£	APRIL IR£	MAY IR£	JUNE IR£	TOTAL FOR JAN.–JUNE IR£
RECEIPTS							
Sales	40,000	40,000	40,000	52,000	52,000	52,000	276,000
EU Grant	—	—			40,000		40,000
Share Capital	—	—				50,000	50,000
A Total Receipts	40,000	40,000	40,000	52,000	92,000	102,000	366,000
Payments							
Light and Heat	1,600	—	1,360		1,360		4,320
Rent	500	500	500	500	500	500	3,000
Wages	2,500	2,500	2,500	2,500	2,500	2,500	15,000
Advertising	—	—			10,000		10,000
Motor Vehicles	—	25,000		30,000			55,000
New Equipment	—	—		170,000			170,000
Purchases	16,000	16,000	17,920	20,070	22,478	25,175	117,643
B Total Payments	20,600	44,000	22,280	223,070	36,838	28,175	374,963
C Net Cash (A – B)	19,400	–4,000	17,720	–171,070	55,162	73,825	–8,963
D Opening Cash	3,000	22,400	18,400	36,120	–134,950	–79,788	3,000
Closing Cash (C + D)	22,400	18,400	36,120	–134,950	–79,788	–5,963	–5,963

ALTERNATIVE

The last entry in the question, 'Purchases will increase each month by 12% beginning in March', may have a different interpretation. If it is understood to be an increase of 12% on February figure of IR£16,000, then the purchases figures for March, April, May and June will be IR£17,920 each month. The figures for total payment, net cash, opening cash and closing cash will have to reflect these figures.

1. (b) *(i) There will be net cash deficits in the months of February (IR£4,000) and April (IR£171,070).*

(ii) There will be an overall net cash deficit of IR£8,963 for period January to June 1994.

(iii) There will be a closing cash deficit of IR£5,963 at the end of the period.

1. (c) *The extra overtime payments of IR£5,000 will increase the net cash deficit at the end of June 1994 from IR£8,963 to IR£13,963.*

Chapter 17 — Commercial Banks and Business

Begin by rereading chapter 8 — Money and Banking.

A. Summary of Services Provided by Commercial Banks for Business

(1) SAVING

Deposit account.

(2) MONEY TRANSFER FACILITIES

(a) **Cheque payments.**
(b) **Bank draft** — a cheque drawn by a bank on its own bank account.
(c) **Standing order** — to make certain fixed payments, e.g. rent, insurance, interest payments.
(d) **Direct debit** — to make variable payments from an account at regular intervals, e.g. ESB, telephone.
(e) **Credit transfer** (bank giro) — to pay ESB or telephone bills, make VAT returns.
(f) **Paypath** — wages transferred directly into employee's bank account.

(3) CARD PAYMENTS

(a) **ATM (Automated Teller Machines)** — a business can lodge, withdraw, request a statement, order a cheque book or pay a bill.
(b) **Company credit cards** — used in business to pay for lunches, hotel accommodation, petrol/diesel.

(4) TRANSFERRING MONEY ABROAD

(a) **Sterling draft/foreign draft** — to pay a creditor abroad.
(b) **Traveller's cheques** — used by salespeople travelling abroad.
(c) **Eurocheques** — used by businesspeople or salespeople anywhere in Europe.

(5) LENDING

(a) **Bank overdraft.**
(b) **Term loan** — given for a **stated reason** for a **specified period of time**, it has an **agreed repayment schedule**.
(c) **Commercial mortgage** — for purchasing property.

(6) SAFE KEEPING

(a) **Strongroom facilities** — a business can store important documents and other valuables in the bank's strongroom.
(b) **Night safe facilities** — money can be lodged in the bank late at night through a chute located in the bank wall. A leather wallet and key is provided.

(7) FOREIGN EXCHANGE

(8) FINANCIAL SERVICES

(a) Financial advice.
(b) Income tax advice.
(c) Facility for **purchase and sale of shares.**
(d) Advice on **insurance** or **assurance.**
(e) Help with **financial planning,** e.g. cash flow statements.

(9) HELP WITH EXPORTING

(a) Foreign currency **exchange.**
(b) Checking **creditworthiness** of foreign customers.
(c) Information on foreign markets.
(d) Arranging **collection of payment** from abroad.
(e) Export credit insurance covers risk of non-payment.
(f) Loans, while firms are waiting for payment from foreign customers.

(10) BANK STATEMENTS AND BANK RECONCILIATION STATEMENTS ARE DEALT WITH FULLY IN CHAPTER 8.

B. Operating a Business Bank Account

(1) Usually two signatures required on all cheques and withdrawal forms.
(2) Record all lodgments and payments in the business bank account.
(3) Request a weekly bank statement.
(4) Prepare bank reconciliation statement regularly.

Chapter 18 — Insurance for Business

There are many risks in business and every business should be adequately insured.

A. Reasons for Business Insurance

(1) **Protection of assets** against fire, theft, etc.
(2) Protection against **legal action** as a result of accidents to the public or staff.
(3) **Legal reasons** — motor insurance.

B. Main Types of Business Insurance

(1) **Motor insurance** — compulsory on all company vehicles.
(2) **Employer's liability** — covers claims by employees arising out of accidents at work.
(3) **Fire insurance** — covers damage to property and contents.
(4) **Burglary/Theft insurance** — covers damage arising from a break-in and theft of contents or property.
(5) **Cash in transit insurance** — covers theft of cash while in transit between the business and the bank.
(6) **Goods in transit insurance** — covers theft or damage to goods while being transported.
(7) **Fidelity guarantee insurance** — compensates an employer for loss of cash arising from the dishonesty of employees.
(8) **Plate glass insurance** — covers the breakages or damage to expensive shop window glass.
(9) **Sprinkler leakage insurance** — covers loss or damage caused to stock by water as a result of accidental switching on of the sprinkler system used for fire-fighting.
(10) **Consequential loss insurance** — covers the firm for loss of profits while a business is closed as a result of a fire or flood.
(11) **Public liability insurance** — covers claims made by members of the public who are injured while on the firm's property.
(12) **Bad debts insurance** — covers a loss arising because a debtor does not pay what he owes.
(13) **Product liability insurance** — provides cover against a claim made by a person that he was harmed or suffered a loss or damage through using the firm's products.
(14) **PRSI (Pay-Related Social Insurance)** — PRSI is a payment to the government. The employee pays a percentage of gross wages, but the employer must also make a contribution for each employee on the payroll.

C. Non-Insurable Risks

(1) Bankruptcy.
(2) Stock becoming obsolete (out of date).
(3) Bad management decisions.

D. Recording the Payment of Insurance in the Books of the Business

When insurance is paid, money goes out of the business.

— Debit insurance account (expense).

— Credit bank account (asset).

Example

A payment of IR£600 was made by cheque for insurance on 1 September 1996.

Bank Account (Asset)

			1/9/96	Insurance	600

Insurance Account (Expense)

1/9/96	Bank	600			

The figure of IR£600 insurance will appear under expenses in the profit and loss account.

Examination-Style Questions and Solutions

Question 1.

Teckno Office Supplies Ltd is not satisfied with its present insurers and has asked HIBO Insurance Co. Ltd to give it a quotation for insuring the following:

Buildings valued IR£180,000; machinery valued IR£60,000; five delivery vans valued IR£15,000 each; stock of office supplies valued IR£280,000; cash held in office IR£1,500.

Hibo Insurance Co. Ltd supplied the following quote for one year's insurance:

Insurance for buildings and machinery IR£3 per IR£1,000 value; motor van insurance third party fire and theft IR£600 per van; stock insurance IR£10 per IR£1,000 value; cash insurance IR£10 per IR£500. New business introductory offer: 10% discount off total premium.

Teckno accepted the quotation and took out insurance on everything at replacement value except buildings, which it insured for IR£120,000.

1. (a) Give two reasons why Teckno should take out insurance. **(6)**

1. (b) Calculate the total cost of the insurance premium. **(8)**

1. (c) In the event of fire damage to buildings of IR£60,000, how much compensation would Teckno receive from the insurance company? Show calculations. **(9)**

1. (d) Teckno paid this premium on 1.7.91 by cheque. Complete this cheque on the blank provided below. **(5)**

Counterfoil		Cheque
Date ______ 19__		**Allied Irish Banks** 93–34–81
To		107/108 MAIN STREET BRAY CO WICKLOW 19
For		
Balance	£ 30,000	Pay ______ or order
Amount Lodged		______ IR£
046 Total	£ 30,000	______ **TECKNO LTD**
Amount this Cheque	______	
Bal. forwd		______ **S. MURRAY**
500046		**"500046" "93"3481" 05001052 "02"**

1. (e) The insurance account in Teckno's ledger has an opening debit balance of IR£3,500. Record the payment to Hibo Insurance Co. in this account in Teckno's ledger. **(6)**

1. (f) Teckno's trading year ends on 29.2.92. Show the relevant extracts of the profit and loss account and balance sheet of Teckno, in respect of the insurance account. **(6)**

Source: Junior Certificate Sample Paper Higher Level. **(40 marks)**

Solution to Question 1.

1. (a) *Two reasons for taking out insurance:*

(i) Insurance helps reduce the risks the business might have.

(ii) The law requires Teckno Office Supplies Ltd to have motor insurance.

(iii) In case of loss due to fire, theft, claims by employees, or claims by members of the public.

1. (b) *Calculate the total cost of the insurance premium.*

PREMIUM CALCULATION:

Buildings	120,000	@	IR£3 per IR£1,000	120 x IR£3	=	IR£360
Machinery	60,000	@	IR£3 per IR£1,000	60 x IR£3	=	IR£180
Five delivery vans	15,000	@	IR£600 per van	5 x IR£600	=	IR£3,000
Stock	280,000	@	IR£10 per IR£1,000	280 x IR£10	=	IR£2,800
Cash	1,500	@	IR£10 per IR£500	3 x IR£10	=	IR£30
						IR£6,370
	Less 10% New Business Introductory Offer					IR£637
	Total cost of premiums to Teckno Office Supplies Ltd					IR£5,733

1. (c) *Compensation for fire damage to buildings of IR£60,000*

Calculation:

Buildings valued @ IR£180,000 insured for IR£120,000, i.e. buildings insured for 2/3 of value. The principle of average clause applies here. The insurance company will pay 2/3 of IR£60,000 = IR£40,000.

Teckno Office Supplies Ltd will receive IR£40,000.

1. (d) *Complete cheque on blank document supplied.*

Counterfoil		Cheque
Date *1 July* 1991		**Allied Irish Banks** 93–34–81
To *Hibo Insurance Ltd*		107/108 MAIN STREET BRAY CO WICKLOW *1/7* 1991
For *Insurance 1/7/91–30/6/92*		Pay *Hibo Insurance Co Ltd* or order
Balance	£ 30,000	*Five thousand seven hundred and thirty three pounds* IR£ *5,733—*
Amount Lodged		TECKNO LTD
046 Total	£ 30,000	*S. Murray*
Amount this Cheque	*£ 5,733*	S. MURRAY
Bal. forwd	*£24,267*	
500046		"500046" "93"3481" 05001052 "02"

1. (e) *Record balance and payment to Hibo Insurance Company in Teckno's ledger.*

Insurance Account

Date	Details	Total
1/7/91	Balance	3,500
1/7/91	Bank	5,733

1. (f) *Extracts from profit and loss account and balance sheet in respect of insurance.*

Profit and Loss Account (Extract) for Year Ending 29 February 1992

Less Expenses		
Insurance	9,233	
Less Insurance Prepaid (1/3)	1,911	7,322

Balance Sheet (Extract) as at 29 February 1992

Current Assets		
Insurance Prepaid		1,911

Question 2.
Answer all sections. This is an Insurance Premium Calculation and Recording Question.

Shopfitters Ltd has decided to change its insurers and has asked Sword Insurers Ltd to give it a quotation for insuring the following:

Buildings IR£135,000; machinery IR£70,000; three delivery vans valued at IR£18,000 each; stock of shopfittings IR£85,000; cash held in the office IR£1,250.

Sword Insurers Ltd supplied the following quotation for one year's insurance:

Insurance for buildings and machinery IR£3.50 per IR£1,000 value; motor van insurance third party fire and theft IR£710 per van; stock insurance IR£11.50 per IR£1,000 value; cash insurance IR£12 per IR£500.
New business introductory offer: 20% discount off total premium.

Shopfitters Ltd accepted the quotation and took out insurance on everything at replacement cost (as stated above) except the machinery, which it insured for IR£50,000.

Shopfitters Ltd paid the premium by cheque on 1 July 1992.

Answer the following:
2. (a) Calculate the amount of the premium paid by Shopfitters Ltd on 1 July 1992. (Show your workings clearly.) **(16)**
2. (b) The Insurance Account in Shopfitters Ltd ledger has an opening debit balance of IR£1,700. Record the payment to Sword Insurers Ltd on 1 July 1992.

Balance the **Insurance Account** on 31 December 1992 (the end of its trading year) showing clearly the amount to be transferred to the Profit and Loss Account. **(12)**

2. (c) In the event of fire damage to machinery of IR£35,000, how much compensation would Shopfitters Ltd receive? (Show your workings.) **(8)**

2. (d) Name two other types of insurance you think Shopfitters Ltd should have. **(4)**

Source: Junior Certificate Higher Level 1993. **(40 marks)**

Solution to Question 2.

2. (a) *Calculate premium paid by Shopfitters Ltd.*

Buildings	IR£135,000 @	IR£3.50 per IR£1,000	135 x IR£3.50 =	IR£472.50
Machinery	IR£50,000 @	IR£3.50 per IR£1,000	50 x IR£3.50 =	IR£175.00
Three delivery vans	IR£18,000 @	IR£710 per van	3 x IR£710 =	IR£2,130.00
Stock	IR£85,000 @	IR£11.50 per IR£1,000	85 x IR£11.50 =	IR£977.50
Cash	IR£1,250 @	IR£12 per IR£500	2.5 x IR£12 =	IR£30.00
				IR£3,785.00
	Less 20% new business introductory offer			IR£757.00
	Total amount of premium paid by Shopfitters Ltd			IR£3,028.00

2. (b) *Insurance Account*

Debit **Insurance Account** **Credit**

Date	Details	Fo	Total	Date	Details	Fo	Total
1/7/92	Balance	B/d	1,700	31/12/92	P & L A/C		3,214
1/7/92	Bank	CB	3,028	31/12/92	Balance	C/d	1,514
			4,728				4,728
1/1/93	Balance	B/d	1,514				

2. (c) *Compensation for fire damage to machinery IR£35,000.*

Calculations:

Machinery valued IR£70,000 is insured for IR£50,000, i.e. it is insured for 5/7 of its value. The average clause principle applies in this partial loss of IR£35,000. The insurance company will pay IR£35,000 x 5/7 = IR£25,000.

2. (d) *Public liability, employer's liability, fidelity guarantee, cash in transit, plate glass, goods in transit, etc.*

Higher Level

Chapter 19 — Communications

Communication is the exchanging of information. The message should be **brief**, **clear** and **simple**.

A. Factors to Be Considered When Choosing a Form of Communication

(1) Cost.
(2) Speed.
(3) Safety.
(4) Written record.
(5) Secrecy.
(6) Destination.
(7) Accuracy.

B. Who Does a Business Communicate With?

(1) Directors, managers, employees, supervisors — **internal communication**.
(2) Customers, public, shareholders, insurance companies, bank, suppliers, tax office — **external communication**.

C. Internal and External Communication

Internal Communication	External Communication
1. Person to person	1. Meeting
2. Notice-board	2. Radio and TV
3. Meeting	3. Trade fairs and exhibitions
4. Intercom	4. Newspapers
5. Paging	5. Publications
6. Walkie-talkie (portable radio)	6. Letters and business documents
7. Memorandum (memo)	7. Computers
8. Internal report	8. Films, slideshows and videos
9. Closed-circuit TV	9. RTE Aertel and BBC Ceefax
10. Computers	10. Telecom Éireann
11. Internal newspapers	11. An Post
12. Graphs, bar charts, pictograms, pie charts	
13. Internal telephone.	

TELECOM ÉIREANN SERVICES

(1) Telephone.
(2) Freephone — 1800 plus the freephone number.
(3) Eircell — mobile phone system.

(4) Chargecard — calls made from any phone are charged to your existing home or office bill.
(5) Eirpage — paging service.
(6) Eirpac — data transmission.
(7) Eirmail — electronic mail service.
(8) Fax (Facsimile) — exact copy of a document can be transmitted over the telephone to another fax machine.
(9) Telex — a message is typed on a telex machine and then sent through the telephone, where it is printed out on the receiver's telex machine.
(10) Minitel — subscription provides access to a wide range of information on matters such as banking, finance, insurance, sports, tourism, transport, travel, weather.
(11) Telemessages — dial 196, give your message and it will be delivered in writing on the next working day.
(12) Tele-Conferencing — a meeting or conference can be held over the telephone.
(13) Video-Conferencing — a way of conducting meetings without travelling to the meeting. Video cameras are used to transmit the picture and sound of the meeting over the telephone.

AN POST

An Post offers a wide range of services in communications.
(1) Collection and Delivery of Letters and Parcels Express Mail.
(2) Publicity Post — delivery of unaddressed leaflets to every household in a specific area for a fee.
(3) Post Aim — allows a business to send letters to all its customers at half-price.
(4) Freepost — allows customers to write to a firm free.
(5) Business Reply Service — the business provides a special business reply envelope.
(6) Registered Post — for sending valuable items through the post.
(7) Fax Post — fax service offered by An Post.

D. Methods of Communication

ORAL	WRITTEN	VISUAL
Person to person Meeting Telephone Intercom Paging Walkie-talkie Video-conferencing Tele-conferencing	Notice-board Memo Report Letter and business documents Newspapers Fax Telex An Post	Films, slides and videos Aertel Ceefax Graphs Bar chart Pictogram Pie charts
Advantage Fast **Disadvantage** No written record	**Advantage** Written record	**Advantages** 1. Easy to understand 2. Very effective

E. Visual Communication/Charts and Graphs

There are four main ways of showing information visually.
Line graph, bar chart, pie chart, pictogram.

(1) LINE GRAPH

A line graph shows a trend, i.e. how things change over time.

Inflation Percentages 1985–1994

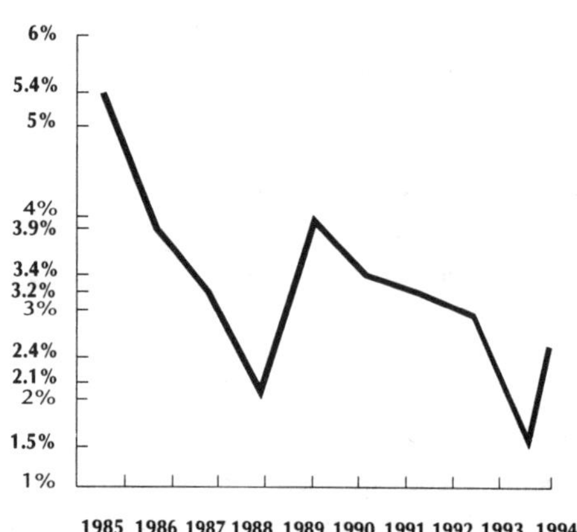

Source: Central Statistics Office.

(2) BAR CHART

A bar chart is very useful when making comparisons. Information is displayed in a series of bars.

Unemployment 1989–1994

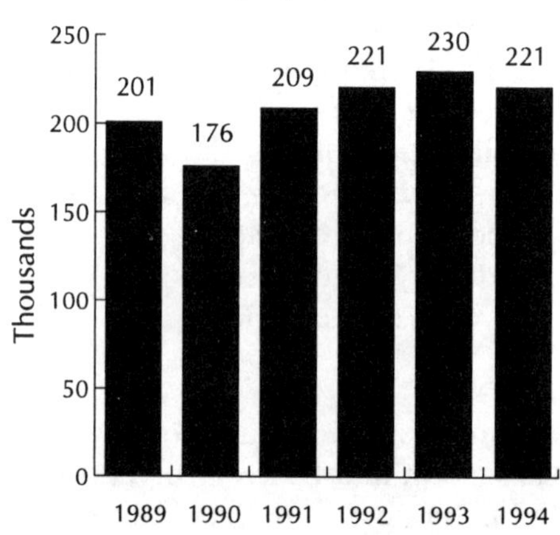

Source: Central Statistics Office.

(3) PIE CHART

A pie chart is a circle divided into sections, each section showing figures as a percentage of the total.

Personal Expenditure 1992

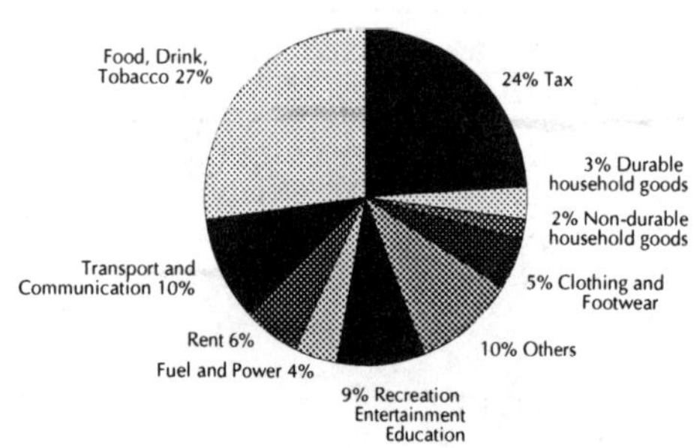

Source: Central Statistics Office.

(4) PICTOGRAM

Here pictures or symbols are used to represent figures.

Some Institutions of the European Union

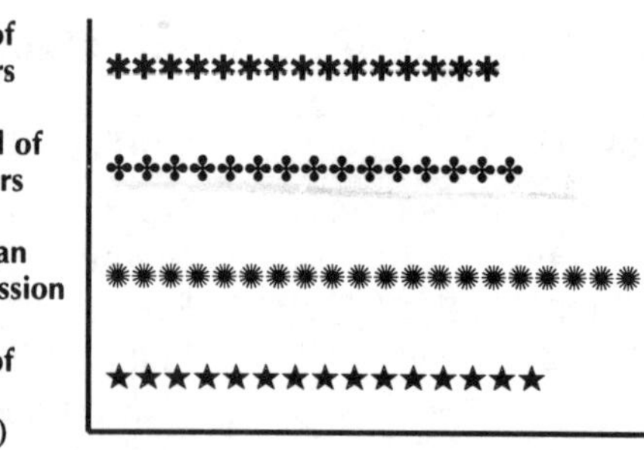

One picture = One member.

PRACTICE QUESTIONS

(i) Question 5, Section A, Ordinary Level, 1993.
(ii) Question 7 (b), (c), (d), Section B, Ordinary Level, 1992.
(iii) Question 6, Paper I, Section A, Higher Level, 1992.

Chapter 20 — Chain of Production and Channels of Distribution

A. Types of Production

(1) **Primary production** (extractive industries), e.g. agriculture, forestry, fishing, mining.
(2) **Secondary production** (manufacturing industries), e.g. brewing, food processing.
(3) **Tertiary production** (service industries), e.g. banking, insurance, transport.

B. Public Sector and Private Sector

Public sector — working for government, e.g. teachers.
Private sector — all other workers not employed by government, e.g. bank officials.

C. Channels of Distribution

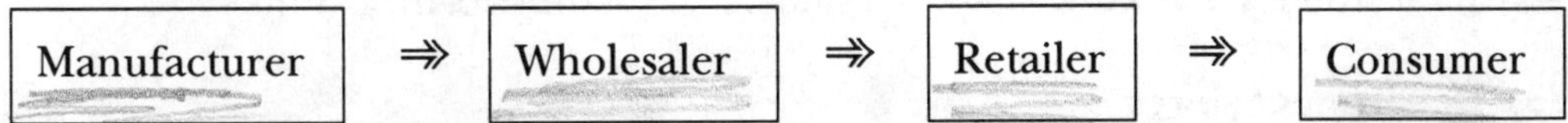

The manufacturer turns raw materials into finished goods.

D. Wholesaler

The wholesaler buys in bulk from manufacturer and sells in smaller quantities to the retailer.

SERVICES TO MANUFACTURER	SERVICES TO RETAILER
(1) Buys in bulk. (2) Blends, grades, packs goods. (3) Advertises manufacturer's goods. (4) Gives information.	(1) Gives credit to retailer. (2) Delivers goods to retailer. (3) Provides wide choice of goods. (4) Informs retailers about new products.

TYPES OF WHOLESALER

(1) Traditional wholesaler
Retailer sends in order. Goods are delivered to retailer's premises. Credit is given.

(2) Specialist wholesaler
Specialises in a certain range of goods.

(3) Cash and carry wholesaler
Sells a wide variety of goods. Retailer goes to the wholesaler's premises, selects and pays for goods and transports them to his premises.

E. Retailer

The retailer buys goods from the wholesaler and sells to the consumer.

FUNCTIONS OF RETAILER

(1) Sells goods or services at a convenient location.
(2) Offers a wide range of goods to the consumer.
(3) May give **credit.**
(4) May **deliver** goods.

TYPES OF RETAILER

(1) Independent shops/Sole traders
- Small shops owned and managed by one person.
- **Examples:** butcher, newsagent.

(2) Multiple shops/Chain stores
- A number of shops/branches owned by same firm.
- Multiple shops **specialise** in a particular type of product.
- Chain stores **sell a wide range** of goods, e.g. Quinnsworth, Dunnes.

(3) Department stores
- Sell a wide range of goods in many different departments.
- **Examples:** Roches Stores, Marks & Spencer.

(4) Supermarkets
- Large self-service stores selling a variety of goods, e.g. Dunnes Stores, Superquinn.

(5) Shopping centres
- A number of shops under one roof usually located on the outskirts of large towns or cities.

(6) Franchising
- Retailer has permission to use name and logo.
- **Examples:** McDonalds, Burgerland.

(7) Voluntary groups
- A number of small retailers link with a wholesaler to form a group.
- **Examples:** Super Valu, Spar.

(8) Mail order
- Customer chooses goods from catalogue.
- **Example:** Family Album.

(9) Vending machines
☛ Machines that sell cigarettes, drinks, sweets.

(10) Petrol stations
☛ Sell a wide range of goods and services.

(11) Street or roadside traders
☛ People who sell from a stall on the street or on the roadside.

(12) Mobile shops
Traders who move around and sell from a van.

(13) Door-to-door sales
People who go from door to door selling, e.g. encyclopaedias, insurance.

DEVELOPMENTS IN RETAILING
(1) Late-night shopping and Sunday trading.
(2) In-store banking.
(3) Bar codes.
(4) Increase in the use of environmentally friendly products.
(5) More foreign competition.
(6) Greater use of credit cards.
(7) Many retailers providing a delivery service.
(8) Growth of franchising.
(9) Increase in the sale of fast foods.
(10) Growth in the number of shopping centres.

Examination-Style Question and Solution

Question 1.
Write in each box whether the following forms of Industry are:

Primary, Secondary or Services

(a) MINING	Primary
(b) BANKING	Services
(c) PEN FACTORIES	Secondary

Source: Junior Certificate Ordinary Level 1994. **(4)**

Chapter 21 — People at Work

A. Work

Performing a task **without payment**.

B. Employment

- Working **for payment.**

C. Nature and Extent of Employment

- People who are employed work in three main areas: agriculture, industry, services.
- People who cannot find employment are said to be unemployed.
- The labour force = those who are employed and those available for work.
- Employment in agriculture and industry is falling.
- Employment in services is increasing.
- Unemployment and the labour force are increasing.

D. Unemployment

People are unemployed when they are willing to work for payment but cannot find a job.

WHY IS UNEMPLOYMENT RISING?

(1) Labour force increasing.
(2) Fall in the number employed in agriculture and industry.
(3) New technology replacing workers.
(4) Firms have reduced staff numbers.
(5) Decrease in the number of foreign firms setting up in Ireland.
(6) Less money being put into job creation.

HOW TO REDUCE UNEMPLOYMENT

(1) Put more money into job creation.
(2) Encourage more enterprise.
(3) Become more competitive abroad and increase sales, thus creating more jobs.
(4) Introduce early retirement and job-sharing schemes.

E. Emigration

Leaving the country in search of employment.

F. Self-Employment

WHY PEOPLE BECOME SELF-EMPLOYED

(1) Cannot find employment.
(2) Made redundant.
(3) See an opportunity to start own business.

REWARDS OF SELF-EMPLOYMENT

(1) Own boss, make your own decisions.
(2) Receive all the profit.
(3) Decide what hours to work.
(4) Decide what to sell.

RISKS OF SELF-EMPLOYMENT

(1) Business may fail.
(2) Work long hours.
(3) Provide all the money (capital).
(4) Overworked.

G. Organisation of the Workplace

ORGANISATION STRUCTURE OF A COMPANY

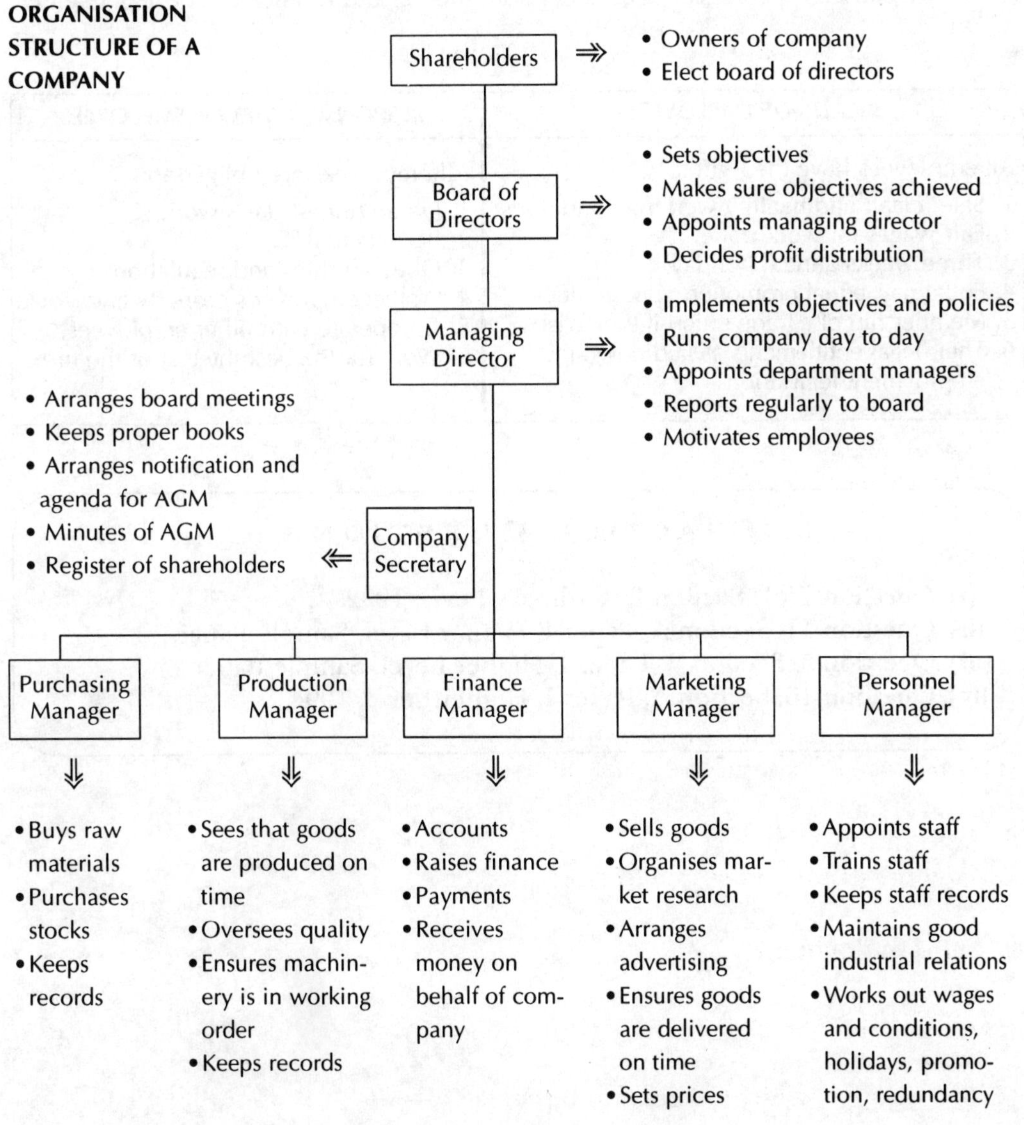
Shareholders
• Owners of company
• Elect board of directors
Board of Directors
• Sets objectives
• Makes sure objectives achieved
• Appoints managing director
• Decides profit distribution
Managing Director
• Implements objectives and policies
• Runs company day to day
• Appoints department managers
• Reports regularly to board
• Motivates employees
Company Secretary
• Arranges board meetings
• Keeps proper books
• Arranges notification and agenda for AGM
• Minutes of AGM
• Register of shareholders
Purchasing Manager
• Buys raw materials
• Purchases stocks
• Keeps records
Production Manager
• Sees that goods are produced on time
• Oversees quality
• Ensures machinery is in working order
• Keeps records
Finance Manager
• Accounts
• Raises finance
• Payments
• Receives money on behalf of company
Marketing Manager
• Sells goods
• Organises market research
• Arranges advertising
• Ensures goods are delivered on time
• Sets prices
Personnel Manager
• Appoints staff
• Trains staff
• Keeps staff records
• Maintains good industrial relations
• Works out wages and conditions, holidays, promotion, redundancy

H. Types of Job

(1) **Services** — providing a service to individuals or to business, e.g. teacher.
(2) **Administration** — in either a management or a supervisory role.
(3) **Artistic/Creative** — using one's imagination or creative abilities, e.g. artist.
(4) **Technical** — understanding how things work, e.g. computer programmer.
(5) **Manual** — physical work, e.g. builder.
(6) **Clerical** — office work.

TYPES OF SKILL

(1) **Unskilled** — no qualifications and no training, e.g. builder's labourer.
(2) **Semi-skilled** — trained to do a particular task, e.g. machine operator.
(3) **Skilled** — trained in a trade, usually having served an apprenticeship, e.g. electrician.
(4) **Professional** — professional qualification, such as a university degree, e.g. teacher.

I.

RIGHTS OF EMPLOYEES	RESPONSIBILITIES OF EMPLOYEES
All employees have the right to: 1. Safe, clean and healthy working conditions. 2. Fair wages for work done. 3. Three weeks annual holidays. 4. Equal pay, equal promotion opportunities. 5. Membership of a trade union if they wish. 6. Their legal entitlements as laid down in employment legislation.	All employees are obliged to: 1. Do an honest day's work. 2. Be punctual. 3. Obey all rules and regulations. 4. Protect employer's property and stock. 5. Co-operate with other employees. 6. Work for the best interest of the firm.

PRACTICE QUESTIONS

(i) Question 7(e), Section B, Ordinary Level, 1992.
(ii) Question 11, Section A, Paper I, Higher Level, Sample Paper.
(iii) Question 5, Section B, Paper I, Higher Level, Sample Paper.
(iv) Question 16, Section A, Paper I, Higher Level, 1994.

Chapter 22 — Being an Employer

A.

RIGHTS OF EMPLOYER	RESPONSIBILITIES OF EMPLOYER
1. To decide on the **objectives** and **policies** of the business. 2. To hire suitable staff. 3. To dismiss dishonest or unsuitable staff. 4. To expect loyalty from staff.	1. To make sure workplace is safe and healthy. 2. To give employees terms of employment in writing. 3. To give proper holidays. 4. To pay agreed wages. 5. Not to discriminate when advertising, recruiting or promoting staff. 6. To give female employees maternity leave. 7. To give equal pay to men and women. 8. To deduct PAYE and PRSI from employees and remit it to Collector General of Taxes.

B. Procedure for Employing Staff

(1) **Draw up** job description.
(2) **Advertise** the job.
(3) **Short-list** candidates.
(4) **Interview** candidates.
(5) **Select** the most suitable candidate.
(6) **Inform** the successful candidate.
(7) Prepare a written **contract of employment.**
(8) New employee is **introduced to the firm**. A **period of training** is organised.
(9) New employee supplies a tax-free allowance certificate. New employee is then registered for PAYE and PRSI.

C. Calculating Wages

Employees are paid by time rate, piece rate or on a commission basis.

(1) TIME RATE
Employees are paid a certain rate per hour or per day.

(2) PIECE RATE
Employees are paid by the number of items produced.

(3) COMMISSION
Calculated as a percentage of sales.

Gross Pay = Basic Pay + Overtime + Commission.

Net Pay = Gross Pay – Deductions.

D. Income Tax Forms

(1) P60

At the end of the tax year each employee receives a P60, which shows amount of pay, tax and PRSI deducted during the tax year.

(2) P45 CESSATION CERTIFICATE

Given to an employee leaving the firm. This shows amount earned and how much tax and PRSI has been paid to date.

(3) P12

Filled up when applying for a tax-free allowance.

E. Wages Slip

When employees are paid they receive their pay plus a payslip. This shows gross pay, deductions and net pay.

Example

Michael Ryan earns a basic wage of IR£250. He earned IR£50 overtime. His TFA is IR£100 per week. His deductions are PAYE 27%, PRSI 10% of gross, union IR£10 and VHI IR£15.

Calculate his net wage and complete the payslip.

Solution

Workings:

(i) Calculation of PAYE (**NB** PAYE is calculated on taxable income)

Gross wage (250 + 50)	= IR£300
– Tax-Free Allowance	IR£100
Taxable income	IR£200
PAYE = 27% of IR£200	= **IR£54**

(ii) Calculation of PRSI (**NB** PRSI is calculated on gross wages)
PRSI = 10% of gross wages = 10% IR£300 = **IR£30**

(iii) Total Deductions
PAYE IR£54 + **PRSI** IR£30 + **Union** IR£10 + **VHI** IR£15 = IR£109
Total deductions: IR£109.

(iv) Find Net Pay

Net Pay = Gross Wages – Deductions.
IR£300 – IR£109 = IR£191 = Net pay.

PAYSLIP

Name	Basic	Pay O/T	Gross	Tax-Free Allowance	PAYE	PRSI	Union	VHI	Total Deductions	Net Pay
MICHAEL RYAN	IR£250	IR£50	IR£300	IR£100	IR£54	IR£30	IR£10	IR£15	IR£109	IR£191

F. Wages Book

The employer will keep a record of all wages/salaries paid in a wages book. From the wages book the employer can calculate the total cost of wages and employer's PRSI. The wages slip is an extract from the wages book.

Example

Wages book of Premier Ltd which employs three people, including Michael Ryan, whose payslip is shown above. Assume employer's rate of PRSI is 12%, employee PRSI 10%, employee PAYE 27%.

WAGES BOOK OF PREMIER LTD

Date	Employee	Basic	O/T	Gross	TFA	PAYE	PRSI	Union	VHI	Total Deductions	Net Pay	Employer PRSI	Total PRSI
20/1/97	Michael Ryan	250	50	300	100	54	30	10	15	109	191	36	66
20/1/97	Mary Lucey	370	30	400	100	81	40	10	20	151	249	48	88
20/1/97	John Murphy	190	10	200	100	27	20	10	12	69	131	24	44
	TOTALS	810	90	900	300	162	90	30	47	329	571	108	198

G. Payment of Wages and Salaries

Wages and salaries may be paid in any one of the following ways:

(1) By cash.

(2) By cheque — safe method of payment.

(3) By credit transfer directly into the bank account of employee (Paypath).

BY CASH

If wages are paid by cash the employer will have to do a cash analysis to show the breakdown of the wages into the various denominations of money required for paying each employee. The following cash analysis will show the exact cash required to pay the three employees of Premier Ltd.

NOTE/COIN ANALYSIS OF PREMIER LTD

NAME	Net Pay	IR£50	IR£20	IR£10	IR£5	IR£1	50p	20p	10p	5p	2p	1p
Michael Ryan	191	3	2	0	0	1	0	0	0	0	0	0
Mary Lucey	249	4	2	0	1	4	0	0	0	0	0	0
John Murphy	131	2	1	1	0	1	0	0	0	0	0	0
Total	571	9	5	1	1	6	0	0	0	0	0	0

H. Recording the Total Cost of Wages in Books of Premier Ltd.

- ➢ Debit wages account. £1,008
- ➢ Credit bank account. £1,008

Gross Wages + Employer's PRSI

Wages Account

20.1.97	Bank	1,008	20.1.97	Profit and Loss Account	1,008

Bank Account

			20.1.97	Wages	1,008

Wages account is closed off to the profit and loss account. Figure will appear under expenses.

Profit and Loss Account for week ending 20.1.97

	Expenses Wages	1,008	

I. Employee Records

Employers keep records on all employees.

(1) Personal details.
(2) Job application form.
(3) Curriculum vitae.
(4) Job performance.
(5) Behaviour — absence, lateness, personal days taken.
(6) Copy of contract of employment.
(7) PAYE and PRSI records.

WHY ARE EMPLOYEE RECORDS KEPT?
(1) A reference if an employee leaves.
(2) Promotion decisions.
(3) PAYE and PRSI records are compulsory.

Examination-Style Question and Solution

Question 1.
Answer (a) and (b) and (c). This is a Person at Work Question.

1. (a) Teresa Clancy recently applied for a job advertised as follows in the Sunday newspapers.

> **MORGAN INSURANCE BROKERS LTD**
> General Insurance Clerk required
> Typing and computer knowledge an advantage.
> Basic Pay IR£140 gross for 39-hour week,
> Overtime also a possibility.
> Subsidised canteen and travel.
> Applications, in writing, should be sent to:
> The Personnel Manager,
> Morgan Insurance Brokers Ltd,
> Cork Road, Waterford.
> Morgan Insurance is an equal opportunities employer.

Explain **any four** of the terms **underlined** in the above advertisement. **(16)**

1. (b) Teresa Clancy got the job. Last week she worked a total of 48 hours.

➢ Overtime is paid at IR£6 per hour. Her tax-free allowances are IR£84 per week. Her rate of tax is 40%, PRSI 10% of gross and her other weekly deductions are union fee IR£3, VHI IR£6.

➢ Calculate her net wage and complete the pay slip, using supplied blank at the end of the question (show your workings). **(18)**

1. (c) State two methods, other than on a time basis, by which an employee can be paid. **(6)**

Name	Basic	Pay O/T	Gross	Tax-Free Allowance	PAYE	PRSI	Union	VHI	Total Deductions	Net Pay
T. Clancy										

Source: Junior Certificate Higher Level 1992. **(40 marks)**

Solution to Question 1.

1. (a) *Basic Pay: Gross pay excluding overtime. Pay for working normal week (usually 39 hours).*
Overtime: Pay for working more than normal hours or for working more than 39 hours a week.
Subsidised: Reduced prices.
Personnel Manager: Person in charge of staff, appointing staff, training staff, staff records.
Equal Opportunities: Job open to both men and women.

1. (b) Document for use with part B

PAYSLIP

Name	Basic	Pay O/T	Gross	Tax-Free Allowance	PAYE	PRSI	Union	VHI	Total Deductions	Net Pay
T. Clancy	*140*	*54*	*194*	*84*	*44*	*19.40*	*3*	*6*	*72.40*	*121.60*

WORKINGS

Basic pay *IR£140 for 39 hours.*

Overtime *9 hours x IR£6 per hour = IR£54.*

Gross pay = *Basic pay IR£140 + O/T IR£54 = IR£194.*

Tax-Free Allowance *IR£84 per week given in question.*

PAYE *is calculated on taxable income.*

Gross pay – TFA = Taxable income.
194 – 84 = 110 x 40% = IR£44.

PRSI = *10% of gross = IR£19.40, union IR£3, VHI IR£6 (see question).*

Total deduction = *PAYE + PRSI + union + VHI*
IR£44 + IR£19.40 + IR£3 + IR£6 = 72.40.

Net pay = *Gross pay 194 – Deductions 72.40 = IR£121.60.*

1. (c) *Piece rate, commission.*

PRACTICE QUESTIONS

(i) Question 14, Section A, Ordinary Level, 1992.
(ii) Question 4, Section B, Ordinary Level, 1994.
(iii) Question 9, Section A, Paper I, Higher Level, 1992.

Chapter 23 — Industrial Relations

A. Introduction

Industrial relations is the term used to describe the relationship between management and employees.

B. What Is a Trade Union?

A trade union is a group of workers who join together to protect their interests and rights and who try to improve their wages and conditions of work.

C. Functions of a Trade Union

(1) To negotiate wages and salaries for members.
(2) To negotiate conditions of work.
(3) To negotiate with employers if a dispute occurs.
(4) To protect members from unfair dismissal.
(5) To negotiate in a redundancy situation.

D. Types of Trade Union

(1) **Industrial unions** — represent all workers in an industry, e.g. Irish Bank Officials' Association (IBOA).
(2) **Craft unions** — members have a trade or craft, e.g. Brick and Stonelayers' Trade Union.
(3) **White-collar unions** — members are usually professional, e.g. teachers' unions: ASTI, TUI, INTO.
(4) **General unions** — members come from a variety of occupations, e.g. SIPTU (Services, Industrial, Professional and Technical Union).

E. How to Join a Trade Union

(1) Contact shop steward (union representative).
(2) Fill up application form.
(3) Pay annual subscription.

F. Functions of a Shop Steward

(1) Acts as intermediary between union members and union head office.
(2) Represents members.
(3) Recruits new members.
(4) Attends union meetings.
(5) Collects subscriptions.

G. Irish Congress of Trade Unions (ICTU)

ICTU represents all trade unions.

H. Irish Business Employers' Confederation (IBEC)

IBEC represents all employers.

I. Management Role

This is very important for good industrial relations. The personnel manager will deal with the shop steward if a dispute arises.

J. What Is a Dispute?

A dispute is a disagreement between employees and management.

K. Main Causes of Disputes

(1) Wages and working conditions.
(2) Dismissal of employees.
(3) Employees being made redundant.
(4) Demarcation — 'who does what?'
(5) Promotion, procedures.

L. Types of Industrial Action (Strikes)

(1) STRIKE

Workers withdraw labour, i.e. refuse to work. There are two types of strike:

(a) Unofficial strike — not approved by trade union.
(b) Official strike — approved by trade union.

(2) ALL-OUT STRIKE

All unions in the firm stop work in support of the union on strike.

(3) WORK TO RULE (I.E. GO SLOW)

Workers go to work but do only the bare essentials.

(4) A 'SIT-IN'

Employees sit in in the premises where they work.

PICKETING

Workers on strike usually **picket** the employer's premises.

M. How to Resolve a Dispute

(1) Discuss problem with supervisor. If no solution:
(2) Discuss problem with shop steward, who will talk to management. If no solution:
(3) Shop steward notifies union head office. If no solution:
(4) A third party may be called in, e.g. Labour Relations Commission.

N. Functions of Labour Relations Commission (LRC)

(1) Conciliation service.
(2) Advisory service.

(3) It appoints **Rights Commissioners**.
(4) It appoints **Equality Officers.**

O. Labour Court

The Labour Court is a court of last resort to help to settle industrial disputes.

P. Equality in Employment

(1) It is illegal to discriminate on the grounds of sex or marital status.
(2) There must be equal pay for men and women.

Q. Business Terms

Arbitrator A person who investigates the dispute and makes a recommendation which both parties have agreed in advance to accept.
ASTI Association of Secondary Teachers of Ireland.
Conciliation A service to try to get both parties to solve the dispute themselves.
Craft Union Members have trade or craft.
Demarcation 'Who Does What' job dispute.
General Union Represents workers from all occupations.
IBEC Irish Business Employers' Confederation — represents employers.
IBOA Irish Bank Officials' Association.
ICTU Irish Congress of Trade Unions — represents all unions in Ireland.
Industrial Relations Relationship between management and employees.
Industrial Union Represents all workers in a particular industry.
INTO Irish National Teachers' Organisation.
Labour Court Court of last resort for solving disputes. Decisions not binding.
Labour Relations Commission Set up to try to settle disputes.
Lightning Strike Sudden stoppage — no warning given.
Lock-Out Employer locks workers out of premises.
Official Strike A strike that union approves.
Overtime Ban Workers refuse to work extra hours.
Picket Workers on strike walking outside business carrying placards.
Promotion Movement to a position of more authority and more responsibility.
Redundancy Workers being 'laid off' — no work.
Token Stoppage Short work stoppage.
Trade Dispute A disagreement between employees and management.
Trade Union Employees join together to protect interests and rights.
TUI Teachers' Union of Ireland.
Union Dues Union subscriptions, i.e. fee paid for union membership.
Unofficial Strike A strike that union does not approve.
White-Collar Unions Professional people who provide services.
Work to Rule Go slow — workers do basic duties only.

PRACTICE QUESTIONS

(i) Question 11, Section A, Paper I, Higher Level, 1993.
(ii) Question 5, Section A, Paper I, Higher Level, 1994.

SECTION THREE — ENTERPRISE

MARKETING AND DISTRIBUTION

Chapter 24 — Marketing

A. Market

A market is a place where goods are bought and sold.

B. Types of Market

(1) Retail Market
(2) Wholesale Market
(3) Street Market
(4) Stock Exchange
(5) Export Market

C. Target Market

The target market is the total number of potential customers for a product or a service, e.g. the target market of pop group Take That is teenage females.

D. Market Segmentation

Producing many different models of the same product to satisfy customers, e.g. Fiat Punto 'European Car of the Year' 1994 SX three-door, SX five-door, or turbo diesel.

E. Marketing

Marketing is concerned with all the stages involved in getting the product or service to the final customer.

F. Five Ps of Marketing/Marketing Mix

(1) Product
(2) Place
(3) Price
(4) Packaging
(5) Promotion.

To be successful a business must have the **right product** on sale in the **right place** at the **right price** in the **right package** using the **right promotion**.

G. Market Research

Market research involves researching, gathering, recording and analysing information about a market. The main objective is to find out information.

H. Reasons for Market Research

To find out:
(1) Who will buy the product.
(2) What price should be charged.
(3) What methods of advertising should be used.
(4) Best packaging to use.
(5) What competition is in the market.

I. Methods of Collecting Information for Market Research

(1) DESK RESEARCH

This involves researching material already in the files.

(2) FIELD RESEARCH

This involves getting information directly from the customer.
(a) Observation
(b) Questionnaire
(c) Telephone interview
(d) Personal interview
(e) Panels.

J. Test Marketing

A new product is tested on a small number of people to find their reaction.

K. Product Development

It is important to **improve existing products** and **develop new products.** If a new product is to be successful it must be

- better quality
- better value
- better presented.

L. Advertising

Advertising is informing consumers about products or services.

M. Aims of Advertising

(1) To give information to consumers.
(2) To persuade consumers to buy.
(3) To launch new products.
(4) To project a good image of the firm.

N. Types of Advertising

(1) **Informative advertising** — giving information to the consumer.
(2) **Persuasive advertising** — trying to convince the consumer.
(3) **Competitive advertising** — comparing with competitors.
(4) **Generic advertising** — industry promotes the product.

O. Advertising Media, i.e. Where to Advertise

(1) Newspapers (Press)
(2) Television
(3) Radio
(4) Posters and Hoardings
(5) Magazines
(6) Cinemas
(7) Trade Fairs and Exhibitions
(8) Leaflets
(9) Window Displays
(10) Vehicle Displays
(11) Shopping Bags
(12) Journals.

P. Steps Involved in an Advertising Campaign

(1) Identify target market, i.e. potential customers.
(2) Choose medium, e.g. radio, TV.
(3) Decide on the message, e.g. song, slogan, cartoon.
(4) Decide on personnel, e.g. pop star, soccer star.

A good advertisement will:

➢ Attract our attention.
➢ Provide information.
➢ Stay in our memories, e.g. 'Magic Moments' for Quality Street.
➢ Create desire.
➢ Stimulate action.

Q. Sales Promotion

This is used to back up advertising and the aim is the same — to increase sales. Techniques include:

(1) Free samples
(2) Special offers
(3) Coupons/Tokens
(4) 'Money-Off Vouchers'
(5) In-store promotions
(6) Competitions and draws.

R. Selling Techniques

(1) BRANDING

Distinguishes product from other similar products, e.g. Levi's, Kerrygold.

(2) LOSS LEADERS

Selling products below cost — illegal.

(3) TRADE MARKS AND LOGOS

A trade mark is the name given to the product or firm while a logo is the symbol, which is usually written in a very distinctive style, e.g.

(4) MERCHANDISING

Arranging products on shelves or in display cabinets for maximum impact on the consumer.

S. Public Relations (PR)

Presenting a good image of the company to the public.

DUTIES OF PUBLIC RELATIONS OFFICER

(1) Issuing press releases.
(2) Arranging trade fairs and exhibitions.
(3) Arranging sponsorship.
(4) Arranging radio and TV coverage of events.
(5) Organising company literature for employees and the public.

T. Sponsorship

Many firms sponsor major events or sports teams. For example, Opel sponsors the Irish international soccer team, Sharp — Manchester United FC.

U. Export Markets

Exports are essential if Irish firms are to survive and expand.
Difficulties in Exporting
(1) Language.
(2) Currency.
(3) Documentation.
(4) Transport costs.
(5) Risk of non-payment is very great.

V. Business Terms

Branded Goods Well-known goods easily identifiable by customers.
Consumer Panel Group of consumers who give reaction to a product.
Desk Research Looking up materials already in files.

Field Research Obtaining information directly from consumers.
Import Substitution Replacing imported product with Irish-made product.
In-Store Promotion Customers taste a product in large stores.
Logo Distinctive style of writing a firm's name.
Loss Leader Selling a product at a loss to attract customers.
Market A place where goods are bought and sold.
Market Research Gathering and recording information about a market.
Market Segmentation Dividing market into different segments.
Marketing All stages in getting product to the consumer.
Marketing Mix Five Ps of marketing: product, place, price, packaging, promotion.
PRO Public Relations Officer.
Product Development Updating and improving existing products and developing new products.
Product Life Cycle Different stages that sales of a product go through.
Sales Promotion Methods other than advertising used to promote products.
Sampling Researching a number of people representative of the whole market.
Sponsorship Where a firm finances an event or team.
TAM Ratings Television Audience Measurement.
Target Market Total number of potential customers for a product.
Test Marketing Testing a product on a few customers.
Trade Mark A name that a firm uses on its products.

Examination-Style Question and Solution

Question 1.
Fitzwear Ltd is a wholesale firm selling fashion clothes for the teenage and early twenties market to shops throughout Ireland. Fitzwear Ltd divides the country into the five regions shown in the table below:

	Total	Dublin	Rest of Leinster	Munster	Connaught	Ulster
1990	IR£200,000	IR£70,000	IR£30,000	IR£40,000	IR£20,000	IR£40,000
1991	IR£230,000	IR£50,000	IR£40,000	IR£60,000	IR£30,000	IR£50,000

The Managing Director, Ms S. Fitzgerald, has stated that she is disappointed with the Dublin sales figures for 1991 and that she has not enough information on this market.

1. (a) Identify the target market for Fitzwear's products from the information above. **(3)**
1. (b) Give two reasons why the company divides the country into regions. **(6)**
1. (c) On graph paper prepare a bar chart illustrating the table above for the two years. **(13)**
1. (d) Give two reasons why you think the Managing Director is disappointed with the Dublin sales figures for 1991. **(4)**

1. **(e)** Assume you are T. Delany, sales manager of the company. Write a report to the Managing Director on 3/1/1992 about the Dublin market, indicating:
   (i) How more information could be obtained about this market, and
   (ii) Three suitable methods for promoting the products. **(14)**

Source: Junior Certificate Sample Paper Higher Level. **(40 marks)**

Solution to Question 1.

1. (a) *Target market — teenagers and people in their early twenties.*

1. (b) Why Divide Country into Regions

(i) Sales representatives can be assigned to a region and they will get to know the area and its needs well.

(ii) Problem areas can be easily identified and catered for.

(iii) You can set up warehouses in each region thus making distribution easier.

1. (c) Bar Chart

Bar Chart Showing Total and Regional Sales for 1990 and 1991

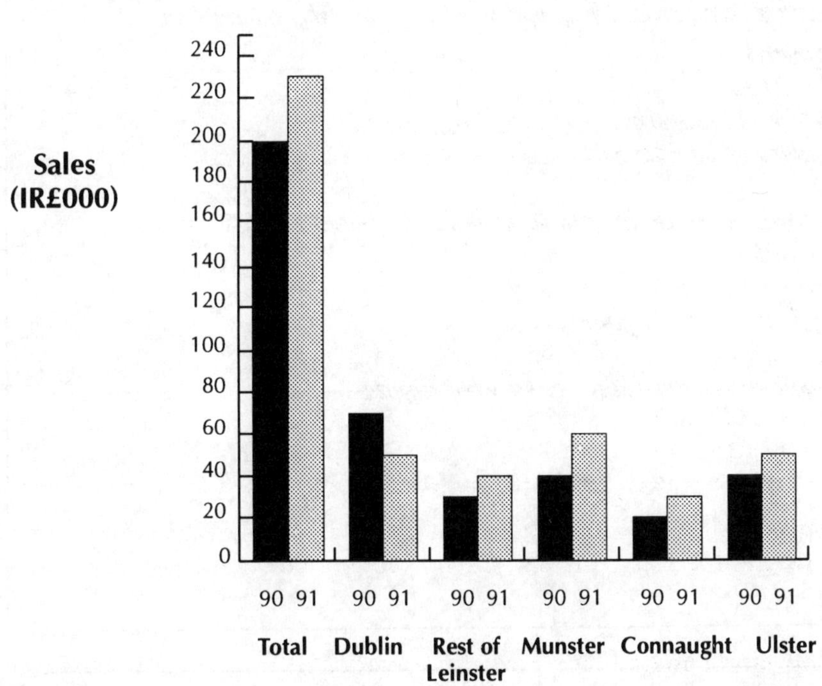

1. (d) Reasons Why Managing Director Is Disappointed with Dublin Sales Figures

(i) Sales in Dublin have fallen in 1991.

(ii) This has taken place in the context of an overall increase in sales and an increase in all other regions in 1991.

1. (e) Report from Sales Manager to Managing Director on the Dublin Market

To: *Managing Director, Ms S. Fitzgerald*

Introduction

I was asked by the Managing Director to prepare a report on the Dublin region indicating
(i) How more information could be obtained about this market, and
(ii) Three suitable methods for promoting the products.

Body of Report

I have spent a number of weeks researching this market and I enclose my findings below.
(a) *Fitzwear can get more information about the market using the following methods:*

(i) Questionnaires
(ii) Observation
(iii) Telephone interviews
(iv) Personal interviews
(v) Panels
(vi) Desk research.

This market research should provide the company with the following information:
(i) The target market.
(ii) The price to charge.
(iii) The competition in the market.
(iv) The best method of advertising to use.

(b) *The following methods should be used to promote the products:*
(i) Local radio advertising.
(ii) Organising a fashion show.
(iii) Advertising in a fashion magazine.

I am available to discuss any of these points when required.

Signed

T. Delany
Sales Manager
3 January 1992

PRACTICE QUESTIONS

(i) Question 16, Section A, Ordinary Level, Sample Paper.
(ii) Question 4, Section B, Ordinary Level, 1993.
(iii) Question 8, Section A, Ordinary Level, 1994.
(iv) Question 14, Section A, Paper I, Higher Level, 1993.

Chapter 25 — Delivery Systems

A. Importance of Delivery in the Chain of Distribution

A good efficient delivery system is important to business.
(1) To deliver raw materials to the manufacturer.
(2) To deliver finished goods.
(3) To transport workers to their jobs.
(4) To transport goods abroad.

B. Factors to Be Considered When Choosing a Delivery System

(1) Cost
(2) Reliability
(3) Speed
(4) Safety
(5) Distance
(6) Type of goods.

C. Types of Delivery System

The following are the main types of delivery system used in Ireland.

TYPES	ADVANTAGES	DISADVANTAGES
ROAD	1. Fast over short distances 2. Door-to-door deliveries 3. Minimum handling 4. Flexible, convenient and cheap	1. Congestion/Poor roads — delays 2. Bad weather — delays 3. Not suitable for bulky goods 4. Slow over long distances
RAIL	1. Fast over long distances 2. Suitable for bulky goods 3. Reliable 4. Cheap for bulky goods	1. Not flexible — fixed timetable 2. Lot of handling 3. Fixed routes 4. Expensive over short distances
SEA	1. Suitable for bulky goods 2. Cheaper than air 3. Suitable for containers 4. Good facilities at ports 5. Modern ships — large loads	1. Slow over long distances 2. Weather conditions — delays 3. Not flexible — fixed timetable 4. Must link with other forms of transport 5. High insurance costs
AIR	1. Fast 2. Suitable for expensive goods 3. Good safety record 4. Less packing — reduced cost 5. Modern aircraft — large loads	1. Expensive 2. Bad weather — delays 3. Must link with other forms of transport 4. Not flexible — fixed timetable 5. Not suitable for bulky goods
PIPELINE	1. Safe 2. Cheap to maintain	1. Expensive to install 2. Suitable only for liquids or gases

D. Modern Developments in Delivery Systems

(1) CONTAINERS
A container is a large metal box into which goods are packed, the container is sealed and loaded on to the mode of transport being used.

(2) REFRIGERATED TRANSPORT
Perishable goods can be transported over long distances.

(3) MOTORWAYS/DUAL CARRIAGEWAYS/RING ROADS
These have been constructed around our major towns and cities, mainly with EC funding.

(4) TOLL ROADS/TOLL BRIDGES
Built by private firms who charge a fee.

(5) COURIERS
Will deliver fast for a fee, e.g. An Post — SDS; Irish Rail — Fastrack.

(6) TACHOGRAPH
A small device attached to commercial vehicles, it records
(a) Distance
(b) Speed
(c) Time.
A driver cannot drive more than four hours continuously or more than eight hours per day.

(7) PALLETS
Pallets are wooden platforms for moving heavy goods.

(8) CHANNEL TUNNEL (CHUNNEL)
Links England and France underground.

(9) RENT-A-VAN
A business can rent a van or truck for a period of time for a fee, e.g. Avis Truck and Van Rental.

(10) ROLL-ON ROLL-OFF (RO-RO)
Ferry service where a vehicle drives on at one port and drives off at port of destination.

(11) EURO TAX DISC
Since 1 January 1995 Irish truckers transporting goods across the Continent have to display a Euro tax disc costing IR£8 per day.

(12) SINGLE EUROPEAN ACT 1992
This has resulted in less documentation and the elimination of customs regulations throughout Europe.

E. Calculating Delivery Time

When calculating delivery time we must:
(1) Work out distance involved (use a distance table).
(2) Calculate average speed of vehicle (km per hour).
(3) Allow for stopovers, traffic delays and time for loading and unloading.

Formula for Calculating Time

$$\frac{\text{Distance}}{\text{Average Speed per Hour (km)}}$$

Examination-Style Question and Solution

Question 1.

Look at the distance table and answer the following questions:

1. (a) How many kilometres from Tralee to Limerick?

Distance Table (km)

Dundalk										
256	Ennis									
238	70	Galway								
240	37	105	Limerick							
92	16	144	148	Mullingar						
246	246	274	210	204	Rosslare					
168	195	138	232	135	326	Sligo				
346	94	162	105	254	290	288	Tralee			
242	164	220	130	170	82	292	210	Waterford		
118	228	254	190	185	19	306	275	62	Wexford	

1. (b) How long would it take for a lorry to travel from Galway to Waterford at an average speed of 44 kilometres per hour? **(5)**

Source: Junior Certificate Ordinary Level 1993.

Solution to Question 1.

1. (a) *105 km.*

1. (b) $\text{Time} = \frac{\text{Distance}}{\text{Av. speed}} = \frac{220 \text{ km}}{44} = 5 \text{ hrs}$

F. Calculating Delivery Costs

As delivery expenses increase the cost of the goods, it is important to choose the cheapest method of transport. It is also important to be able to calculate the cost of delivery accurately. Cost of delivery will depend on whether:

(1) Firm uses its own vehicles

OR

(2) Firm uses a courier.

(1) FIRM USES OWN VEHICLES

When using own vehicles there are two costs involved.

Fixed costs must be paid no matter how much the vehicle is used and must be divided out over each day the vehicle is used in the year, e.g. maintenance, road tax, vehicle insurance.

Variable costs vary with the usage of the vehicle and are associated with a particular delivery, e.g. petrol/diesel, wages.

Sample Question and Solution on Cost of Delivery

Question

Calculate the total cost of a journey from Cork to Dublin and back to Cork from the following data:

- ➢ Distance from Cork to Dublin 260 km.
- ➢ Diesel van will do 10 km per litre of diesel.
- ➢ Cost of diesel is 50p per litre.
- ➢ Van driver's wages are IR£50 a day.
- ➢ Annual van tax is IR£250.
- ➢ Annual van insurance is IR£750.
- ➢ Annual repairs IR£500.
- ➢ The company operates 250 days in the year.

Solution — Cost of Delivery Calculation

	Total distance	260 km x 2 (return journey)	= 520 km
	Number of litres used	$\frac{520}{10}$	= 52 litres
Variable Costs	Cost of diesel	= 52 litres x 50p	= IR£26
	Driver's wages		= IR£50
Fixed Costs	Motor tax per day	= $\frac{\text{IR£250}}{\text{250 days}}$	= IR£1
	Insurance per day	= $\frac{\text{IR£750}}{\text{250 days}}$	= IR£3
	Repairs per day	= $\frac{\text{IR£500}}{\text{250 days}}$	= IR£2
	Total cost of delivery		= IR£82

(2) FIRM USES A COURIER

A pharmacy needs to send a small parcel of 10 kgs urgently from Dublin to New Ross. It wishes to use a courier. DHL International quotes the following collection fee and fee per kilogram (kg):

	Dublin	Rest of Leinster
Collection Fee	IR£18	IR£24
Fee per Kg	50p	70p

Courier Cost

Collection fee	=	IR£18
Fee per kg 50p x 10 kgs	=	IR£5
Cost of courier delivery	=	IR£23

G. Business Terms

Aer Lingus State-owned Irish airline.

C & F — Carriage and Freight Price quoted includes all costs to the port of destination — except insurance.

Chartering Renting/Hiring a ship for a specific journey or a specific time.

CIF — Carriage Insurance Freight Price quoted includes all costs to the port of destination.

Coastal Shipping Transports goods around coast from one port to another.

Ex-Works Price quoted assumes buyer must collect the goods from seller's premises. All costs of transport must be paid for by the buyer.

FAS — Free Alongside Ship Price quoted includes delivery as far as ship.

Ferries Carry passengers and vehicles.

FOB — Free On Board Price quoted includes delivery as far as ship plus loading.

Juggernaut Articulated truck.

Liner Carries passengers and cargo — travels on a fixed route.

Lo-Lo — Lift-On Lift-Off Containers on ships or trucks.

Pipeline Used to transport water, gas, oil, sewage.

Refrigerated Truck A truck with cold-storage facilities.

Road Tax Money paid by vehicle owners to government for upkeep of roads.

Ro-Ro — Roll-On Roll-Off Ferry service.

Ryanair Privately owned Irish airline.

Specialised ships Built to carry specific cargo, e.g. oil tanker.

Tramp Ship No fixed timetable or route.

Examination-Style Question and Solution

Question 1.

Answer all sections. This is a Distribution of Goods/Cost of Transport Question.

1. (a) The wholesaler plays an important role in the distribution of goods.
State three services the wholesaler provides to the manufacturer and three services the wholesaler provides to the retailer. **(12)**

1. (b) Transport is very important in the distribution of goods.
List four factors a business should take into account when deciding on what type of transport to use. **(8)**

1. (c) (i) Murphy Electric Ltd asks you to calculate the total cost of a journey from Galway to Dublin and back again to Galway on 20 May 1993 from the following data:

- The distance from Galway to Dublin is 216 km.
- Their diesel van can do 8 km per litre of diesel.
- The cost of diesel is 45p per litre.
- The van driver's wages are IR£60 per day.
- The Annual Motor Tax is IR£450.
- The Annual Motor Insurance is IR£925.
- The Annual Repairs are IR£625.
- The company operates 250 working days in the year. **(14)**

(ii) The invoice value of the goods delivered to Dublin is IR£18,460. Express the total cost of the return journey as a percentage of this figure. **(3)**

(iii) Give one reason why it is important to know this percentage. **(3)**

Source: Junior Certificate Higher Level 1993. **(40 marks)**

Solution to Question 1.

1. (a) Services Wholesaler Provides to Manufacturer

(i) Buys in bulk from manufacturer.
(ii) Stores the goods until they are sold.
(iii) Advises manufacturer of the opinions of retailers about the products.

Services Wholesaler Provides to Retailer

(i) Sells goods in small quantities to retailer.
(ii) Gives credit to retailer.
(iii) Provides a delivery service to retailer.
(iv) Provides retailer with a wide variety of goods.

1. (b) Four Factors in Deciding on Type of Transport

(i) Cost
(ii) Reliability
(iii) Speed
(iv) Safety
(v) Distance
(vi) Type of goods.

1. (c) (i) Cost of Delivery Calculation

	o Total distance (216 km x 2)		=	432 km
	o Number of litres of diesel used	$\frac{432}{8}$	=	54 litres
Variable Costs	o Cost of diesel	54 litres x 45p	=	IR£24.30
	o Wages		=	IR£60
Fixed Costs	o Motor tax per day	$\frac{\text{IR£450}}{\text{250 days}}$	=	1.80
	o Insurance per day	$\frac{\text{IR£925}}{\text{250 days}}$	=	3.70
	o Repairs per day	$\frac{\text{IR£625}}{\text{250 days}}$	=	2.50
	Total cost of delivery		=	IR£92.30

(ii) Cost of Delivery as a Percentage of Value of Goods Delivered

Formula = $\frac{\text{Cost of Delivery} \times 100}{\text{Value of Goods Delivered}} = \frac{\text{IR£92.30} \times 100}{\text{IR£18,460}} = 0.5\%$

(iii) Reason Why It Is Important to Know This Percentage

It costs 0.5% of the value of the goods to deliver the goods. Other methods of transporting the goods should be looked at to find out whether they could be delivered more cheaply.

PRACTICE QUESTIONS

(i) Question 15, Section A, Ordinary Level, 1992.
(ii) Question 8, Section B, Ordinary Level, 1994.
(iii) Question 15, Section A, Ordinary Level, Sample Paper.
(iv) Question 1, Section A, Paper I, Higher Level, Sample Paper.
(v) Question 5, Section A, Paper I, Higher Level, 1993.

BUSINESS TRANSACTIONS AND BUSINESS DOCUMENTS

Chapter 26 — Purchases and Sales

1. PURCHASES

A. Effective Purchasing

Purchasing the **right goods** in the **right quantity** at the **right price** at the **correct time**.

B. Enquiring About Goods and Services

When suitable suppliers are identified, contact can be made by letter, telephone, fax or personal call. A number of suppliers may be contacted with **an enquiry** about prices, quality, delivery terms, discount terms and payment terms. Most suppliers will reply by means of **a quotation** and on comparing these a decision can be made from which company to **order** the goods.

C. Prices

(1) Price list — a list of all goods and their price.
(2) Catalogue — a book containing details and descriptions of all goods for sale.
(3) Quotation — contains details about the price at which the seller is prepared to supply his goods.

D. Delivery Terms

(1) Carriage paid — price quoted includes all transport costs (paid by seller).
(2) Ex-works/Ex-factory — buyer pays for delivery.
(3) Free on rail — price quoted includes delivery of goods by the seller to the nearest railway station.

E. Discount Terms

(1) TRADE DISCOUNT

Discount given by the seller to the buyer off the list price of the goods to enable the buyer to make a profit when he resells the goods. Trade discount is deducted on the invoice.

(2) CASH DISCOUNT

Discount given to the buyer to encourage him to pay promptly.

F. Payment Terms

(1) CWO (Cash With Order) — customer must pay when ordering.
(2) COD (Cash On Delivery) — customer must pay on delivery.

G. VAT — Value Added Tax

VAT is a tax on goods and services sold. Businesses with a certain turnover must register for VAT. They will pay VAT on their purchases and must charge VAT on their sales.

---

2. SALES

A. Selling on Credit

A credit sale is where goods are sold and the customer pays for them at a later date.

B. Stock Control (Higher Level)

It is very important for a business to have the correct level of stock at all times. This is the optimum stock level.

OVERSTOCKING COSTS	UNDERSTOCKING COSTS
1. Cash tied up. 2. More storage space required. 3. Higher insurance costs. 4. More security staff required. 5. Risk of pilferage. 6. Risk of stock becoming obsolete.	1. Loss of orders. 2. Loss of sales. 3. Loss of customers. 4. Loss of profit.

To ensure that a firm has always the correct amount of stock, it is important to have a proper stock control system.

SETTING UP A STOCK CONTROL SYSTEM

(1) Code every item in stock.
(2) Decide the correct level of stock for each item.
(3) Develop a method of recording stock.
(4) Carry out regular stocktaking.

C. Computerised Stock Control

When a business is computerised the computer will give an automatic update on stock position. Each time a product is sold the bar code on the product is passed over a scanner and the stock count of the product is reduced by one.

D. Mark-Up and Margin (Higher Level)

Aim of being in business is to make a profit. A business will buy goods at cost and add on its profit to give the selling price.

COST + PROFIT = SELLING PRICE

Mark-up and margin are expressed as percentages.

Example Cost price IR£100 Selling price IR£120 ∴ Profit = IR£20

Mark-up — Profit expressed as a percentage of cost.

$$\text{Mark-Up} = \frac{\text{Profit x 100}}{\text{Cost Price}} = \frac{\text{IR£20 x 100}}{\text{IR£100}} = 20\%$$

Margin — Profit expressed as a percentage of selling price.

$$\text{Margin} = \frac{\text{Profit x 100}}{\text{Selling Price}} = \frac{\text{IR£20 x 100}}{\text{IR£120}} = 16.66\%$$

E. Filing

Filing is the storing of documents so that they can be easily and quickly found when required. There are many methods of filing. The most common are alphabetical and numerical.

(1) ALPHABETICAL

This is where the customer files are arranged in the filing cabinet in alphabetical order. Steel cabinets are used. A folder is used for each customer and the name of the customer is written on a tab.

(2) NUMERICAL

Each customer file is given a number rather than the customer name. Files are arranged in the filing cabinet in numerical sequence. A card index system showing each customer's name and address and file number is used in conjunction with numerical filing.

It is very important to file all business documents carefully, so that they can be found when needed.

Examination-Style Questions and Solutions

Question 1.

Given a cost price of IR£40 and a selling price of IR£45.60, calculate the percentage mark-up. **(4)**

Solution to Question 1.

ANSWER
14%

Workings

$$\text{Mark-Up} = \frac{\text{Profit x 100}}{\text{Cost Price}}$$

$$= \frac{\text{IR£5.60 x 100}}{\text{IR£40.00}} = 14\%$$

Source: Junior Certificate Higher Level 1993.

Question 2.
Given a buying price of IR£50 and a selling price of IR£60 calculate the percentage profit 'margin'. **(4)**

Solution to Question 2.

ANSWER
16.66%

Workings

$$\text{Profit Margin} = \frac{\text{Profit} \times 100}{\text{Selling Price}}$$

$$= \frac{\text{IR£10} \times 100}{\text{IR£60.00}} = 16.66\%$$

Source: Junior Certificate Higher Level 1992.

PRACTICE QUESTIONS

(i) Question 6, Section A, Paper I, Higher Level, Sample Paper.
(ii) Question 11, Section A, Paper I, Higher Level, Sample Paper.
(iii) Question 10, Section A, Paper I, Higher Level, 1994.

Chapter 27 — Business Letters / Report Writing

Business letters are an important form of communication. A letter will reveal what a business is like. A good business letter should be accurate, brief and clear.

Examination-Style Question and Solution

Question 1.
This question is about writing a Letter.
(To be completed in your Answer Book.)

Sarah McKenna is Treasurer of Fairways Golf Club, Links Road, Cork. The annual subscription for members is IR£100. On 20 April 1994 she received a cheque for IR£30 from Jack Palmer, one of the members, who lives at 29 Salt Road, Mallow. Mr Palmer stated that he would pay the rest of the annual subscription in September.

Sarah immediately wrote a letter to Mr Palmer, thanking him for the IR£30 and enclosing a Receipt. In the letter, she pointed out that the Golf Club was not in a position to wait until September for the rest of his annual subscription as this would not be fair to all the other members who had already paid in full. She also stated that, according to the rules, anyone whose full annual subscription was not paid by 1 May would no longer be a member of the club. She hoped that Mr Palmer would forward the balance due before that date.

1. (a) Assume you are Sarah McKenna. Write the letter that Sarah sent to Mr Jack Palmer.

Source: Junior Certificate Ordinary Level 1994. **(45)**

Solution to Question 1. LETTER

[1] Fairways Golf Club
Links Road
Cork

Tel (021) 926311

[2] 20 April 1994

[3] Mr Jack Palmer
29 Salt Road
Mallow

[4] Re: Annual Subscription

[5] Dear Mr Palmer

[6] I wish to **thank you for your cheque** of IR£30, for which a receipt is enclosed. Unfortunately, the Golf Club **is not in a position to wait until September for the rest of your annual subscription** as this would not be fair to all the other members who have paid in full. **[7]**

According to the rules, **anyone whose full subscription is not paid before the first of May will cease to be a member** of this club.

[8] I hope you can **forward the balance due of IR£70** before that date.

[9] Yours sincerely

[10] Sarah McKenna
Treasurer.

[11] ENC 1

LAYOUT OF A BUSINESS LETTER

[1] Address of sender — This is printed information on the top of company or club notepaper as follows:

Full name and address of company or club, telephone number, fax number and VAT number.

[2] **Date** — The most acceptable order for the date in a business letter is day, month, year.

[3] **Inside address** — This is the person to whom the letter is addressed.

[4] **Re — Regarding** — This outlines what the letter is about.

[5] **Salutation** — This is the greeting with which every letter begins, i.e. Dear Sir, Dear Madam.

[6] **Introduction** — If the letter is a reply to a letter received thank the writer and briefly mention the subject-matter (state what the letter is about).

[7] **Body of the Letter** — The body of the letter should be written in clear concise English. It should be divided into paragraphs.

[8] **Follow-up** — Stating what should happen next.

[9] **Complimentary Close** — This is the ending of a business letter and must match the salutation. The most used are Yours faithfully/Yours truly, Yours sincerely.

[10] **Signature and position/Title** of letter writer

[11] **Enc — Enclosures 1** — This shows that something else has been enclosed with the letter, e.g. receipt, and the number of items.

WHAT MARKS ARE AWARDED FOR IN BUSINESS LETTERS

(1) Format/Layout — Address of sender, date, inside address, salutation, Yours sincerely, signature, regarding, enclosures.
(2) Content/Body of Letter — Generally four points of information are required as bold underlined in the solution.
(3) English — Marks are awarded for paragraphs, punctuation, grammar, spelling.
(4) Presentation/Neatness — Marks will be awarded for a well-presented and neat letter.

LAYOUT OF A REPORT

1. Title of report
2. Address of report writer
3. Date
4. Who the report is for
5. Introduction — reasons for report and how the information was collected
6. Main body of report — conclusions and recommendations
7. Follow-up — report writer available to discuss report
8. Signature of report writer
9. Position/Title of report writer
   (see reports on pages 146, 232, 265, 277 and 283)

Chapter 28 — Business Transactions and Business Documents

A. Cash Transaction

A cash transaction is where goods are purchased and payment is made at the time of purchase either by cash or by cheque.

B. Credit Transaction

A credit transaction is where goods are purchased and payment is made at a later date.

C. Business Documents

Business documents are a very efficient way of putting business transactions on paper. They give both the buyer and the seller a written record of the transaction.

(1) LETTER OF ENQUIRY

A letter of enquiry is sent to a supplier enquiring about the prices, terms and conditions under which he is prepared to supply his goods.

SAMPLE TRANSACTION

Murphy TV, Hi-Fi & Video Ltd wish to enquire about electrical equipment from Panasonic Ireland Ltd.

LETTER OF ENQUIRY

Murphy TV, Hi-Fi & Video Ltd
10 Princess Street — Cork

Tel (021) 639425
Fax (021) 639426

VAT Reg. No.: 258364X

Panasonic Ireland Ltd
Sandyford Industrial Est.
Dublin 18

10 May 1996

Dear Sir or Madam

Please send me a quotation for the following goods:

50 Panasonic 21″ Nicam Stereo TVs
50 Panasonic HD Nicam Videos
50 Panasonic Mini Hi-Fi Systems

Yours sincerely

John Murphy

Purchasing Director

NB Murphy TV, Hi-Fi & Video Ltd may send letters of enquiry to a few different suppliers.

(2) QUOTATION

A quotation is a document from a supplier stating the prices and the details of discounts, delivery and VAT. The following is the quotation sent by Panasonic Ireland Ltd.

QUOTATION No. 205

PANASONIC IRELAND LTD
Sandyford Industrial Est.
Dublin 18

Tel (01) 9986241
Fax (01) 9986242

Vat. Reg. No. 924651N

Murphy TV, Hi-Fi & Video Ltd
10 Princess Street
Cork

13 May 1996

Dear Sir

Thank you for your enquiry. Our quotation is as follows:

Quantity	Description	Unit Price	Delivery
50	Panasonic 21″ Nicam Stereo TVs	IR£499	Ready
50	Panasonic HD Nicam Videos	IR£459	Ready
50	Panasonic Mini Hi-Fi Systems	IR£279	Ready

Yours sincerely

Gary Richards

Sales Director

TERMS OF SALE:
VAT 21% on all models. Trade Discount 10%. Carriage Paid.

This quotation will be compared with other quotations before a supplier is decided on.

(3) ORDER

An order is a document sent by the buyer ordering the goods required.

ORDER No. 648

Murphy TV, Hi-Fi & Video Ltd
10 Princess Street
Cork

Tel (021) 639425 **Vat Reg. No.: 258364X**
Fax (021) 639426

Panasonic Ireland Ltd
Sandyford Industrial Est.
Dublin 18

17 May 1996

Please supply the following goods:

Quantity	Description	Unit Price
50	Panasonic 21″ Nicam Stereo TVs	IR£499
50	Panasonic HD Nicam Videos	IR£449
50	Panasonic Mini Hi-Fi Systems	IR£279

Signed *John Murphy*

Purchasing Director

Treatment of incoming orders

(a) Date-stamp order.
(b) Get goods ready for delivery.
(c) Send order to office for preparation of invoice and delivery docket.
(d) File order.

(4) DELIVERY NOTE

When the goods are delivered the buyer will sign the delivery docket. It gives a list of the goods delivered. If any goods are missing or damaged it should be noted on the delivery docket. It is made out in duplicate, one copy given to the buyer and the second copy kept by seller as proof of delivery.

The goods were delivered to Murphy TV, Hi-Fi & Video Ltd on 20 May 1996.

DELIVERY NOTE **No. 74**

PANASONIC IRELAND LTD
Sandyford Industrial Est.
Dublin 18

Tel (01) 9986241
Fax (01) 9986242

VAT Reg. No. 924651N

Murphy TV, Hi-Fi & Video Ltd
10 Princess Street
Cork

20 May 1996

Quantity	Description
50	Panasonic 21″ Nicam Stereo TVs
50	Panasonic HD Nicam Videos
50	Panasonic Mini Hi-Fi Systems

Received the above goods in perfect condition.

Signed: *John Murphy*

Purchasing Director

(a) The delivery note should be checked against the order to ensure that the goods received were ordered.

(b) The delivery note should be carefully filed so that it can be checked against the invoice when it arrives.

(5) INVOICE

An invoice is sent from the seller to the buyer. It is the bill for the goods. It shows the quantity, description and price of the goods, details of trade discount and VAT and the total due to the seller.

The invoice is the source document for recording credit sales and credit purchases.

(a) The **seller** writes up his **Sales Day Book** from **invoices sent**.
(b) The buyer writes up his **Purchases Day Book** from **invoices received**.

The invoice received will be checked against the delivery docket to make sure that the buyer received what he is being charged for.

What Seller Should Do Before Sending Invoices/Treatment of Outgoing Invoices
1. Compare prices with the quotation given. 2. Check calculations for accuracy. 3. Check address of customer. 4. Write up sales day book. 5. File a copy of invoice.
What Buyer Should Do on Receiving Invoices/Treatment of Incoming Invoices 1. Compare with order and delivery docket. 2. Check accuracy of prices and calculations. 3. Write up purchases day book. 4. File invoice.

The following invoice was sent by Panasonic Ireland Ltd to Murphy TV, Hi-Fi & Video Ltd on 21 May 1996. (See p. 166.)

INVOICE **No. 61**

PANASONIC IRELAND LTD
Sandyford Industrial Est.
Dublin 18

Tel (01) 9986241
Fax (01) 9986242 **VAT Reg. No.** 924651N

21 May 1996

Murphy TV, Hi-Fi & Video Ltd
10 Princess Street
Cork

Quantity	Description	Unit Price	Total (Ex. VAT)
50	Panasonic 21″ Nicam Stereo TVs	IR£499	IR£24,950
50	Panasonic HD Nicam Videos	IR£449	IR£22,450
50	Panasonic Mini Hi-Fi Systems	IR£279	IR£13,950
	Total (ex. VAT)		IR£61,350
	Less Trade Discount 10%		IR£6,135
			IR£55,215
	Add VAT 21%		IR£11,595.15
	Total Due		IR£66,810.15

Terms of Sale:
Carriage paid.

E & O E

NOTES

(i) The design and layout of invoices may vary.
(ii) E & O E means Errors and Omissions Excepted. This gives the seller the right to correct any errors discovered later.
(iii) On the invoice always deduct the trade discount before adding VAT.

RECORDING INVOICES SENT IN THE SALES DAY BOOK OF SELLER

Books of Panasonic Ireland Ltd (Seller)

SALES DAY BOOK

Date	Details	Inv. No.	Fo	Net	VAT	Total
21/5/96	Murphy TV, Hi-Fi & Video Ltd	61		55,215	11,595.15	66,810.15

RECORDING INVOICES RECEIVED IN PURCHASES DAY BOOK OF BUYER

Books of Murphy TV, Hi-Fi & Video Ltd (Buyer)

PURCHASES DAY BOOK

Date	Details	Inv. No.	Fo	Net	VAT	Total
21/5/96	Panasonic Ireland Ltd	61		55,215	11,595.15	66,810.15

(6) DEBIT NOTE

A debit note is sent from seller to buyer if

(a) The seller **undercharged** the buyer on the invoice.
(b) The seller **omitted some items** from the invoice.

NB The debit note increases the amount of money buyer owes seller.

If we compare the quotation and the invoice we will see that Panasonic Ireland Ltd **undercharged** Murphy TV, Hi-Fi and Video Ltd by IR£10 each on the 50 Panasonic HD Nicam Videos (quoted price IR£459, invoice price IR£449).

A debit note is issued by Panasonic Ireland Ltd to the buyer as follows.

DEBIT NOTE **No. 104**

PANASONIC IRELAND LTD
Sandyford Industrial Est.
Dublin 18

Tel (01) 9986241
Fax (01) 9986242

VAT Reg. No. 924651N

22 May 1996

Murphy TV, Hi-Fi & Video Ltd
10 Princess Street
Cork

Quantity	Description	Unit Price	Total (Ex. VAT)
50	Panasonic HD Nicam Videos Less Trade Discount 10%	10	500 50
			450
	Add VAT 21%		94.50
	Total Additional Amount Due:		IR£544.50

Undercharge on Invoice No. 61

RECORDING DEBIT NOTES IN SALES DAY BOOK OF SELLER

The seller will record debit notes sent out in his sales day book.

SALES DAY BOOK (SELLER)

Date	Details	Inv. No.	Fo	Net	VAT	Total
22/5/96	Murphy TV, Hi-Fi & Video Ltd	DN 104		450	94.50	544.50

(7) CREDIT NOTE

A credit note is sent from seller to buyer if:

(a) The buyer has been **overcharged** on the invoice.

(b) The **buyer returns goods** to the seller and the seller issues a credit note to the buyer.

REASONS FOR RETURNING GOODS

- ➢ Damaged in transit.
- ➢ Not ordered.
- ➢ Faulty.
- ➢ Out of date.

NB The credit note reduces the amount of money buyer owes seller.

Let us assume that Murphy TV, Hi-Fi & Video Ltd returned two Panasonic Mini Hi-Fi Systems because they were faulty.

A credit note is issued by Panasonic Ireland Ltd to the buyer as follows:

CREDIT NOTE **No. 140**

PANASONIC IRELAND LTD
Sandyford Industrial Est.
Dublin 18

Tel (01) 9986241
Fax (01) 9986242

VAT Reg. No. 924651N

24 May 1996

Murphy TV, Hi-Fi & Video Ltd
10 Princess Street
Cork

Quantity	Description	Unit Price	Total (Ex. VAT)
2	Panasonic Mini Hi-Fi Systems	279	558
	Total (Ex. VAT)		558
	Less Trade Discount 10%		55.80
			502.20
	Add VAT 21%		105.46
	Total		607.66

Faulty Goods Ref. Inv. No. 61
E & O E

NOTES

(i) If trade discount was deducted on the original invoice it must be deducted on the credit note and debit note.

(ii) If VAT was paid on the original invoice it must be added in the credit note and debit note.

The credit note is the source document for recording Sales Returns and Purchases Returns.
(a) The seller writes up his **Sales Returns Day Book** from credit notes sent.
(b) The buyer writes up his **Purchases Returns Day Book** from credit notes received.

RECORDING CREDIT NOTES SENT IN SALES RETURNS DAY BOOK OF SELLER

SALES RETURNS DAY BOOK — OF PANASONIC IRL. LTD (SELLER)

Date	Details	Credit Note No.	Fo	Net	VAT	Total
24/5/96	Murphy TV Hi-Fi & Video Ltd	140		502.20	105.46	607.66

RECORDING CREDIT NOTES RECEIVED IN PURCHASES RETURNS DAY BOOK OF BUYER

PURCHASES RETURNS DAY BOOK — OF MURPHY TV, HI-FI & VIDEO LTD (BUYER)

Date	Details	Credit Note No.	Fo	Net	VAT	Total
24/5/96	Panasonic Ireland Ltd	140		502.20	105.46	607.66

(8) STATEMENT OF ACCOUNT

A statement of account is a document sent from the seller to the buyer at the end of a period of time (usually one month).

It outlines the transactions that took place between the seller and the buyer and shows how much the buyer owes at the end of the period.

Let us assume that Panasonic Ireland Ltd sent a statement of account to Murphy TV, Hi-Fi & Video Ltd on 31 May 1996 as follows.

STATEMENT OF ACCOUNT **No. 210**

PANASONIC IRELAND LTD
Sandyford Industrial Est.
Dublin 18

Tel (01) 9986241
Fax (01) 9986242

VAT Reg. No. 924651N

31 May 1996

Murphy TV, Hi-Fi & Video Ltd
10 Princess Street
Cork

Date	**Details**	**Debit**	**Credit**	**Balance**
21/5/96	Invoice No. 61	66,810.15		66,810.15
22/5/96	Debit Note No. 104	544.50		67,354.65
24/5/96	Credit Note No. 140		607.66	66,746.99

AMOUNT DUE

NOTES

(i) The statement of accounts is presented on the continuous balance format — thus you get a new balance after each transaction.
(ii) Invoices and debit notes are put into the debit column and are added to the balance figure, increasing the amount owed by the buyer.
(iii) Credit notes and payments (cash or cheque) are put into the credit column and are subtracted from the balance figure, reducing the amount owed by the buyer.

What Seller Should Do Before Sending Statements/Treatment of Outgoing Statements	What Buyer Should Do on Receiving Statements/Treatment of Incoming Statements
1. Check that all transactions are correct — compare with copies of relevant documents. 2. Check all calculations. 3. Check name and address of buyer. 4. File copy of statement.	1. Compare statement transactions with relevant documents. 2. Compare statement with account of seller in creditors ledger. 3. Check all calculations. 4. Pay seller amount due. 5. File statement.

(9) PAYMENT

The buyer will usually pay the statement of account promptly by cheque.

Assume Murphy TV, Hi-Fi & Video Ltd pays Panasonic Ireland Ltd by cheque on 5 June 1996.

CHEQUE

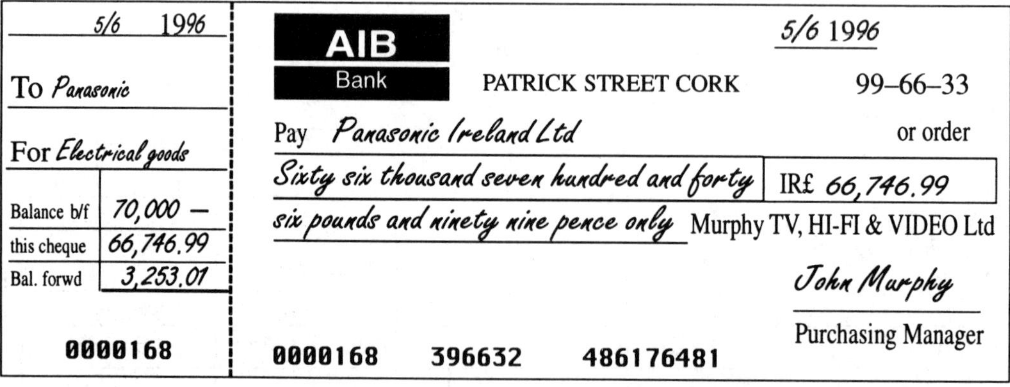

5/6 1996
To Panasonic
For Electrical goods

Balance b/f	70,000 —
this cheque	66,746.99
Bal. forwd	3,253.01

0000168

AIB Bank PATRICK STREET CORK 5/6 1996 99–66–33

Pay Panasonic Ireland Ltd or order

Sixty six thousand seven hundred and forty six pounds and ninety nine pence only IR£ 66,746.99

Murphy TV, HI-FI & VIDEO Ltd
John Murphy
Purchasing Manager

0000168 396632 486176481

NB Balance B/f IR£70,000 — Assume Murphy TV, Hi-Fi & Video Ltd had IR£70,000 in its account before writing this cheque.

(10) RECEIPT

When the seller receives the payment it is usual to issue a receipt to the buyer. This acknowledges payment and when it is received by the buyer it should be filed as proof of payment.

Assume Panasonic Irl Ltd issued a receipt on 10 June 1996.

RECEIPT **No. 802**

PANASONIC IRELAND LTD
Sandyford Industrial Est.
Dublin 18

Received with thanks, Date *10 June 1996*

The sum of *Sixty six thousand seven hundred and forty six pounds and ninety nine pence.* IR£ *66,746.99*

FROM *Murphy TV, Hi-Fi & Video Ltd*
10 Princess Street – Cork.

Signed *Jim Kelly*
Accounts Dept

Examination-Style Questions and Solutions

Question 1.

Answer all sections. This is a Business Document Question.

William Lyons is the Manager of the Purchasing Department in Office Supplies Ltd. On 21 April 1993 he received the following quotation:

QUOTATION **No. 759**

DESKMAKERS LTD
Industrial Estate, Castlebar, Co. Mayo.

To: Office Supplies Ltd
Canal Road
Roscommon

Date: 20 April 1993
Tel: 094–79555
Fax: 094–89755
Vat No.: IE644311

Model	Description	IR£ Price Each	Delivery
D42	Office Desks	240.00	Ready
CS6	Swivel Chairs	75.00	Ready
T21	Typewriters	145.00	Ready
F44	Filing Cabinets	280.00	Ready
	VAT 20% extra on all goods. Carriage Paid. For acceptance within 30 days.		

William decides that the typewriters are too costly, but he sends an Order (No. 94) to Deskmakers Ltd for five office desks, ten swivel chairs and six filing cabinets. These goods are delivered in a truck to Office Supplies Ltd on 6 May 1993. William checks the goods when they arrive and finds everything correct. After he signs the Delivery Note he is handed an Invoice (No. 732) for the goods by the driver of the truck.

1. (a) From the above details complete Invoice Number 732, using the blank invoice supplied at the end of the question. **(30)**

1. (b) In the space provided (at the end of the question), give one reason why William should check the invoice against the quotation before paying for the goods. **(10)**

On behalf of Office Supplies Ltd, William then writes out a cheque in full payment and hands the cheque to the driver to bring back to Deskmakers Ltd.

1. (c) Complete the cheque and counterfoil using the blank supplied at the end of the question. **(20)**

Documents for Question 1.

1. (a) Invoice

INVOICE — No. 732

DESKMAKERS Ltd
Industrial Estate, Castlebar, Co. Mayo

To:

Date
Tel: 094–79555
Fax: 094–89755
Vat No.: IE644311
ORDER NO.:

Quantity	Description	Model No.	Price Each	Total
			Total (Excluding VAT)	
			VAT	
			Total (Including VAT)	

E & O E

1. (b) Reason

Quotation

1. (c) Cheque

19	**AIB Bank** MAIN STREET, ROSCOMMON 19 93–77–99
To	Pay or order
For	IR£
Balance 6,315 00	OFFICE SUPPLIES LTD
Am't Lodged	
Total	
Am't this chq.	
Bal. forwd	Purchasing Manager
2355217	2355217 937799 65477822

Source: Junior Certificate Ordinary Level 1993. **(60 marks)**

Solution to Question 1.

Documents for Question 1.

1. (a) Invoice

INVOICE **No. 732**

DESKMAKERS Ltd
Industrial Estate, Castlebar, Co. Mayo

To: *Office Supplies Ltd*
Canal Road
Roscommon

Date *6 May 1993*
Tel: 094–79555
Fax: 094–89755
Vat No.: IE644311
ORDER NO.: *94*

Quantity	Description	Model No.	Price Each	Total
5	*Office Desks*	*D42*	*240.00*	*1,200.00*
10	*Swivel Chairs*	*CS6*	*75.00*	*750.00*
6	*Filing Cabinets*	*F44*	*280.00*	*1,680.00*
		Total (Excluding VAT)		*3,630.00*
		VAT		*726.00*
		Total (Including VAT)		*4,356.00*

E & O E

1. (b) Reason

Quotation To see if he was charged the correct prices as on the quotation.

1. (c) Cheque

6 May 1993	AIB Bank — 6 May 1993
To Deskmakers	MAIN STREET, ROSCOMMON 93–77–99
For Goods	Pay DESKMAKERS LTD or order
Balance 6,315 00	Four thousand, three hundred and fifty six pounds only — IR£ 4,356.00
Am't Lodged	OFFICE SUPPLIES LTD
Total	
Am't this chq. 4,356 00	William Lyons
Bal. forwd 1,959 00	Purchasing Manager
2355217	2355217 937799 65477822

Question 2.

Answer all sections. This is an Integrated Invoice/Document Question.

On 10 April A. & P. Lawlor Ltd, Furniture Suppliers, Galway, received an order No. 3 from J. Donnelly Ltd, 2 Dublin Road, Sligo for the following goods:

10 pine tables	@	IR£350	each excluding VAT
15 TV cabinets	@	IR£90	each excluding VAT
30 kitchen chairs	@	IR£8	each excluding VAT
60 bedroom lockers	@	IR£6	each excluding VAT

A. & P. Lawlor Ltd sent an invoice No. 91 on 13/4/92 to J. Donnelly Ltd. The invoice stated that the trade discount would be 30% of the retail price, and the goods would be delivered by A. & P. Lawlor Ltd on 16/4/92. Furniture is subject to VAT at 20%.

On delivery J. Donnelly Ltd examined the furniture and found that one of the TV cabinets was damaged, and ten of the bedroom lockers had faulty doors. These were returned in the supplier's lorry and A. & P. Lawlor Ltd issued a credit note No. 65 on 18/4/92. At the end of April A. & P. Lawlor Ltd sent an appropriate document to J. Donnelly Ltd.

2. (a) Complete the invoice of 13/4/92 and the credit note of 18/4/92 on the blank document sheet supplied with this paper. **(22)**

2. (b) Record the invoice and credit note issued in the books of first entry of A. & P. Lawlor Ltd. **(10)**

2. (c) Name the document sent by A. & P. Lawlor Ltd to J. Donnelly Ltd at the end of April. **(2)**

2. (d) Outline how J. Donnelly Ltd should treat incoming invoices. **(6)**

2. (a) **INVOICE CASH/CREDIT**

A. & P. LAWLOR LTD
Furniture Suppliers
Galway

No.: 91
Telephone: (091) 21354
VAT Reg.: 3174L
Date:

Order No.:
Terms:

Quantity	Description	Unit Price IR£	Total (Ex. VAT) IR£
		Total (Ex. VAT)	
		Less: Trade Discount	
		Add: VAT	
		Total Due	

E & O E

2. (a) **CREDIT NOTE**

A. & P. LAWLOR LTD
Furniture Suppliers
Galway

No.: 65
Telephone: (091) 21354
VAT Reg.: 3174L
Date:

Order No.:
Terms:

Quantity	Description	Unit Price IR£	Total (Ex. VAT) IR£
		Total (Ex. VAT)	
		Less: Trade Discount	
		Add: VAT	
		Total Due	

E & O E

Source: Junior Certificate Higher Level 1992. **(40 marks)**

Solution to Question 2.

2. (a) **INVOICE CASH/CREDIT**

J. Donnelly Ltd
2 Dublin Road Sligo
Order No.: 3
Terms: Delivery Free

A. & P. LAWLOR LTD
Furniture Suppliers
Galway

No.: 91
Telephone: (091) 21354
VAT Reg.: 3174L
Date: 13/4/92

Quantity	Description	Unit Price IR£	Total (Ex. VAT) IR£
10	Pine Tables	350.00	3,500.00
15	TV Cabinets	90.00	1,350.00
30	Kitchen Chairs	8.00	240.00
60	Bedroom Lockers	6.00	360.00
		Total (Ex. VAT)	5,450.00
		Less: Trade Discount	1,635.00
			3,815.00
		Add: VAT	763.00
		Total Due	4,578.00

E & O E

2. (a) **CREDIT NOTE**

J. Donnelly Ltd
2 Dublin Road Sligo
Order No.: 3
Terms: Delivery Free

A. & P. LAWLOR LTD
Furniture Suppliers
Galway

No.: 65
Telephone: (091) 21354
VAT Reg.: 3174L
Date: 18/4/92

Quantity	Description	Unit Price IR£	Total (Ex. VAT) IR£
1	TV Cabinet	90.00	90.00
10	Bedroom Lockers (Damaged Goods)	6.00	60.00
		Total (Ex. VAT)	150.00
		Less: Trade Discount	45.00
			105.00
		Add: VAT	21.00
		Total Due	126.00

E & O E

2. (b) **SALES DAY BOOK**

Date	Details	Invoices	Fo	Net	VAT	Total
13/4/92	J. Donnelly	91	CL/1	3,815	763	4,578
30/4/92	Credit Sales and VAT A/C			3,815	763	4,578

SALES RETURNS DAY BOOK

Date	Details	Credit Note No.	Fo	Net	VAT	Total
18/4/92	J. Donnelly	65	CL/1	105	21	126
30/4/92	Debit Sales Returns and VAT A/C			105	21	126

2. (c) Document Sent by A. & P. Lawlor at End of April

Statement of account.

2. (d) Treatment of Incoming Invoices

(1) Compare with order and delivery docket.
(2) Check accuracy of prices and calculations.
(3) Write up purchases day book.
(4) File invoice.

Question 3.

Answer all sections. This is an Integrated Business Documents Question.

The following details refer to the sale of goods on credit by FAHY LTD to DELFWARE LTD, 10 HIGH ST, CAVAN for the month of May 1993.

On 1 May 1993 there was a balance due of IR£350 in Delfware's account in Fahy Ltd books.

1993

4 May	Fahy sent Invoice No. 6 to Delfware for	IR£10,000
7 May	Fahy sent Invoice No. 19 to Delfware for	IR£25,000
11 May	Fahy received Cheque from Delfware for	IR£29,000
13 May	Fahy sent Credit Note No. 68 to Delfware for goods returned	IR£700 + 15% VAT
17 May	Fahy sent Invoice No. 34 to Delfware for	IR£23,000
23 May	Fahy sent Credit Note No. 72 to Delfware for goods returned	IR£1,900 + 15%VAT
27 May	Fahy sent Invoice No. 41 to Delfware for	IR£20,000

- On 31 May 1993 Fahy Ltd sent a Statement of Account to Delfware Ltd.
- Delfware paid the amount due on the Statement by cheque.
- Fahy Ltd issued a Receipt on 19 June 1993, signed by Henry Fahy.

You are required to:

3. (a) Record the two credit notes sent on 13 and 23 May 1993 in the appropriate book of first entry of Fahy Ltd. **(7)**

3. (b) Complete the Statement sent by Fahy Ltd on 31st May 1993 on the blank statement document supplied. **(17)**

3. (c) Complete the receipt issued by Fahy Ltd on 19 June 1993 on the blank receipt document supplied. **(10)**

3. (d) In the case of Delfware Ltd suggest two checks that their book-keeper should carry out before paying the amount due on the Statement. **(6)**

For Use with Question 3. (Part B)

STATEMENT

FAHY LTD
TUAM RD., GALWAY

To:

Tel: (091) 46377
VAT No. IE43156
Account No. 39

Date:

Date	Details	Debit	Credit	Balance

↑
AMOUNT DUE

For use with Question 3. (Part C)

RECEIPT **No. 658**

FAHY LTD, TUAM ROAD, GALWAY.

Received with thanks, Date__________

The sum of ____________________

IR£

FROM

Signed __________

Accounts Dept

Source: Junior Certificate Higher Level 1993. **(40 marks)**

Solution to Question 3.

SALES RETURNS BOOK

Date	Details	Credit Note No.	Fo	Net	VAT	Total
13/5/93	Delfware	68	DL11	700	105	805
23/5/93	Delfware	72	DL11	1,900	285	2,185
31/5/93	Debit Sales Returns and VAT A/C			2,600	390	2,990

For Use with Question 3. (Part B)

STATEMENT

FAHY LTD
TUAM RD, GALWAY

To: Delfware Ltd
10 High Street
Cavan

Tel: (091) 46377
VAT No. IE43156
Account No. 39

Date: 31 May 1993

Date	Details	Debit	Credit	Balance
1 May	Balance			350
4 May	Invoice No. 6	10,000		10,350
7 May	Invoice No. 19	25,000		35,350
11 May	Cheque		29,000	6,350
13 May	Credit Note No. 68		805	5,545
17 May	Invoice No. 34	23,000		28,545
23 May	Credit Note No. 72		2,185	26,360
27 May	Invoice No. 41	20,000		46,360

↑ AMOUNT DUE

For use with Question 3. (Part C)

RECEIPT **No. 658**

FAHY LTD, TUAM ROAD, GALWAY.

Received with thanks, Date 19 June 1993

The sum of Forty six thousand three hundred and sixty pounds

IR£ 46,360

FROM Delfware Ltd
10 High Street
Cavan

Signed Henry Fahy
Accounts Dept

3. (d) (i) Check arithmetical accuracy.
(ii) Compare Statement with creditors ledger.
(iii) Check that terms agreed were given.

PRACTICE QUESTIONS

(i) Question 5, Section B, Ordinary Level, Sample Paper.
(ii) Question 5, Section B, Ordinary Level, 1994.
(iii) Question 5, Section B, Ordinary Level, 1992.
(iv) Question 3, Paper II, Higher Level, Sample Paper.
(v) Question 19, Section A, Paper I, Higher Level, 1993.
(vi) Question 18, Section A, Paper I, Higher Level, 1992.
(vii) Question 3, Section A, Paper I, Higher Level, Sample Paper.

Chapter 29 — Introduction to Double Entry Book-Keeping, Day Books and Ledger

A. Book-Keeping

Book-keeping is the art of recording business transactions in a systematic manner so that the business will have a permanent record.

B. Double Entry Book-Keeping

Double Entry Principle: Every business transaction has a twofold aspect: **giving** and **receiving**.

C. Fundamental Rule of Double Entry Book-Keeping

Debit	Receiver
Credit	Giver

D. An Account in the Ledger

An account is a space in the ledger set aside for a particular purpose, e.g. cash account, computer account.

Example I

On 1 May a firm spends IR£2,000 cash on the purchase of a computer.

- ➢ Money goes out of the business — cash account is giving — **Credit Giving Account.**
- ➢ Computer comes into the business — computer account is receiving — **Debit Receiving Account.**

Our two entries are:

(1) Debit computer account.

(2) Credit cash account.

Debit **Computer A/C** **Credit**

Date	Details	Total	Date	Details	Total
1 May	Cash	IR£2,000			

Cash A/C

Date	Details	Total	Date	Details	Total
			1 May	Computer	IR£2,000

Example II
10 Jan. Purchased machinery on credit from John Keane IR£10,000.
➢ Two accounts are machinery and John Keane.
(1) Debit machinery account (machinery account — receiving).
(2) Credit John Keane account (John Keane account — giving).

LEDGER

Debit **Machinery A/C** **Credit**

Date	Details	Total	Date	Details	Total
10 Jan.	John Keane	IR£10,000			

John Keane A/C

Date	Details	Total	Date	Details	Total
			10 Jan.	Machinery	IR£10,000

E. Day Books

(1) **Purchases Day Book** — for recording goods purchased on credit for resale.
(2) **Purchases Returns Day Book** — for recording goods returned by the purchaser.
(3) **Sales Day Book** — for recording goods sold on credit.
(4) **Sales Returns Day Book** — for recording goods returned to the seller.
(5) **Cash Book** — Cash receipts and bank lodgments are entered on the debit side. Cash payments and cheque payments are entered on the credit side.
(6) **General Journal** — used to record transactions which are not recorded in other books of first entry.

F. Source Documents for Day Books

(1) Seller writes up his sales day book from invoices sent. Purchaser writes up his purchases day book from invoices received.
(2) Seller writes up his sales returns day book from details on credit notes sent. Purchaser writes up his purchases returns day book from credit notes received.

SOURCE DOCUMENTS FOR CASH BOOK

Cash receipts — from cash register, tally roll, or copy of receipts given to cash customers.

Bank lodgments — written up from bank lodgments, counterfoils, bank statements showing receipts paid directly into bank.

Cash payments — written up from cash vouchers showing what the payment was for.

Cheque payments — written up from cheque counterfoils or from bank statements.

G. Layout of Books of First Entry

Layout of the Sales Day Book and Purchases Day Book

Date	Details	Inv. No.	Fo	Net	VAT	Total

NB Exactly same layout for returns day books, except credit note number replaces invoice number.

Layout of Cash Book

Layout Number 1: Use analysed cash receipts and lodgments book and analysed cash and cheque payments book, combined with a cash account and a bank account in the ledger.

Layout Number 2: This layout combines the above two books into what is known as The Analysed Cash Book.

H. The Ledger

Every debit entry will have a corresponding credit entry. The ledger is divided into three sections:

(1) Debtors Ledger — accounts of people and firms that owe us money.
(2) Creditors Ledger — accounts of people and firms to whom we owe money.
(3) General Ledger — accounts of a non-personal nature such as expenses, gains, assets and liabilities.

I. Trial Balance

A Trial Balance is a list of all balances standing on the ledger accounts and cash books of a business at the end of the period. Debit balances go to the debit column, credit balances go to the credit column. When totalled the debit total should correspond to the credit total, thus the entries on the accounts are **arithmetically** correct.

J. Business Terms

Account A page in the ledger in which all transactions relating to a particular person or firm are recorded.
Assets Items that a business **owns.**
Balance The difference between two sides of an account.
Credit An entry on the right-hand side of an account.
Creditor A person or firm to whom money is owed.
Debit An entry on the left-hand side of an account.
Debtor A person or firm who owes money.
Liabilities Items that a business **owes.**
Trial Balance A list of balances from the ledger.

Examination-Style Questions and Solutions

Question 1.
Your total takings in cash in your grocery business on 22 May are IR£500. Show how you would enter the IR£500 in both of the following accounts of your business:

Debit **Cash Account** **Credit**

Date	Details	Total	Date	Details	Total
22 May	Sales	500			

Sales Account

Date	Details	Total	Date	Details	Total
			22 May	Cash	500

Source: Junior Certificate Ordinary Level 1992. **(5)**

Question 2.
Larkin & Co. Ltd paid for repairs to its computer on 4 June with a cheque for IR£850. Show how you would enter the payment of IR£850 in both of the following accounts of Larkin & Co. Ltd:

Debit **Bank Account** **Credit**

Date	Details	Total	Date	Details	Total
			4 June	Repairs to computer	850

Sales Account

Date	Details	Total	Date	Details	Total
4 June	Bank	850			

Source: Junior Certificate Ordinary Level 1993. **(5)**

Question 3.
In the spaces provided, name the two accounts (in A.N.G. Ltd's books) affected by the following transaction:

> A.N.G. Ltd (Engineering Works) purchased a delivery truck from Roches Garage Ltd by cheque on 1 May 1992.

Debit the *Delivery Van* Account. Credit the *Bank* Account.

Source: Junior Certificate Higher Level 1992. **(4)**

Question 4.

Answer either **(a)** or **(b)**:

4. (a) Balance the following Bank Account and bring down the balance:

Debit				**Bank Account**			**Credit**
Date	**Details**	**F**	**IR£**	**Date**	**Details**	**F**	**IR£**
1 May	Balance	B/d	850	9 May	Wages	GL8	639
4 May	Sales	GL4	755	17 May	Purchases	GL3	247
				31 May	*Balance*	*C/d*	*719*
			1,605				*1,605*
31 May	*Balance*	*B/d*	*719*				

OR

4. (b) Complete the last 3 lines of the 'Balance' column in the following Bank Account:

Bank Account					
Date	**Details**	**F**	**Dr**	**Cr**	**Balance**
1 May	Balance	B/d			850
4 May	Sales	GL4	755		*1,605*
9 May	Wages	GL8		639	*966*
17 May	Purchases	GL3		247	*719*

Source: Junior Certificate Ordinary Level 1993. **(5)**

Question 5.

Show how the following transaction would be recorded in the ledger of Cablelines Ltd, a TV company.

Cablelines Ltd sold a delivery van on credit to O'Brien Transport Ltd for IR£4,700.

Debit *O'Brien Transport Ltd* Account

Credit *Delivery Van* Account

Source: Junior Certificate Higher Level 1993. **(4)**

Question 6.
In the space provided, name the two accounts affected by the following transaction in the ledger of Kilcara Hardware Ltd.

Kilcara Hardware Ltd purchased goods for resale on credit from Smith Ltd.

Debit *Purchases* Account

Credit *Smith Ltd* Account

Source: Junior Certificate Higher Level 1994. **(4)**

PRACTICE QUESTIONS

(i) Question 13, Section A, Ordinary Level, Sample Paper.
(ii) Question 18, Section A, Ordinary Level, Sample Paper.
(iii) Question 18, Section A, Ordinary Level, 1994.
(iv) Question 20, Section A, Ordinary Level, 1994.
(v) Question 7, Section A, Paper I, Higher Level, 1993.
(vi) Question 8, Section A, Paper I, Higher Level, 1994.

Chapter 30 — Purchases Day Book and Purchases Returns Day Book

Higher Level

A. Purchases Day Book (PDB)

The purchases day book is used to record goods bought on credit. When you purchase goods you receive an invoice. The purchases day book is written up from invoices received.

B. Purchases Returns Day Book (PRDB)

The purchases returns day book is used to record the return of goods purchased on credit by a business. When goods are returned the buyer receives a credit note. The purchases returns day book is written up from the credit notes received.

C. Source Documents for Recording Purchases Day Book and Purchases Returns Day Book

Invoices Received ——➤	Purchases Day Book
Credit Notes Received ——➤	Purchases Returns Day Book

Sample Question and Solution

Question

Write up the purchases day book, purchases returns day book, post to the ledger, balance the accounts and extract a trial balance.

- ➢ 1 Feb. Purchased goods on credit from Motorola Ltd. Invoice No. 186 IR£2,000 + VAT @ 21%.
- ➢ 8 Feb. Returned goods to Motorola Ltd. Received credit note No. 41 IR£400 + VAT @ 21%.
- ➢ 15 Feb. Received invoice No. 149 from Kestrel Ltd IR£6,000 + VAT @ 21%.
- ➢ 24 Feb. Received credit note No. 201 from Kestrel Ltd IR£200 + VAT @ 21%.

Solution

(1) Day Books

Purchases Day Book **Page 1**

Date	Details	Invoice No.	Fo	Net	VAT	Total
1 Feb.	Motorola Ltd	186	CL/1	2,000	420	2,420
15 Feb.	Kestrel Ltd	149	CL/2	6,000	1,260	7,260
28 Feb.	Debit Purchases and VAT A/Cs			8,000	1,680	9,680
				GL/1	GL/2	

Purchases Returns Day Book **Page 2**

Date	Details	Credit Note No.	Fo	Net	VAT	Total
8 Feb.	Motorola Ltd	41	CL/1	400	84	484
24 Feb.	Kestrel Ltd	201	CL/2	200	42	242
28 Feb.	Credit Purchases Returns and VAT A/Cs			600	126	726
				GL/3	GL/2	

CL = Creditors Ledger **GL** = General Ledger

(2) Rules for Posting to Ledger

Posting Purchases Day Book	Posting Purchases Returns Day Book
Debit Purchases account with net amount. **Debit** VAT account with VAT amount. **Credit** Personal accounts with total amount, **i.e.** Credit Motorola Ltd with IR£2,420. Credit Kestrel Ltd with IR£7,260.	**Debit** Personal accounts with total amount, **i.e.** Debit Motorola Ltd with IR£484. Debit Kestrel Ltd with IR£242. **Credit** Purchases returns account with net amount. **Credit** VAT account with VAT amount.

GENERAL LEDGER

Debit **Purchases A/C No. 1** **Credit**

Date	Details	Fo	Total	Date	Details	Fo	Total
28 Feb.	Total PDB	PDB1	8,000				

Debit **VAT A/C No. 2** **Credit**

Date	Details	Fo	Total	Date	Details	Fo	Total
28 Feb.	Total PDB	PDB1	1,680	28 Feb.	Total PRDB	PRDB2	126
				28 Feb.	Balance	C/d	1,554
			1,680				1,680
28 Feb.	Balance	B/d	1,554				

Debit **Purchases Returns A/C No. 3** **Credit**

Date	Details	Fo	Total	Date	Details	Fo	Total
				28 Feb.	Total PRDB	PRDB2	600

CREDITORS LEDGER

Debit **Motorola Ltd A/C No. 1** **Credit**

Date	Details	Fo	Total	Date	Details	Fo	Total
8 Feb.	Purchases Returns	PRDB2	484	1 Feb.	Purchases	PDB1	2,420
28 Feb.	Balance	C/d	1,936				
			2,420				2,420
				28 Feb.	Balance	B/d	1,936

Debit **Kestrel Ltd A/C No. 2** **Credit**

Date	Details	Fo	Total	Date	Details	Fo	Total
24 Feb.	Purchases Returns	PRDB2	242	15 Feb.	Purchase	PDB1	7,260
28 Feb.	Balance	B/d	7,018				
			7,260				7,260
				28 Feb.	Balance	B/d	7,018

BALANCING THE ACCOUNTS

All accounts with more than one entry must be balanced off. Balance in VAT account is IR£1,554. Balance in Motorola Ltd account is IR£1,936 and balance in Kestrel Ltd account is IR£7,018. If an account has only one entry there is no need to balance it off.

THE TRIAL BALANCE

- ➢ The trial balance is a list of balances from the ledger.
- ➢ Debit balances go into the Debit column.
- ➢ Credit balances go into the Credit column.

Trial Balance as on 28 February

Date	Details	Fo	Debit	Credit
	Purchases	GL1	8,000	
	VAT	GL2	1,554	
	Purchases Returns	GL3		600
	Motorola Ltd	CL1		1,936
	Kestrel Ltd	CL2		7,018
			9,554	9,554

PRACTICE QUESTION

Write up the purchases day book and purchases returns day book, post to the ledger, balance the accounts and extract a trial balance.

1 Mar. Purchased goods on credit from Nelson Ltd. Invoice No. 214 IR£7,600 + VAT @ 21%.
10 Mar. Returned goods to Nelson Ltd. Received credit note No. 388 IR£200 + VAT @ 21%.
16 Mar. Received invoice No. 260 from Experto Ltd. IR£10,000 + VAT @ 21%.
24 Mar. Received credit note No. 181 from Experto Ltd. IR£600 + VAT @ 21%.

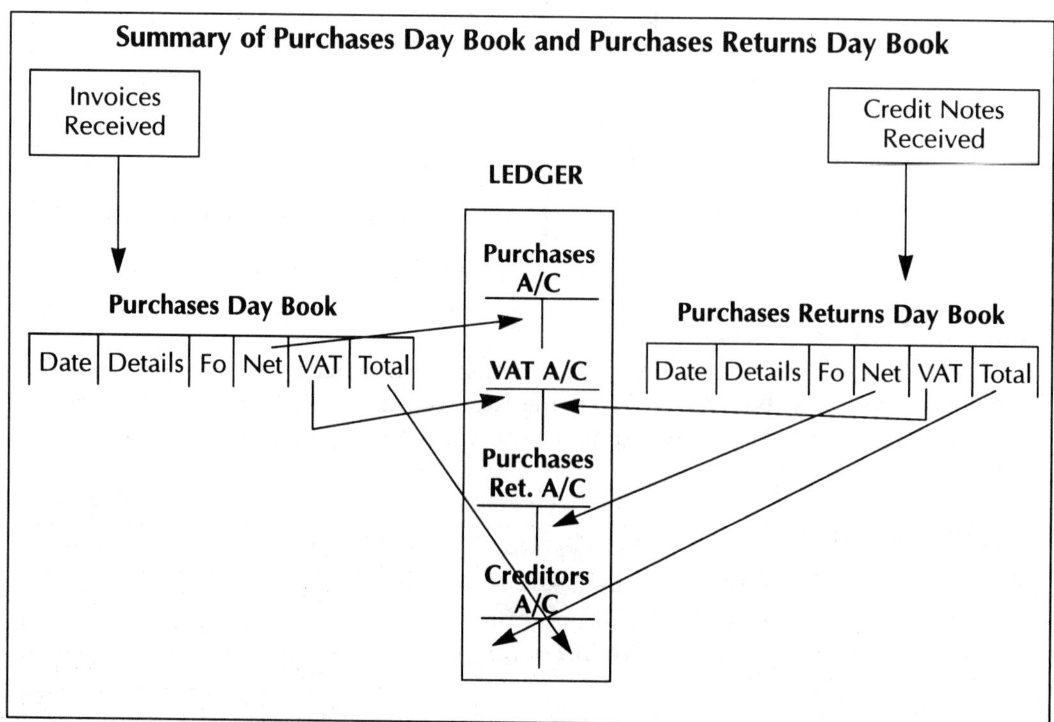

Chapter 31 — Sales Day Book and Sales Returns Day Book

Higher Level

A. Sales Day Book (SDB)

The sales day book is used to record goods sold on credit. When a firm sells goods on credit it sends an invoice to the buyer. The sales day book is written up from invoices sent.

B. Sales Returns Day Book (SRDB)

The sales returns day book is used to record goods returned to the business previously sold on credit. When goods are returned the seller issues a credit note. The sales returns day book is written up from credit notes issued.

C. Source Documents for Recording Sales Day Book and Sales Returns Day Book

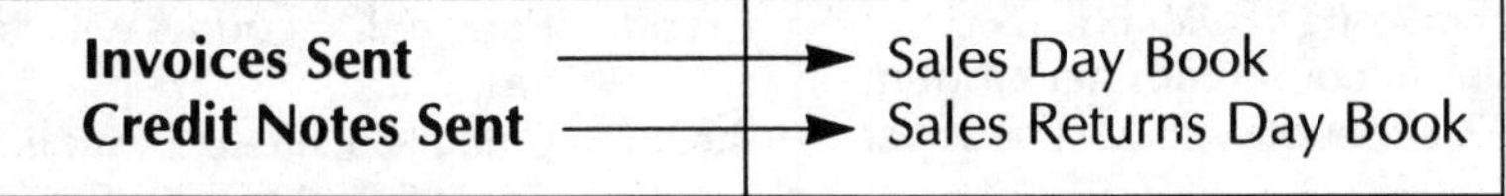

Sample Question and Solution

Question

- ➢ Write up the sales day book and sales returns day book, post to the ledger, balance the accounts and extract a trial balance.
- ➢ 1 Apr. Sold goods on credit to Sapphire Ltd. Invoice No. 238 IR£9,000 + Vat @ 21%.
- ➢ 6 Apr. Sent a credit note No. 412 to Sapphire Ltd for damaged goods IR£200 + VAT @ 21%.
- ➢ 15 Apr. Sent invoice No. 324 to Scott Ltd IR£6,000 + VAT @ 21%.
- ➢ 22 Apr. Sent credit note No. 202 to Scott Ltd for damaged goods IR£500 + VAT @ 21%.

Solution

(1) Day Books

Sales Day Book **Page 1**

Date	Particulars	Invoice No.	Fo	Net	VAT	Total
1 Apr.	Sapphire Ltd	238	DL/1	9,000	1,890	10,890
15 Apr.	Scott Ltd	324	DL/2	6,000	1,260	7,260
30 Apr.	Credit Sales and VAT A/Cs			15,000	3,150	18,150
				GL/1	GL2	

Sales Returns Day Book **Page 2**

Date	Details	Credit Note No.	Fo	Net	VAT	Total
6 Apr.	Sapphire Ltd	412	DL/1	200	42	242
22 Apr.	Scott Ltd	202	DL/2	500	105	605
30 Apr.	Debit Sales Returns and VAT A/Cs			700	147	847
				GL/3	GL/2	

DL = Debtors Ledger **GL** = General Ledger

(2) Rules for Posting to Ledger

Posting Sales Day Book	Posting Sales Returns Day Book
Debit Personal accounts with total amount, **i.e.** Debit Sapphire Ltd with IR£10,890. Debit Scott Ltd with IR£7,260. **Credit** Sales account with net amount. **Credit** VAT account with VAT amount.	**Debit** Sales Returns account with net amount. **Debit** VAT account with VAT amount. **Credit** Personal accounts with total amount, **i.e.** Credit Sapphire Ltd with IR£242. Credit Scott Ltd with IR£605.

GENERAL LEDGER

Debit **Sales A/C No. 1** **Credit**

Date	Details	Fo	Total	Date	Details	Fo	Total
				30 Apr.	Total as per SDB	SDB1	15,000

Debit **VAT A/C No. 2** **Credit**

Date	Details	Fo	Total	Date	Details	Fo	Total
30 Apr.	Total as per SRDB	SRDB2	147	30 Apr.	Total as per SDB	SDB1	3,150
30 Apr.	Balance	C/d	3,003				
			3,150				3,150
				30 Apr.	Balance	B/d	3,003

Debit — **Sales Returns A/C No. 3** — Credit

Date	Details	Fo	Total	Date	Details	Fo	Total
30 Apr.	Total as per SRDB	SRDB2	700				

DEBTORS LEDGER

Debit — **Sapphire Ltd A/C No. 1** — Credit

Date	Details	Fo	Total	Date	Details	Fo	Total
1 Apr.	Sales	SDB1	10,890	6 Apr.	Sales Returns	SRDB2	242
				30 Apr.	Balance	C/d	10,648
			10,890				10,890
30 Apr.	Balance	B/d	10,648				

Debit — **Scott Ltd A/C No. 2** — Credit

Date	Details	Fo	Total	Date	Details	Fo	Total
15 Apr.	Sales	SDB1	7,260	22 Apr.	Sales Returns	SRDB2	605
				30 Apr.	Balance	B/d	6,655
			7,260				7,260
30 Apr.	Balance	B/d	6,655				

BALANCING THE ACCOUNTS

All accounts with more than one entry must be balanced off. Balance in VAT account is IR£3,003. Balance in Sapphire Ltd account is IR£10,648 and balance in Scott Ltd account is IR£6,655. If an account has only one entry there is no need to balance it off.

THE TRIAL BALANCE

- ➢ The trial balance is a list of balances from the ledger.
- ➢ Debit balances go into the Debit column.
- ➢ Credit balances go into the Credit column.

Trial Balance as on 30 April

Date	Details	Fo	Debit	Credit
	Sales	GL1		15,000
	VAT	GL2		3,003
	Sales Returns	GL3	700	
	Sapphire Ltd	DL1	10,648	
	Scott Ltd	DL2	6,655	
			18,003	18,003

PRACTICE QUESTION

Write up the sales day book and sales returns day book, post to the ledger, balance the accounts and extract a trial balance.

1 May Sold goods on credit to Rainbow Ltd. Invoice No. 425 IR£8,000 + VAT @ 21%.

7 May Sent a credit note No. 553 to Rainbow Ltd for damaged goods IR£800 + VAT @ 21%.

21 May Sent invoice No. 411 to Goldstar Ltd. IR£7,000 + VAT @ 21%.

23 May Sent credit note No. 901 to Goldstar Ltd for damaged goods IR£200 + VAT @ 21%.

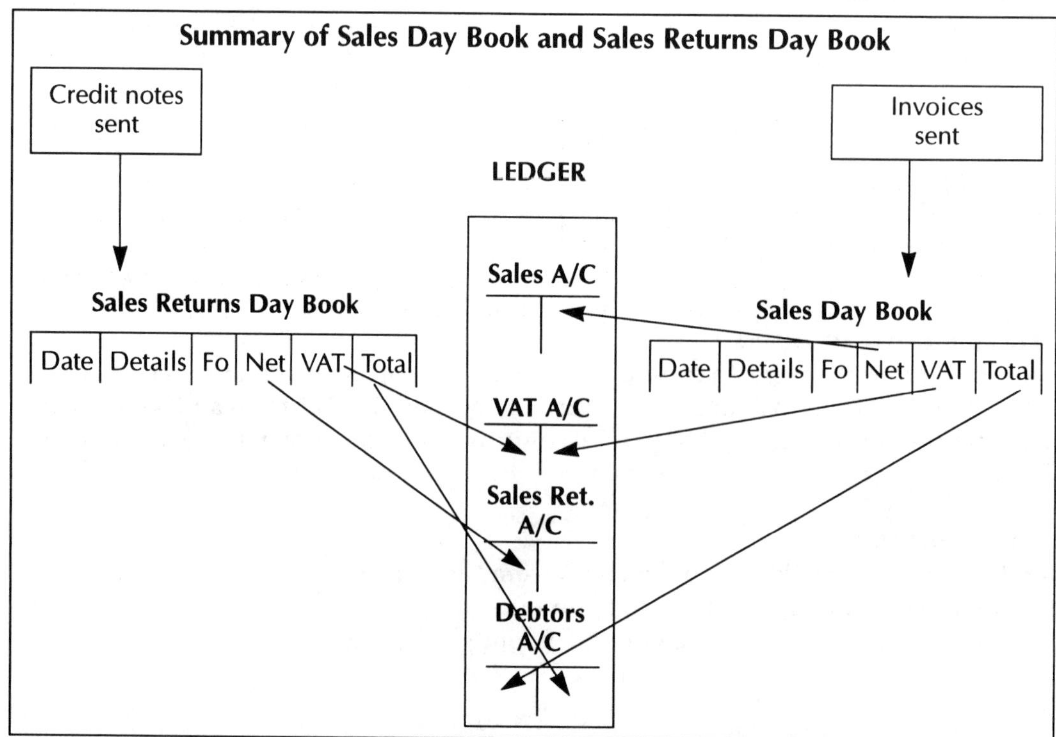

Chapter 32 — Cash Book (Including VAT)

A. Cash Book

The cash book is used to record money received by the business and money paid out by the business. Cash transactions are entered in the cash column and transactions by cheque are entered in the bank column.

B. Format of Cash Book

The layout of the cash book may vary from one business to another.

METHOD I — TWO SEPARATE CASH BOOKS

Use analysed cash receipts and lodgments book and analysed cash and cheque payments book, plus a cash account and bank account in the ledger.

OR

METHOD II — ANALYSED CASH BOOK

This combines the above two books.

(1) Information in the analysed cash receipts and lodgments book would appear on the debit side of the analysed cash book.
(2) Information in the analysed cash and cheque payment book would appear on the credit side of the analysed cash book.

No cash account or bank account are needed in the ledger as the cash and bank columns are balanced in the analysed cash book.

NB Either method will answer any question at Junior Certificate Business Studies.

RULES FOR WRITING UP CASH BOOKS

(1) Any money coming into the business goes into analysed cash receipts book, or debit side of analysed cash book.
(2) Any money going out of the business goes into the analysed cash and cheque payments book, or credit side of analysed cash book.

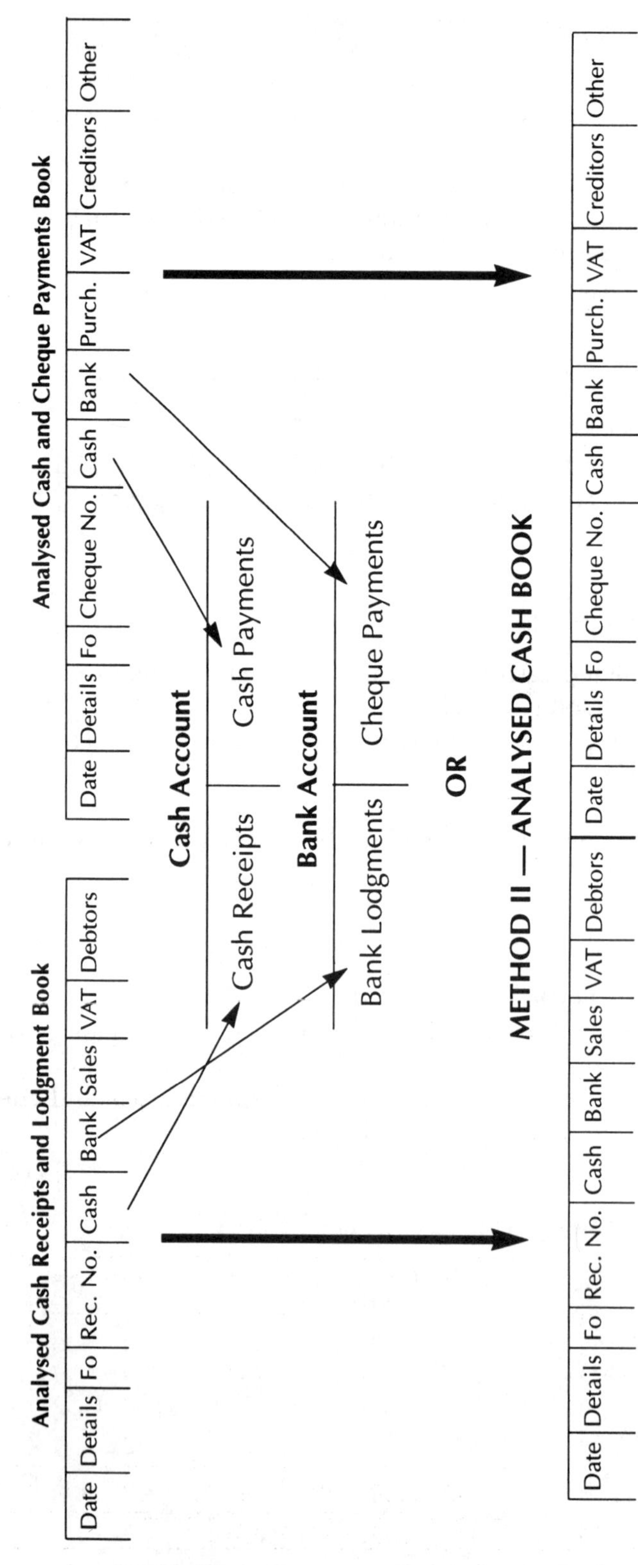

NO CASH OR BANK ACCOUNT IS USED AS CASH AND BANK COLUMNS ARE BALANCED IN ANALYSED CASH BOOK.

Sample Question and Solution

Question

Record the following transactions for the month of June in the appropriate books of first entry, post relevant figures to the ledger, extract a trial balance as on 30 June.

NOTE

Analyse the cash and bank transactions using the following money column headings:

Debit (Receipts) Side: Cash, Bank, VAT, Sales.
Credit (Payments) Side: Cash, Bank, Purchases, VAT, Creditors, Wages, Other.
Transactions

1 June Cash balance IR£3,000, Bank balance IR£10,000
4 June Cash sales lodged IR£6,000, this includes VAT of IR£1,041 (receipt No. 1)
10 June Paid wages cheque No. 41 IR£900
12 June Purchased goods cheque No. 42 IR£800 + VAT @ 21%
15 June D. Creedon Ltd (debtor) settled his account of IR£8,000 by cheque and it was lodged (receipt No. 2)
20 June Paid J. Shorthall Ltd (creditor) by cheque No. 43 IR£2,000
23 June Paid office expenses by cash IR£200
28 June Cash sales IR£10,000. This includes VAT of IR£1,736 (receipt No. 3)

Solution

METHOD I — TWO CASH BOOKS

Analysed Cash Receipts and Lodgment Book **Page 1**

Date	Details	Fo	Rec. No.	Cash	Bank	Sales	VAT	Debtors
4 June	Sales		1		6,000	4,959	1,041	
15 June	D. Creedon Ltd	DL1	2		8,000			8,000
28 June	Sales		3	10,000		8,264	1,736	
30 June	Debit Cash and Bank A/Cs			10,000	14,000	13,223	2,777	8,000
					GL1	GL2	GL3	GL4

Analysed Cash and Cheque Payment Book **Page 1**

Date	Details	Fo	Chq. No.	Cash	Bank	Purch.	VAT	Cred.s	Wages	Other
10 June	Wages	GL/6	41		900				900	
12 June	Purchases		42		968	800	168			
20 June	J. Shorthall Ltd	CL/1	43		2,000			2,000		
23 June	Office Expenses	GL/7		200						200
30 June	Credit Cash and Bank A/Cs			200	3,868	800	168	2,000	900	200
				GL/1	GL/2	GL/5	GL/4			

Rules for Posting Cash Book to Ledger

(1) Any item in the analysed cash receipts and lodgment book, i.e. debit side of analysed cash book, is posted to the credit side of ledger.

(2) Any item in the analysed cash and cheque payment book, i.e. credit side of analysed cash book, is posted to debit side of ledger.

GENERAL LEDGER

Cash Account **No. 1**

Date	Details	Fo	Total	Date	Details	Fo	Total
1 June	Balance		3,000	30 June	Payments	CB1	200
30 June	Receipts	CB1	10,000	30 June	Balance	C/d	12,800
			13,000				13,000
30 June	Balance	B/d	12,800				

Bank Account **No. 2**

Date	Details	Fo	Total	Date	Details	Fo	Total
1 June	Balance		10,000	30 June	Payments	CB1	3,868
30 June	Receipts	CB1	14,000	30 June	Balance	C/d	20,132
			24,000				24,000
30 June	Balance	B/d	20,132				

Sales Account **No. 3**

Date	Details	Fo	Total	Date	Details	Fo	Total
				30 June	Cash Book	CB1	13,223

Capital Account

Date	Details	Fo	Total	Date	Details	Fo	Total
				1 June	Cash Book		13,000

VAT Account **No. 4**

Date	Details	Fo	Total	Date	Details	Fo	Total
30 June	Cash Purchases	CB1	168	30 June	Cash Sales	CB1	2,777
30 June	Balance	C/d	2,609				
			2,777				2,777
				30 June	Balance	B/d	2,609

Purchases Account **No. 5**

Date	Details	Fo	Total	Date	Details	Fo	Total
12 June	Bank	CB1	800				

Wages Account **No. 6**

Date	Details	Fo	Total	Date	Details	Fo	Total
10 June	Bank	CB1	900				

Office Expenses Account **No. 7**

Date	Details	Fo	Total	Date	Details	Fo	Total
23 June	Cash	CB1	200				

DEBTORS LEDGER

D. Creedon Ltd Account **No. 1**

Date	Details	Fo	Total	Date	Details	Fo	Total
				15 June	Bank	CB1	8,000

CREDITORS LEDGER

J. Shorthall Ltd Account **No. 1**

Date	Details	Fo	Total	Date	Details	Fo	Total
20 June	Bank	CB1	2,000				

NOTES

(i) Cash balance and bank balance are entered in the cash account and bank account on the debit side (overdrawn balance is entered on credit side).

(ii) The credit entry for these balances is in the capital account.

Trial Balance	
	Debit Balance → Debit Column
	Credit Balance → Credit Column

Trial Balance as on 30 June

Date	Details	Fo	Debit	Credit
	Cash		12,800	
	Bank		20,132	
	Sales			13,223
	Capital			13,000
	VAT			2,609
	Purchases		800	
	Wages		900	
	Office Expenses		200	
	D. Creedon Ltd			8,000
	J. Shorthall Ltd		2,000	
			36,832	36,832

METHOD II — ANALYSED CASH BOOK

Analysed Cash Book

Debit																		Credit
Date	Details	Fo	Rec. No.	Cash	Bank	Sales	VAT	Debtors	Date	Details	Fo	Chq. No.	Cash	Bank	Purch.	VAT	Crs	Wages	Other
1 June	Balance			3,000	10,000				10 June	Wages	GL/6	41		900				900	
4 June	Sales	GL3	1		6,000	4,959	1,041		12 June	Purchases	GL/5	42		968	800	168			
15 June	D. Creedon Ltd	DL1	2		8,000			8,000	20 June	J. Shorthall Ltd	CL/1	43		2,000			2,000		
28 June	Sales	GL3	3	10,000		8,264	1,736												
									23 June	Office Exp.	GL/7		200						200
									30 June	Balance	C/d		12,800	20,132					
				13,000	24,000	13,223	2,777	8,000					13,000	24,000	800	168	2,000	900	200
						↑ GL /3	↑ GL/4								↑ GL/5	↑ GL/4			
30 June	Balance	B/d		12,800	20,132														

NOTE

The analysed cash book will contain the same figures as in the analysed cash receipts and lodgments book and the analysed cash and cheque payments book, as well as the opening and closing balances in the cash account and bank account in the ledger, i.e. cash and bank accounts are balanced in the analysed cash book.

C. Opening Balances

(1) The opening balance in the cash account must be on the debit side.
(2) The opening balance in the bank account can be on the debit side (i.e. business has money in the bank)**OR** it can be on the credit side (i.e. business has an overdraft).

NB Opening balances are not posted to the ledger.

D. Contra Entries

A Contra Entry is where
(1) Cash is being lodged to the bank.

OR

(2) Cash is being withdrawn from the bank for use in office.

(1) Lodged cash in bank	Take money from cash. Credit cash. Put money into bank. Debit bank.
(2) Withdrew cash from bank	Take money from bank. Credit bank. Put money into cash. Debit cash.

NB A contra entry involves cash account and bank account only. A contra entry is not posted to the ledger. To denote a contra entry a 'c' is put in the folio column.

E. Overheads of a Business

Overheads are the expenses involved in the running of a business. **When they are paid they are recorded in the analysed cash and cheque payments book/credit side of analysed cash book.** To complete the double entry **debit the appropriate ledger account**. The main overheads of a business are:

Rent	**Postage and Stationery**	**Wages and Salaries**
Rates	**Telephone**	**Interest on Loans**
Insurance	**Advertising**	**Light and Heat**

PRACTICE QUESTION

Record the following transactions for the month of July in the appropriate books of first entry, post relevant figures to the ledger, extract a trial balance as on 31 July.

NOTE

Analyse the cash and bank transactions using the following money column headings:

Debit (Receipts) Side: Cash, Bank, VAT, Sales.
Credit (Payments) Side: Cash, Bank, Purchases, VAT, Creditors, Wages, Other.
Transactions

1 July Cash balance IR£5,000, Bank balance IR£15,000
3 July Cash sales lodged IR£8,000, this includes VAT of IR£1,389 (receipt No. 1)
4 July Paid wages cheque No. 80 IR£1,200
8 July Purchased goods cheque No. 81 IR£1,500 + VAT @ 21%
12 July Kennedy Ltd (debtor) settled its account of IR£10,000 by cheque and it was lodged (receipt No. 2)
15 July Paid Horgan Ltd (creditor) by cheque No. 82 IR£600
23 July Paid office expenses by cash IR£600
25 July Cash sales IR£9,000. This includes VAT of IR£1,562 (receipt No. 3)
26 July Purchased equipment by cheque No. 83 IR£6,000

Chapter 33 — Petty Cash Book

A. Introduction

The petty cash book is used to record small cash payments, e.g. postage stamps, bus fares, envelopes. It has a debit side which records the petty cash float, and the credit side records payments. The credit side is analysed to give a breakdown of the payments.

B. Imprest System

The petty cash book operates on the Imprest System, which works as follows:

(1) Chief cashier gives Petty cashier a sum of money called Float which it is estimated will cover petty cash expenses for the month. It is shown on the debit side of the petty cash book.
(2) During the month this float is used to pay small expenses. A petty cash voucher is completed by the person requiring the money. Payments are recorded on the credit side of petty cash book.
(3) At the end of month petty cash book is balanced and amount spent is calculated.
(4) Chief cashier gives petty cashier a sum equivalent to amount spent to restore imprest to original level so that petty cashier can start next month with the same float.

C. Petty Cash Voucher

If an employee needs money to purchase something small he will complete a petty cash voucher giving:

(1) Date
(2) Amount
(3) Reason for money required
(4) Signature of claimant
(5) Signature of supervisor.

The payment is recorded in the credit side of the petty cash book.

Examination-Style Question and Solution

Question 1.
Answer (a), (b) and (c). This is a Petty Cash Question.
Mary Sweeney is the Office Manager in a company called Waldorf Ltd. She uses a Petty Cash Book to keep an account of small office expenses. At the beginning of each month, she starts off with an imprest of IR£100.

Here is what happened in May 1993:

- 1 May Balance (imprest) on hand IR£100.
- 2 May She paid IR£3 for postage — Petty Cash Voucher No. 101
- 4 May She bought envelopes for IR£2 — Petty Cash Voucher No. 102
- 6 May She paid IR£12 to Mr John Power to repair a broken typewriter — Petty Cash Voucher No. 103
- 7 May She bought writing paper (stationery) for IR£7 — Petty Cash Voucher No. 104
- 8 May She paid train fare IR£11 for sales representative — Petty Cash Voucher No. 105
- 9 May She paid the office cleaner IR£16 — Petty Cash Voucher No. 106
- 11 May She paid IR£6 for postage — Petty Cash Voucher No. 107
- 14 May She paid IR£5 out of petty cash to a local charity for a sponsored walk — Petty Cash Voucher No. 108
- 17 May She posted a parcel — the stamp cost IR£3 — Petty Cash Voucher No. 109
- 19 May She paid IR£4 taxi fare for sales manager — Petty Cash Voucher No. 110
- 23 May She paid the office cleaner IR£13 — Petty Cash Voucher No. 111
- 28 May She purchased computer paper (stationery) for IR£14 — Petty Cash Voucher No. 112

1. (a) A blank Petty Cash Voucher (No. 103) is supplied at the end of the question. Use it to enter the transaction of 6 May (only). **(15)**
1. (b) In your answer book, write up the Petty Cash Book for the month of May, using the following analysis columns:

POSTAGE STATIONERY CLEANING TRAVEL SUNDRIES

Total each analysis column and balance the Petty Cash Book at the end of May. **(40)**
1. (c) How much money will Mary receive from the chief cashier to enable her to start next month with an imprest of IR£100? **(5)**

1. (a) Document for Question 1. (a) PETTY CASH VOUCHER

WALDORF LTD			
PETTY CASH VOUCHER		No. 103	
Details		Amount	
		IR£	p
Signature			
Date			

Source: Junior Certificate Ordinary Level 1993. **(60 marks)**

Solution to Question 1.

1. (a) Document for Question 1. (a) PETTY CASH VOUCHER

WALDORF LTD			
PETTY CASH VOUCHER		No. 103	
Details		Amount	
John Power *Repairs to broken typewriter*		IR£	p
		12	*00*
Signature	*Mary Sweeney*		
Date	*6 May 1993*		

1. (b) PETTY CASH BOOK Page 1

Date	Details	Total	Date	Details	Voucher No.	Total	Postage	Stationery	Cleaning	Travel	Sundries
1 May	Balance	100.–	2 May	Postage	101	3.00	3.00				
			4 May	Envelopes	102	2.00		2.00			
			6 May	J. Power	103	12.00					12.00
			7 May	Writing Paper	104	7.00		7.00			
			8 May	Train Fare	105	11.00				11.00	
			9 May	Office Cleaner	106	16.00			16.00		
			11 May	Postage	107	6.00	6.00				
			14 May	Sponsored Walk	108	5.00					5.00
			17 May	Parcel Post	109	3.00	3.00				
			19 May	Taxi	110	4.00				4.00	
			23 May	Office Cleaner	111	13.00			13.00		
			28 May	Computer Paper	112	14.00		14.00			
						96.00	12.00	23.00	29.00	15.00	17.00
							GL/1	GL/2	GL/3	GL/4	GL/5
			31 May	Balance	C/d	4.00					
		100.–				100.00					
31 May	Balance B/d	4.–									
1 June	Bank	96.–									

1. (c) *Mary will receive from chief cashier IR£96.00.*

D. Posting Petty Cash Book to Ledger

At the end of month the analysis columns are totalled and the Petty Cash Book is balanced. An account for each analysis column is opened in the general ledger and the total of each account is posted to the **debit side** of the relevant account.

GENERAL LEDGER

Postage Account **No. 1**

Date	Details	Fo	Total	Date	Details	Fo	Total
31 May	Petty Cash Book	PCB1	12.00				

Stationery Account **No. 2**

Date	Details	Fo	Total	Date	Details	Fo	Total
31 May	Petty Cash Book	PCB1	23.00				

Cleaning Account **No. 3**

Date	Details	Fo	Total	Date	Details	Fo	Total
31 May	Petty Cash Book	PCB1	29.00				

Travel Account **No. 4**

Date	Details	Fo	Total	Date	Details	Fo	Total
31 May	Petty Cash Book	PCB1	15.00				

Sundries Account **No. 5**

Date	Details	Fo	Total	Date	Details	Fo	Total
31 May	Petty Cash Book	PCB1	17.00				

PRACTICE QUESTIONS

(i) Answer **(a)**, **(b)** and **(c)**. This is a Petty Cash Question.

Mary Murphy is office manager in a company called Sherwood Ltd. She uses a petty cash book to keep an account of small office expenses. At the beginning of each month she starts off with an Imprest of IR£150.

Here is an account of transactions for March 1996.

- 1 March Balance (Imprest) on hand IR£150.
- 3 March She paid IR£2 for postage stamps — Petty Cash Voucher No. 201
- 5 March She purchased envelopes for IR£2 — Petty Cash Voucher No. 202
- 8 March She paid for cleaning office IR£5 — Petty Cash Voucher No. 203
- 10 March She paid bus fares IR£6 — Petty Cash Voucher No. 204
- 16 March She purchased copying paper IR£12 — Petty Cash Voucher No. 205
- 18 March She purchased stationery IR£6 — Petty Cash Voucher No. 206
- 22 March She paid for cleaning office IR£5 — Petty Cash Voucher No. 207
- 25 March She donated IR£6 to charity — Petty Cash Voucher No. 208
- 29 March She paid for bus fares IR£6 — Petty Cash Voucher No. 209
- 30 March Purchased postage stamps IR£10 — Petty Cash Voucher No. 210

(i) (a) On the blank Petty Cash Voucher No. 203 supplied below enter the transaction of 8 March (only).

SHERWOOD LTD			
PETTY CASH VOUCHER		No. 203	
Details		Amount	
		IR£	p
Signature			
Date			

(i) (b) In your answer book, write up the petty cash book for the month of March, using the following analysis columns:

POSTAGE STATIONERY CLEANING TRAVEL SUNDRIES

Total each analysis column and balance the petty cash book at end of March.

(i) (c) How much money will Mary receive from the chief cashier to enable her to start next month with an Imprest of IR£150?

(i) (d) Post the totals of the analysis columns to the appropriate ledger accounts.

(ii) Question 7, Section A, Ordinary Level, 1994.

Chapter 34 — General Journal

Higher Level

A. Introduction

The General Journal is used to record transactions which cannot be recorded in any other book of first entry.

These transactions are:
(1) Opening entries.
(2) Purchase and sale of fixed assets on credit.
(3) Bad debts written off.
The General Journal is also posted to the Ledger.

B. Layout of General Journal

GENERAL JOURNAL

Date	Details	Fo	Debit	Credit
	Names of Accounts and Narration (Explanation of Transaction)		A/C to be Debited	A/C to be Credited

(1) OPENING ENTRIES

A list of **Assets** and **Liabilities** at the start of the trading period.

Assets — Debit Column
Liabilities — Credit Column

The difference is called Share Capital and is entered in the Credit Column, i.e. money owed to owners/shareholders.

Assets – Liabilities = Share Capital

Narration — a brief explanation of the transaction.

Sample Question and Solution

Question

Kavanagh Ltd had the following Assets and Liabilities on 1 January. Enter these in the General Journal and post to the ledger.

Assets: Cash IR£10,000 Bank IR£20,000 Buildings IR£150,000
Debtor: Seamus McCarthy IR£6,000
Liabilities Creditor: Patrick Hennessey IR£3,000
Share Capital: IR£183,000

Solution

GENERAL JOURNAL **Page 1**

Date	Details	Fo	Debit	Credit
1 Jan.	Assets			
	Cash	CB1	10,000	
	Bank	CB1	20,000	
	Buildings	GL1	150,000	
	Debtor: Seamus McCarthy	DL1	6,000	
	Liabilities			
	Creditor: Patrick Hennessey	CL1		3,000
	Share Capital	GL2		183,000
			186,000	186,000
	Assets, Liabilities and Share Capital of Kavanagh Ltd on 1 Jan.			

Posting opening entries to ledger

- *Assets which are in the Debit Column of the General Journal are **Debit Balances** in the Ledger.*
- *Liabilities and Share Capital which are in the **Credit Column** of the General Journal are **Credit Balances** in the Ledger.*

GENERAL LEDGER

Building Account **No. 1**

Date	Details	Fo	Total	Date	Details	Fo	Total
1 Jan.	Balance	GJ1	150,000				

Share Capital Account **No. 2**

Date	Details	Fo	Total	Date	Details	Fo	Total
				1 Jan.	Balance	GJ1	183,000

DEBTORS LEDGER

Seamus McCarthy Account **No. 1**

Date	Details	Fo	Total	Date	Details	Fo	Total
1 Jan.	Balance	GJ1	6,000				

CREDITORS LEDGER

Patrick Hennessey Account **No. 1**

Date	Details	Fo	Total	Date	Details	Fo	Total
				1 Jan.	Balance	GJ1	3,000

CASH BOOK

Date	Details	Fo	Cash	Bank	Date	Details	Fo	Cash	Bank
1 Jan.	Balance	GJ1	10,000	20,000					

---

(2) PURCHASE AND SALE OF FIXED ASSETS ON CREDIT

Sample Question and Solution

Question

➢ 2 Jan. Purchased office equipment on credit from Munster Business Equipment for IR£3,000 + VAT @ 21%

➢ 3 Jan. Sold office equipment on credit to Frank Boland for IR£500 + VAT @ 21%

Solution — Explanation

➢ *2 Jan.* ***Debit*** *office equipment account IR£3,000 – receiving account*
Debit *VAT account IR£630*
Credit *Munster Business Equipment – IR£3,630 – giving account*

➢ *3 Jan.* ***Debit*** *Frank Boland account – IR£605 – receiving account*
Credit *office equipment account – IR£500 – giving account*
Credit *VAT account – IR£105*

GENERAL JOURNAL				Page 1
Date	Details	Fo	Debit	Credit
2 Jan.	Office Equipment A/C	GL1	3,000	
	VAT A/C	GL2	630	
	Munster Business Equipment A/C	CL1		3,630
	Purchase of Office Equipment on Credit			
3 Jan.	Frank Boland A/C	DL1	605	
	Office Equipment A/C	GL1		500
	VAT A/C	GL2		105
	Sale of Office Equipment on Credit			

GENERAL LEDGER

Office Equipment Account

Date	Details	Fo	Total	Date	Details	Fo	Total
2 Jan.	Munster Business Equipment	GJ1	3,000	3 Jan.	Frank Boland	GJ1	500

VAT Account

Date	Details	Fo	Total	Date	Details	Fo	Total
2 Jan.	Munster Business Equipment	GJ1	630	3 Jan.	Frank Boland	GJ1	105

DEBTORS LEDGER

Frank Boland Account

Date	Details	Fo	Total	Date	Details	Fo	Total
3 Jan.	Office Equipment	GJ1	605				

CREDITORS LEDGER

Munster Business Equipment Account

Date	Details	Fo	Total	Date	Details	Fo	Total
				2 Jan.	Office Equipment	GJ1	3,630

(3) BAD DEBTS WRITTEN OFF

A bad debt arises when goods are sold on credit to a debtor and the debtor fails to pay the money owed. The business will then write the figure off as a bad debt.

Sample Question and Solution

Question

5 Feb. Jim Lawlor (debtor) owes IR£600 and has been declared bankrupt and can pay only IR£200. The remaining IR£400 is to be written off as a bad debt.

Solution

Debit bank account with IR£200 — amount received.
Debit bad debts account IR£400 — amount of bad debt.
Credit Jim Lawlor — IR£600 — to close his account.

GENERAL JOURNAL **Page 2**

Date	Details	Fo	Debit	Credit
5 Feb.	Bank A/C	CB1	200	
	Bad Debts A/C	GL1	400	
	Jim Lawlor A/C	DL1		600
	Jim Lawlor declared bankrupt. Paid IR£200, balance owed written off as a bad debt.			

CASH BOOK **Page 1**

Date	Details	Fo	Cash	Bank	Date	Details	Fo	Cash	Bank
5 Feb.	Jim Lawlor	GJ2	200						

GENERAL LEDGER

Bad Debts Account **No. 1**

Date	Details	Fo	Total	Date	Details	Fo	Total
5 Feb.	Jim Lawlor	GJ2	400				

DEBTORS LEDGER

Jim Lawlor Account **No. 1**

Date	Details	Fo	Total	Date	Details	Fo	Total
1 Feb.	Balance	GJ2	600	5 Feb.	Bank	GJ2	200
				5 Feb.	Bad Debts	GJ2	400
			600				600

PRACTICE QUESTION

Colour Printing Ltd runs a small business. Enter the following opening balances and transactions in the general journal and post to the ledger.

1 MAR.

Assets

Cash IR£5,000, Bank IR£10,000

Stock IR£290,000 Motor Vehicles, IR£25,000

Debtors: Print and Design Ltd IR£200

Graphic Print Ltd IR£800

Liabilities

Creditors: Kerry Printers Ltd IR£2,000

ABC Printers Ltd IR£1,000

Share Capital IR£48,000

3 MAR. Purchased printing equipment on credit from Kerry Printers Ltd for IR£15,000 + VAT @ 21%

5 MAR. Sold printing equipment on credit to Graphic Print Ltd for IR£2,000 + VAT @ 21%

10 MAR. Print and Design Ltd (debtor) has been declared bankrupt, owes IR£200 and can pay only IR£50. Remaining IR£150 to be written off as a bad debt.

Chapter 35 — Book-Keeping Revision

Higher Level

In this chapter we will summarise briefly the books of first entry and work a question from a Junior Certificate paper (Higher Level).

BOOKS OF FIRST ENTRY — SUMMARY

Books of First Entry	Type of Transaction Book Is Used For	Source Documents	Rules for Posting to Ledger
Purchases day book	Goods purchased on credit	Invoices received	DR — Purchases A/C Net DR — VAT A/C — VAT CR — Personal A/C — Total
Purchases returns day book	Returns of goods purchased on credit	Credit notes received	DR Personal A/C — Total CR Purch. Ret. A/C — Net CR VAT A/C — VAT
Sales day book	Goods sold on credit	Invoices sent	DR Personal A/C — Total CR Sales A/C — Net CR Vat A/C — VAT
Sales returns day book	Return of goods previously sold on credit	Credit notes sent	DR Sales Ret. A/C — Net DR VAT A/C — VAT CR Personal A/C — Total
Cash book	Cash receipts ⟶ Bank lodgments ⟶	Cash register/+ receipts given Lodgment counterfoils/ + bank statements	Debit side of cash book ⟶ Credit side of ledger
	Cash payments ⟶ Cheque payments ⟶	Cash vouchers Cheque counterfoils/ + bank statements	Credit side of cash book ⟶ Debit side of ledger
Petty cash book	Small items of expenditure	Petty cash vouchers	Total of each analysis column is posted to Debit side of ledger A/C
General journal	(1) Opening entries	Relevant invoices, etc.	(1) DR Assets — CR Liabilities
	(2) Purchase of assets on credit		(2) DR — Asset A/C DR — VAT A/C CR — Personal A/C
	(3) Sale of assets on credit		(3) DR — Personal A/C CR — Asset A/C CR — VAT A/C
	(4) Bad debts written off		(4) DR — Bank A/C DR — Bad Debts A/C CR — Personal A/C

Examination-Style Question and Solution

Question 1.

Answer (a), (b) and (c). This is a book of First Entry and Ledger Question.

Sunshine Paints Ltd had the following balances in its General Journal on 1 May 1993.

GENERAL JOURNAL				
Date	**Details**	**F**	**Dr**	**Cr**
1 May	Premises	GL1	70,000	
	Motor Vans	GL2	30,000	
	Bank		5,000	
	Debtor: J.J. Builders Ltd	DL1	3,000	
	Creditor: Throne Paints Ltd	CL1		48,000
	Ordinary Share Capital	GL3		60,000
			108,000	108,000

The following transactions took place during the month of May 1993:

CREDIT TRANSACTIONS

4/5/93	Purchased paint for resale on credit from Throne Paints Ltd	Invoice No. 361 IR£40,000 + VAT 20%
10/5/93	Sold paint on credit to Brushwell Ltd	Invoice No. 120 IR£5,000 + VAT 20%
17/5/93	Sold paint on credit to J.J. Builders Ltd	Invoice No. 121 IR£25,000 + VAT 20%

BANK TRANSACTIONS

6/5/93	Cash sales lodged		IR£9,000. (This includes IR£1,500 VAT.)
8/5/93	Paid wages	(Cheque No. 75)	IR£1,050
15/5/93	Purchased paint	(Cheque No. 76)	IR£1,200 + VAT 20%
22/5/93	J.J. Builders Ltd settled their account in full by cheque and it was lodged.		
28/5/93	Paid Throne Paints Ltd	(Cheque No. 77)	IR£35,000

You are required to:

1. (a) Post the balances on 1 May given in the General Journal to the relevant accounts. **(7)**

1. (b) Record the transactions for the month of May in the appropriate books of first entry. Post relevant figures to the ledger.

NOTE

Analyse the bank transactions using the following money column headings:
Debit (Receipts) Side: Bank, Sales, VAT, Debtors.
Credit (Payments) Side: Bank, Purchases, VAT, Creditors, Wages. (25)

1. (c) Balance the accounts on 31 May 1993 and extract a Trial Balance as on that date. (8)

Source: Junior Certificate Higher Level 1993. **(40 marks)**

Solution to Question 1.

PURCHASES DAY BOOK

Date	Details	Inv. No.	Fo	Net	VAT	Total
4/5/93	Throne Paints Ltd	361	CL9	40,000	8,000	48,000
31/5/93	Debit Purchases and VAT A/Cs			40,000	8,000	48,000

SALES DAY BOOK

Date	Details	Inv. No.	Fo	Net	VAT	Total
10/5/93	Brushwell Ltd	120	DL2	5,000	1,000	6,000
17/5/93	J.J. Builders Ltd	121	DL1	25,000	5,000	30,000
31/5/93	Credit Sales and VAT A/Cs			30,000	6,000	36,000

Analysed Cash Book (1)

Date	Details	Fo	Bank	Sales	VAT	Debtors	Date	Details	Fo No.	Chq.	Bank	Purch.	VAT	Crs	Wages
1/5/93	Balance	GJ1	5,000				8/5/93	Wages	GL4	75	1,050				1,050
6/5/93	Sales	GL1	9,000	7,500	1,500		15/5/93	Purch.	GL2	76	1,440	1,200	240		
22/5/93	J.J. Builders	DL1	33,000			33,000	28/5/93	Throne Paints	GL9	77	35,000			35,000	
							31/5/93	Bal.	C/d		9,510				
			47,000	7,500	1,500	33,000					47,000	1,200	240	35,000	1,050
31/5/93	B/d		9,510												

OR

Analysed Cash Receipts and Lodgments Book

Date	Details	Fo	Bank	Sales	VAT	Debtors
6/5/93	Sales	GL1	9,000	7,500	1,500	
22/5/93	J.J. Builders	DL1	33,000			33,000
31/5/93	Debit Bank A/C		42,000	7,500	1,500	33,000

AND

Analysed Cheque Payments Book

Date	Details	Fo	Ch. No.	Bank	Purch.	VAT	Cdts	Wages
8/5/93	Wages	GL4	75	1,050				1,050
15/5/93	Purchases	GL2	76	1,440	1,200	240		
28/5/93	Throne Paints	GL9	77	35,000			35,000	
31/5/93	Credit Bank A/C			37,490	1,200	240	35,000	1,050

AND

Bank Account No. 1

Date	Details	Fo	Total	Date	Details	Fo	Total
1/5/93	Balance	GJ1	5,000	31/5/93	Cheque Payments Book	CPB1	37,490
31/5/93	Cash Receipts and Lodgments	CRLB1	42,000	31/5/93	Balance	C/d	9,510
			47,000				47,000
31/5/93	Balance	B/d	9,510				

GENERAL LEDGER

Premises Account

Date	Details	Fo	Total	Date	Details	Fo	Total
1/5/93	Balance	GJ1	70,000				

Motor Vans Account

Date	Details	Fo	Total	Date	Details	Fo	Total
1/5/93	Balance	GJ1	30,000				

Ordinary Share Capital Account

Date	Details	Fo	Total	Date	Details	Fo	Total
				1/5/93	Balance	GJ1	60,000

Wages Account

Date	Details	Fo	Total	Date	Details	Fo	Total
8/5/93	Bank	CB1	1,050				

Sales Account

Date	Details	Fo	Total	Date	Details	Fo	Total
				31/5/93	Sales Day Book	SB1	30,000
				31/5/93	Bank	CB1	7,500
							37,500

Purchases Account

Date	Details	Fo	Total	Date	Details	Fo	Total
31/5/93	Purchases Day Book	PB1	40,000				
31/5/93	Bank	CB1	1,200				
			41,200				

VAT Account

Date	Details	Fo	Total	Date	Details	Fo	Total
31/5/93	Credit Purchases	PB1	8,000	31/5/93	Credit Sales	SB1	6,000
31/5/93	Cash Purchases	CB1	240	31/5/93	Cash Sales	CB1	1,500
				31/5/93	Balance	C/d	740
			8,240				8,240
1/6/93	Balance	C/d	740				

DEBTORS LEDGER

J.J. Builders Ltd Account

Date	Details	Fo	Total	Date	Details	Fo	Total
1/5/93	Balance	GJ1	3,000	22/5/93	Bank	CB1	33,000
17/5/93	Sales	SB1	30,000				
			33,000				33,000

Brushwell Ltd Account

Date	Details	Fo	Total	Date	Details	Fo	Total
10/5/93	Sales	SB1	6,000				

CREDITORS LEDGER

Throne Paints Ltd Account

Date	Details	Fo	Total	Date	Details	Fo	Total
28/5/93	Bank	CB1	35,000	1/5/93	Balance	GJ1	48,000
31/5/93	Balance	C/d	61,000	4/5/93	Purchases	PB1	48,000
			96,000				96,000
				1/6/93	Balance	B/d	61,000

Trial Balance as on 31/5/93

Date	Details	Fo	Debit	Credit
31/5/93	Premises		70,000	
	Motor Vans		30,000	
	Ordinary Share Capital			60,000
	Wages		1,050	
	Sales			37,500
	Purchases		41,200	
	VAT		740	
	Brushwell Ltd		6,000	
	Throne Paints Ltd			61,000
	Bank		9,510	
			158,500	158,500

PRACTICE QUESTIONS

(i) Question 1, Paper II, Higher Level, Sample Paper.
(ii) Question 1, Paper II, Higher Level, 1992.
(iii) Question 1, Paper II, Higher Level, 1994.
(iv) Question 2, Paper II, Higher Level, 1994.
(v) Question 15, Section A, Paper I, Higher Level, 1994.

Higher Level

Chapter 36 — Control Accounts

We can check on the accuracy of the debtors and creditors ledger — by Control accounts (Total accounts).

A. Principles of Control Accounts

(1) Entries in a control account are exactly the same as in personal accounts **but they are in total.**
(2) Items **debited** in a personal account are **debited** in total in a control account. Items **credited** in a personal account are **credited** in total in a control account.
(3) The control account is prepared by taking the **totals from the day books.**

B. Types of Control Account

(1) Debtors Control Account ↓ Checks Debtors (Sales) Ledger	**(2)** Creditors Control Account ↓ Checks Creditors (Purchases) Ledger

There are two types:

(1) DEBTORS CONTROL ACCOUNT

The debtors control account is a total account and is prepared by taking totals of sales day book, sales returns book and total cash/cheques received from debtors. The balance in the debtors control account should be equal to the total of the balances on **all** personal accounts in the debtors ledger, thus providing evidence of the accuracy of the debtors ledger.

Consider the entries in the personal account of a debtor.

Debit		**A Debtor A/C**			**Credit**
	ENTRIES	**SOURCE**		**ENTRIES**	**SOURCE**
	Balance (amount due from debtor) →	General Journal		Sales returns →	Sales Returns Day Book
	Credit sales →	Sales Day Book		Cash/cheques received from debtor →	Cash Book
				Balance C/d (amount due from debtor)	

And now look at the control account.

DEBTORS CONTROL (TOTAL) ACCOUNT						
	ENTRIES	SOURCE		ENTRIES	SOURCE	
	Balance (total amount due from all debtors) →	General Journal		Total sales returns →	Sales Returns Day Book	
				Total cash/cheques received from debtors →	Cash Book	
	Total credit sales →	Sales Day Book		Balance C/d (balance due from all debtors)		

NB Total debtors account is prepared from totals of books of first entry (SDB, SRDB, CB).

Sample Question and Solution

Question

Complete and balance the debtors control account from the following data.

- Balance as on 1 June 1996 IR£2,000
- Total cash received from debtors in June IR£10,000
- Total sales on credit in June IR£15,000
- Total sales returns in June IR£1,000

Solution

'T' ACCOUNT FORMAT

Debtors Control Account

Date	Details	Fo	Total	Date	Details	Fo	Total
1 June	Balance B/d	GJ	2,000	30 June	Cash rec. from debtors	CB	10,000
30 June	Credit sales	SB	15,000	30 June	Sales returns	SRB	1,000
				30 June	Balance	C/d	6,000
			17,000				17,000
30 June	Balance	B/d	6,000				

OR

CONTINUOUS BALANCING FORMAT

Debtors Control A/C					
Date	Details	Fo	Debit	Credit	Balance
1 June	Balance B/d	GJ			2,000
30 June	Credit sales	SB	15,000		17,000
30 June	Cash received from debtors	CB		10,000	7,000
30 June	Sales returns	SRB		1,000	6,000

(2) CREDITORS CONTROL ACCOUNT

The creditors control account is also a total account and is prepared by taking the totals of purchases day book, purchases returns book and total cash/cheques paid to creditors from the cash book. The balance in the creditors control account should be equal to the total of the balances on **all** personal accounts in the creditors ledger, thus providing evidence of the accuracy of the creditors ledger.

Consider the entries in a personal account of a creditor.

Debit		**A Creditor A/C**			**Credit**
	ENTRIES	**SOURCE**		**ENTRIES**	**SOURCE**
	Purchases returns →	Purchases Returns Book		Balance (amount due to creditor) →	General Journal
	Cash/cheques paid to creditor →	Cash Book		Credit purchases →	Purchases Day Book
	Balance C/d (amount due to creditor)				

And now look at the control account.

CREDITORS CONTROL (TOTAL) ACCOUNT					
	ENTRIES	**SOURCE**		**ENTRIES**	**SOURCE**
	Total purchases returns →	Purchases Ret. Book		Balance (total amount due to all creditors) →	General Journal
	Total cash/cheques paid to creditors →	Cash Book		Total credit purchases →	Purchases Day Book
	Balance C/d (amount due to all creditors)				

NB Total creditors account is prepared from totals of books of first entry (PDB, PRDB, CB).

Sample Question and Solution

Question

Complete and balance the creditors control account from the following data.

- Balance as on 1 July 1996 IR£4,000
- Total purchases on credit in July IR£20,000
- Total payments (by cheque) during July to creditors IR£15,000
- Total payments (by cash) during July to creditors IR£1,000
- Total purchases returns during July IR£3,000

Solution

'T' ACCOUNT FORMAT

Creditors Control Account

Date	Details	Fo	Total	Date	Details	Fo	Total
31 July	Payments to creditors – cheques	CB	15,000	1 July	Balance B/d	GJ	4,000
31 July	Payments to creditors – cash	CB	1,000	31 July	Total credit purchases	PB	20,000
31 July	Purchases returns	PRB	3,000				
31 July	Balance	C/d	5,000				
			24,000				24,000
				31 July	Balance B/d		5,000

OR

CONTINUOUS BALANCING FORMAT

Creditors Control A/C					
Date	**Details**	**Fo**	**Debit**	**Credit**	**Balance**
1 July	Balance	GJ			4,000
31 July	Credit purchases	PB		20,000	24,000
31 July	Payments to creditors – cheques	CB	15,000		9,000
31 July	Payments to creditors – cash	CB	1,000		8,000
31 July	Purchases returns	PRB	3,000		5,000

PRACTICE QUESTIONS

(i) Question 10, Section A, Paper I, Higher Level, Sample Paper.
(ii) Question 18, Section A, Paper I, Higher Level, Sample Paper.
(iii) Question 4, Section A, Paper I, Higher Level, 1992.

Higher Level

Chapter 37 — Continuous Presentation of Ledger Accounts

A. Types of Presentation

There are two ways of presenting ledger accounts.

(1) 'T' ACCOUNT FORMAT

This has the debit side on the left and the credit side on the right.

(2) CONTINUOUS BALANCING FORMAT

This has a debit column, a credit column and a balance column. The balance column is adjusted after each transaction so we can see immediately the balance on a particular day.

NB Students may opt to do ledger accounts either 'T' account format or continuous balancing format. But higher level students must be able to convert from 'T' account format to continuous balancing format or vice versa.

Conversion of a Debtor's Account from 'T' Account Format to Continuous Balancing Format

Sample Question and Solution

Question

Convert the following account in the debtors ledger into continuous balancing format.

DEBTORS LEDGER

DR ↑ **Patrick Gallagher Account** **CR ↓**

Date	Details	Fo	Total	Date	Details	Fo	Total
1 Jan.	Balance	GJ	2,000	15 Jan.	Cash	CB	2,000
10 Jan.	Sales	SB	15,000	18 Jan.	Bank	CB	9,000
22 Jan.	Sales	SB	11,000	25 Jan.	Sales returns	SRB	1,000
				31 Jan.	Balance	C/d	16,000
			28,000				28,000
31 Jan.	Balance	B/d	16,000				

Solution

DEBTORS LEDGER

Patrick Gallagher A/C					
Date	**Details**	**Fo**	**Debit +**	**Credit –**	**Balance**
1 Jan.	Balance	GJ			2,000
10 Jan.	Sales	SB	15,000		17,000
15 Jan.	Cash	CB	–	2,000	15,000
18 Jan.	Bank	CB	–	9,000	6,000
22 Jan.	Sales	SB	11,000	–	17,000
25 Jan.	Sales Returns	SRB	–	1,000	16,000

NB In Debtors Ledger

Figures in Debit column increase the balance.
Figures in Credit column reduce the balance.

Conversion of a Creditor's Account from 'T' Account Format to Continuous Balancing Format

Sample Question and Solution

Question
Convert the following account in the creditors ledger into continuous balancing format.

CREDITORS LEDGER

DR ↓ **John Molloy Account** **CR ↑**

Date	Details	Fo	Total	Date	Details	Fo	Total
10 Feb.	Cash	CB	3,000	1 Feb.	Balance	GJ	10,000
15 Feb.	Bank	CB	6,000	6 Feb.	Purchases	PB	15,000
24 Feb.	Purchases returns	PRB	3,000	17 Feb.	Purchases	PB	2,000
28 Feb.	Balance	C/d	15,000				
			27,000				27,000
				28 Feb.	Balance	B/d	15,000

Solution

CREDITORS LEDGER

John Molloy A/C					
Date	**Details**	**Fo**	**Debit –**	**Credit +**	**Balance**
1 Feb.	Balance	GJ			10,000
6 Feb.	Purchases	PB		15,000	25,000
10 Feb.	Cash	CB	3,000		22,000
15 Feb.	Bank	CB	6,000		16,000
17 Feb.	Purchases	PB		2,000	18,000
24 Feb.	Purchases returns	PRB	3,000		15,000

NB In Creditors Ledger

Figures in the Credit column increase the balance.
Figures in the Debit column reduce the balance.

PRACTICE QUESTIONS

(i) Question 7, Section A, Paper I, Higher Level, Sample Paper.
(ii) Question 9, Section A, Paper I, Higher Level, 1993.

FINAL ACCOUNTS OF A PRIVATE LIMITED COMPANY

Chapter 38 — Trading Account

A. Purpose of a Trading Account

The purpose of a trading account is to find the gross profit or gross loss made by a business in the trading period.

B. Trading Period

The trading period is the account period. It is usually twelve months (i.e. 1 January 1995–31 December 1995) but it could also be for six months.

C. Gross Profit/Gross Loss

The gross profit/gross loss is the difference between sales and cost of sales.

D. Contents of a Trading Account

(1) **Sales** — Value of all sales during the year/turnover.
(2) **Sales Returns/Returns Inwards** — Goods returned to us by debtors.
(3) **Opening Stock** — Value of stock at start of year.
(4) **Purchases** — Goods bought for resale during the year.
(5) **Purchases Returns/Returns Outwards** — Goods returned to our suppliers.
(6) **Carriage Inwards** — Transport costs of purchases.
(7) **Customs Duty/Import Duty** — Tax on goods coming into the country.
(8) **Manufacturing Wages/Direct Wages** — Wages paid to manufacturing workers.
(9) **Closing Stock** — Value of stock at end of year.

Net Sales/Turnover = Sales – Sales Returns.

Net Purchases = Purchases – Purchases Returns.

Cost of Sales = Opening Stock + Purchases + Carriage Inwards + Customs Duty + Manufacturing Wages – Closing Stock.

Gross Profit = Net Sales – Cost of Sales.

Sample Question and Solution

Question
From the following information prepare the trading account of Bobbit Enterprises Ltd for year ending 31 December 1995.

- ➢ Sales IR£200,000
- ➢ Purchases IR£80,000
- ➢ Carriage inwards IR£6,000
- ➢ Manufacturing wages IR£3,000
- ➢ Sales returns IR£1,000
- ➢ Purchases returns IR£2,000
- ➢ Opening stock (1 January 1995) IR£10,000
- ➢ Closing stock (31 December 1995) IR£15,000
- ➢ Import duty IR£2,000

Solution

Trading Account of Bobbit Enterprises Ltd for Year Ending 31 December 1995

	Sales		200,000	
	Less sales returns		1,000	
	Net sales/turnover			199,000
	Deduct Cost of Sales			
	Stock 1/1/95		10,000	
	Purchases	80,000		
	Less purchases returns	2,000	78,000	
	Carriage inwards		6,000	
	Import duty		2,000	
	Manufacturing wages		3,000	
	Cost of goods available for sale		99,000	
	Less closing stock 31/12/95		15,000	
	Cost of Sales			84,000
	Gross Profit			115,000

E. Interpretation of Information Presented in a Trading Account

The trading account gives the owner(s) of a business a lot of valuable information. (Refer to trading account of Bobbit Enterprises Ltd.)

(1) NET SALES/TURNOVER
IR£199,000

(2) COST OF SALES
IR£84,000

(3) RATE OF STOCK TURNOVER

This tells us how many times the stock is replaced in the business during the year.

$$\text{Formula} = \frac{\text{Cost of Sales}}{\text{Average Stock}} \qquad \frac{84{,}000}{12{,}500} = 6.72 \text{ Times}$$

$$\text{Average Stock} = \frac{\text{Opening Stock} + \text{Closing Stock}}{2}$$

$$\frac{10{,}000 + 15{,}000}{2}$$

$$= \frac{25{,}000}{2} = 12{,}500 = \text{Average Stock}$$

This business has a stock turnover of 6.72 times which means that it replaces its stock every 54 days approx. (365 ÷ 6.72).

(4) GROSS PROFIT MARGIN/GROSS PROFIT PERCENTAGE

This rate shows how much gross profit was made on each IR£1.00 of sales.

$$\text{Formula} = \frac{\text{Gross Profit x 100}}{\text{Sales}} \qquad \frac{115{,}000 \times 100}{199{,}000} = 57.78\%$$

This firm is making a gross profit of 57.78p on every IR£1.00 of sales. The gross profit percentage can be compared with
(a) Previous year's gross profit margin.
(b) Other firms in the same industry.
(c) The industry average.

F. Trading and Non-Trading Stock

Trading stock is the stock of goods for resale to customers. Non-trading stock is stock of goods not for resale to customers, e.g. stock of heating, stock of stationery, stock of packing materials.

G. Stocktaking — Higher Level

The aim of stocktaking is to find out the value of goods in the business on a particular day. Stocktaking involves only trading stock.

(1) REASONS FOR STOCKTAKING

(a) To find the value of closing stock required for the trading account and balance sheet.
(b) To identify slow-moving items and damaged goods.
(c) To find out whether goods have been stolen.

(2) MANUAL STOCKTAKING PROCEDURE

(a) Close business on the day.
(b) Divide store into sections.
(c) Assign two stocktakers to each section: one will count the goods, the other will record the information on the stock sheets.
(d) On completion of task, stocksheets will be returned to office for valuation of stock on hand.

(3) VALUATION OF STOCK

Stock is valued at the **lowest** of (a) cost price or (b) replacement price or (c) selling price.

(4) STOCKTAKING REPORT

STOCKTAKING REPORT DECEMBER 1996

To: Declan O'Brien Accounts Department
From: George Sutton Stock Supervisor
Date: 10 January 1997

Introduction: I was asked by you to report on the stocktaking on 31 December 1996.

Body of Report:

(a) Stocktaking took place on 31 December 1996 commencing at 10.00 a.m. and finishing at 5.00 p.m. The store was closed for business on the day.
(b) The task was performed accurately, a number of spot checks were taken and all stock sheets were accurate.
(c) Some items of stock are slow-moving (see stock sheets Nos. 6 and 10). Some stock is also damaged (see stock sheet No. 14). This stock needs urgent attention.
(d) I am satisfied that this stock count is correct.

I am available to discuss this report if required.

Signed: George Sutton, Stock Supervisor.

PRACTICE QUESTIONS

(i) Question 12, Section A, Ordinary Level, 1992.
(ii) Question 5, Section A, Ordinary Level, 1994.
(iii) Question 5, Section A, Paper I, Higher Level, Sample Paper.
(iv) Question 11, Section A, Paper I, Higher Level, 1994.

Chapter 39 — Profit and Loss Account

A. Purpose of a Profit and Loss Account

The purpose of a profit and loss account is to find the net profit or net loss made by a business in the trading period — profit after all expenses are deducted.

Net Profit/Net Loss = Gross Profit + Gains – Expenses

B. Gains

Gains are income other than trading income received by a business, e.g. rent received, discount received, interest received, insurance received, bad debt recovered.

C. Expenses/Overheads

Overheads are the expenses involved in the running of a business on a daily basis, e.g. rent, insurance, wages, telephone.

D. Finding Net Profit/Net Loss

(1) Add gains to gross profit.
(2) Subtract total expenses.

E. Monitoring Overheads — Higher Level

Firms must curtail overheads as much as possible otherwise their net profit will be substantially reduced. All overheads must be recorded carefully.
(1) Establish whether the expense is necessary.
(2) Record the payment carefully.
(3) Check all bills for accuracy before payment.
(4) Eliminate wastage in the business, i.e. unnecessary telephone calls.

F. Recording Overheads — Higher Level

All overheads when paid are entered in the analysed cash book **credit side**. The relevant account is **debited** in the ledger.

Example
10 Jan. Paid insurance IR£2,000 by cheque.

Analysed Cash Book

Date	Details	Fo	Cash	Bank	Date	Details	Fo	Cash	Bank
					10 Jan.	Insurance			2,000

Insurance A/C

Date	Details	Fo	Bank	Date	Details	Fo	Bank
10 Jan.	Bank		2,000	31 Jan.	P + L A/C		2,000

At end of year all overheads are closed off to the profit and loss account.

Debit P + L A/C (show under expenses).
Credit Overhead A/C (Insurance in above example).

G. Difference Between a Trading A/C and a Profit and Loss A/C

Trading A/C shows	Profit and Loss A/C shows
(1) Sales (2) Opening stock, purchases and closing stock (3) Purchasing expenses (4) Gross profit/gross loss	(1) Gains (2) All expenses (3) Net profit/net loss

H. Capital Expenditure and Revenue Expenditure — Higher Level

Capital Expenditure — Purchasing fixed assets which will last a number of years, e.g. equipment, machinery, premises, motor vehicles. These assets are recorded in the **balance sheet** and not in the profit and loss account.

Revenue Expenditure — Expenses involved in the day-to-day running of the business, e.g. wages, rent, insurance, advertising, telephone. These expenses are recorded in the **profit and loss account.**

Examination-Style Question

Question 1.

Classify the following items of expenditure under Capital or Revenue for a Delivery Van manufacturing business:

A. Stock of Heating Oil; **B.** Machinery; **C.** Wages; **D.** Repairs to Machinery; **E.** Delivery Vans for Resale; **F.** Repayment of Bank Term Loan; **G.** Carriage Outwards; **H.** Factory Extension.

Place appropriate letter under Capital or Revenue Expenditure in table below.

CAPITAL EXPENDITURE	REVENUE EXPENDITURE

Source: Junior Certificate Sample Paper Higher Level. **(4)**

Sample Question and Solution

Question

From the following prepare a profit and loss account of Bobbit Enterprises Ltd for year ending 31 December 1995.

Gross profit	IR£115,000	Advertising	IR£1,600
Postage and telephone	IR£8,150	Audit fees	IR£4,000
Rent received	IR£6,800	Insurance received	IR£4,600
Bank charges	IR£200	Marketing expenses	IR£1,500
Loan interest	IR£6,500	Carriage outwards	IR£900
Bad debts W/o	IR£2,000	Sales staff's salaries	IR£10,400
Packing materials	IR£8,000	Travelling expenses	IR£9,000
Rent	IR£200	Showroom expenses	IR£2,500
Insurance	IR£2,500		

Solution

Profit and Loss Account of Bobbit Enterprises Ltd for Year Ending 31 December 1995

	Gross Profit		115,000
	Add Gains		
	Insurance received	4,600	
	Rent received	6,800	11,400
			126,400
	Less Expenses		
	Postage and telephone	8,150	
	Bank charges	200	
	Loan interest	6,500	
	Bad debts W/o	2,000	
	Packing materials	8,000	
	Rent	200	
	Insurance	2,500	
	Advertising	1,600	
	Audit fees	4,000	
	Marketing expenses	1,500	
	Carriage outwards	900	
	Sales staff's salaries	10,400	
	Travelling expenses	9,000	
	Showroom expenses	2,500	57,450
	Net Profit		68,950

I. Interpretation of Information Presented in a Profit and Loss Account

The profit and loss account gives the owner(s) of a business a lot of valuable information. (Refer to profit and loss account of Bobbit Enterprises Ltd.)

(1) TOTAL EXPENSES
IR£57,450

(2) NET PROFIT
IR£68,950

(3) NET PROFIT MARGIN/NET PROFIT PERCENTAGE
This ratio shows how much net profit was made on each IR£1.00 of sales.

$$\text{Formula} = \frac{\text{Net Profit x 100}}{\text{Sales}} \qquad \frac{68{,}950 \text{ x } 100}{199{,}000} = 34.64\%$$

This firm is making a net profit of 34.64p on every IR£1.00 of sales. The net profit percentage can be compared with

(a) Previous year's net profit margin.
(b) Other firms in the same industry.
(c) The industry average.

PRACTICE QUESTIONS

(i) Question 12, Section A, Ordinary Level, Sample Paper.
(ii) Question 8, Section A, Paper I, Higher Level, 1992.

Chapter 40 — Profit and Loss Appropriation Account

A. Purpose of Profit and Loss Appropriation Account

The purpose of the profit and loss appropriation account is to show how the profit made is distributed (shared out). The board of directors will recommend to the shareholders how the profit should be shared.

B. Ordinary Share Dividend

Profit made in a company belongs to the shareholders. Profit distributed to shareholders is called ordinary share dividend.

C. Retained Earnings

It is normal practice to retain some profit for future use in the business. This is called retained earnings.

Ordinary Share Dividend is amount of profit given to shareholders.

Retained Earnings is amount of profit retained by the company for future use.

D. Calculation of Ordinary Share Dividend — Higher Level

The dividend is calculated as a percentage of the issued share capital of the company and not a percentage of net profit.

Sample Question and Solution

Question

Bobbit Enterprises Ltd has an issued capital of IR£100,000 ordinary shares @ IR£1 each. Net profit for year ending 31 December 1995 was IR£68,950. The directors declared a dividend of 10%.

(1) Calculate the ordinary share dividend.
(2) Prepare the profit and loss appropriation account.

Solution

(1) *Calculation of ordinary share dividend*

Dividend = 10% of IR£100,000 (issued share capital) = IR£10,000

NB The balance of the profit, i.e. IR£58,950, is retained by the company for future use.

Each shareholder will get 10p per share owned, e.g. John, who owns 2,000 shares, will get a dividend cheque of (2,000 x 10p) = IR£200.

(2) Profit and Loss Appropriation Account of Bobbit Enterprises Ltd for Year Ending 31 December 1995

	Net profit			68,950
	Ordinary share dividend			10,000
	Retained earnings			58,950

E. Ledger Account to Record Ordinary Share Dividend and Retained Earnings

Ordinary Share Dividend Account

Date	Details	Fo	Total	Date	Details	Fo	Total
				31/12/95	Profit and Loss App. A/C		10,000

Retained Earnings Account

Date	Details	Fo	Total	Date	Details	Fo	Total
				31/12/95	Profit and Loss App. A/C		58,950

(1) The ordinary share dividend is a **liability** of the business until it is paid — it will be entered in the balance sheet under current liabilities.

When the dividend is paid

Debit ordinary share dividend account.

Credit bank account.

When the dividend is paid there is no liability thus there will be no entry in the balance sheet.

(2) The retained earnings will be entered in the balance sheet in the financed by section under the heading 'Reserves'.

Chapter 41 — Balance Sheet

A. Balance Sheet

A balance sheet is a statement of assets, liabilities and share capital of a business on a particular day.

Assets — Property or things that a business owns.
Liabilities — Debts that a business owes.
Share Capital — Money invested in the company by its owners/shareholders (money owed to shareholders).

B.

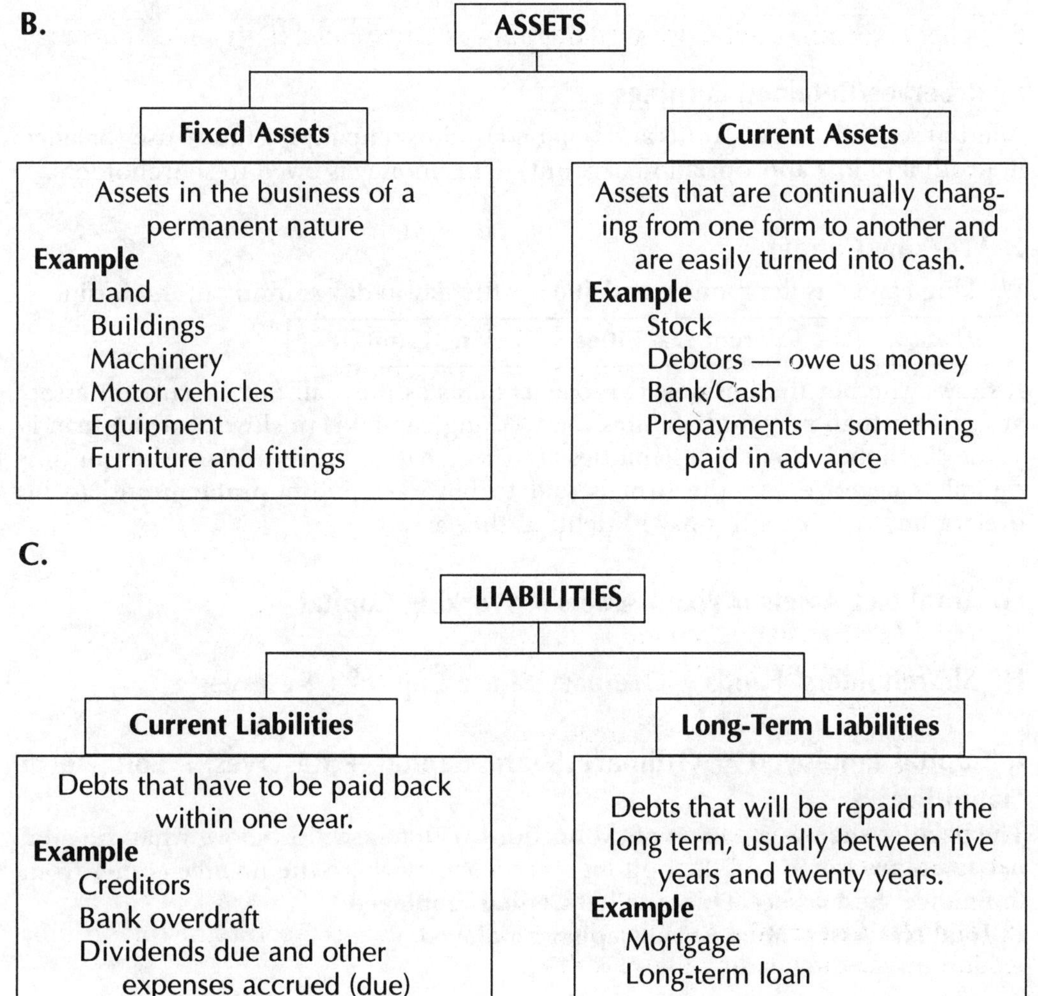

ASSETS
Fixed Assets
Assets in the business of a permanent nature
Example
Land
Buildings
Machinery
Motor vehicles
Equipment
Furniture and fittings
Current Assets
Assets that are continually changing from one form to another and are easily turned into cash.
Example
Stock
Debtors — owe us money
Bank/Cash
Prepayments — something paid in advance
C.
LIABILITIES
Current Liabilities
Debts that have to be paid back within one year.
Example
Creditors
Bank overdraft
Dividends due and other expenses accrued (due)
Long-Term Liabilities
Debts that will be repaid in the long term, usually between five years and twenty years.
Example
Mortgage
Long-term loan

D.

SHARE CAPITAL

Money invested in the company by the shareholders
(i.e. money is owed to shareholders)

Authorised Share Capital	Issued Share Capital
Maximum amount of capital that company can raise through selling shares.	Actual amount of shares sold to shareholders.

E. Reserves/Retained Earnings

Amount set aside out of profits and retained by the company for future use (balance in profit and loss appropriation account). This money is owed to shareholders.

F. Working Capital

Working capital is the money available for the day-to-day running of the business.

(Current assets – Current Liabilities = Working Capital)

It shows whether the business can pay its debts as they fall due. If current assets are greater than current liabilities the working capital is **positive** and the firm is said to be **liquid**. If current liabilities are greater than current assets the working capital is **negative** and the firm is said to have a **liquidity problem** and to be **overtrading** (i.e. it cannot pay its debts as they arise).

G. Total Net Assets = Fixed Assets + Working Capital

H. Shareholders' Funds = Ordinary Share Capital + Reserves

I. Capital Employed = Ordinary Share Capital + Reserves + Long-Term Liabilities

The balance sheet is made up of two sections. The top section shows what the **total net assets are worth** and the bottom section shows where the finance comes from to finance these assets. This is called **Capital Employed**.

Total Net Assets Must Equal Capital Employed.

Sample Question and Solution

Question

From the following information prepare the balance sheet of Bobbit Enterprises Ltd as on 31 December 1995.

FB	Authorised share capital	IR£200,000	Ordinary shares at IR£1 each
FB	Issued share capital	IR£100,000	Ordinary shares at IR£1 each
FA	Land	IR£115,950	
CA	Closing stock	IR£15,000	
CL	Bank overdraft	IR£6,000	
CA	Debtors	IR£18,000	
FA	Buildings	IR£60,000	
FA	Machinery	IR£20,000	
RES	Retained earnings	IR£58,950	
CA	Bank	IR£6,000	
CL	Creditors	IR£10,000	
CA	Cash	IR£2,000	
CA	Prepayments	IR£1,000	
FA	Motor vehicles	IR£10,000	
CL	Dividends due	IR£10,000	
CL	Wages due	IR£3,000	
LTL	Long-term loan	IR£60,000	

Key

FB = Financed By
FA = Fixed Asset
CA = Current Asset
CL = Current Liability
RES = Reserves
LTL = Long-Term Liability

Solution

Balance Sheet of Bobbit Enterprises Ltd as on 31 December 1995

		Cost	Depre-ciation	Net Book Value
	Fixed Assets			
	Land	115,950		115,950
	Buildings	60,000		60,000
	Machinery	20,000		20,000
	Motor vehicles	10,000		10,000
		205,950		205,950
	Current Assets			
	Closing stock	15,000		
	Debtors	18,000		
	Bank	6,000		
	Cash	2,000		
	Prepayments	1,000	42,000	
	Less Current Liabilities			
	Bank overdraft	6,000		
	Creditors	10,000		
	Dividends due	10,000		
	Wages due	3,000	29,000	
	Working capital			+13,000
	Total net assets			218,950
	FINANCED BY			
	Authorised share capital			
	200,000 ordinary shares @ IR£1 each			200,000
	Issued Share Capital			
	100,000 ordinary shares @ IR£1 each			100,000
	Reserves			
	Retained earnings			58,950
	Long-Term Liabilities			
	Long-term loan			60,000
	Capital employed			218,950

J. Business Terms

Accruals Expenses due at end of trading period.
Appreciation Assets increasing in value.
Assets Items of value owned by a business.
Balance Sheet A summary of assets and liabilities on a particular date.
Capital Employed Total money used in business. It is ordinary shares + reserves + long-term liabilities.
Current Assets Assets easily converted into cash.
Current Liabilities Debts that must be repaid within one year.
Depreciation Reduction in the value of fixed assets due to usage, wear and tear, and age.
Dividends Profit distributed to shareholders.
Fixed Assets Assets of a permanent nature in the business not for resale.
Liability A debt the business owes.
Liquidity Ability of firm to pay debts as they fall due.
Long-Term Liabilities Amount borrowed by a business that will be repaid in the long term.
Net Worth Fixed assets + (current assets – current liabilities).
Overtrading Negative working capital.
Prepayments Expenses paid in advance at end of year.
Retained Earnings Amount of profit retained by company.
Secured Loan Some asset is given as security/collateral for the loan.
Share Capital Money invested by owners of a company.
Term Loan A medium-term loan repayable over a one- to five-year period.
Working Capital Current assets – current liabilities.

PRACTICE QUESTIONS

(i) Question 17, Section A, Ordinary Level, Sample Paper.
(ii) Question 19, Section A, Ordinary Level, Sample Paper.
(iii) Question 17, Section A, Ordinary Level, 1992.
(iv) Question 3, Section A, Ordinary Level, 1993.
(v) Question 7, Section A, Paper I, Higher Level, 1992.
(vi) Question 1, Section A, Paper I, Higher Level, 1993.
(vii) Question 17, Section A, Paper I, Higher Level, 1993.
(viii) Question 15, Section A, Paper I, Higher Level, Sample Paper.
(ix) Question 20, Section A, Paper I, Higher Level, 1994.

Chapter 42 — Revision Trading, Profit and Loss Account, Appropriation Account and Balance Sheet (Without Adjustments)

A. Type of Question on Final Account at Ordinary Level

This question on the Junior Certificate examination requires the preparation of a full set of final accounts from information presented in a trial balance with closing stock listed underneath the trial balance. There also may be one or two other theory questions included.

PROCEDURE

(1) Examine each item in the trial balance and establish where it will go in the accounts.

> **NB** Debit column contains Assets and Expenses.
> Credit column contains Liabilities and Gains.

(2) Write down on the question where each item goes, i.e. T (Trading A/C), P & L (Profit and Loss A/C), App. (Appropriation A/C), B/S (Balance Sheet).
(3) Tick off each item as you enter it in the accounts.

Examination-Style Question and Solution

Question 1.
Answer (a), (b) and (c). This is a Final Accounts and Balance Sheet Question.

➢ Furnish Ltd is a company that sells furniture. Its Authorised Capital is 150,000 Ordinary Shares at IR£1 each.

➢ The following Trial Balance has been taken from the books of Furnish Ltd as at 31 December 1992 — the end of the financial year.

		Dr IR£	Cr IR£
B/S	Issued Share Capital in IR£1 Shares		120,000
T	Cash Sales		480,000
T	Cash Purchases for Resale	312,000	
T	Opening Stock at 1/1/92	22,000	
T	Carriage Inwards	4,500	
App.	Dividend Paid	25,000	
P&L	Insurance	13,150	
P&L	Wages and Salaries	49,500	
P&L	Interest on Bank Overdraft	850	
P&L	Light and Heat	15,300	
P&L	Telephone	1,200	
B/S	Bank Overdraft		18,000
B/S	Cash in Hand	9,500	
B/S	Premises	80,000	
B/S	Machinery	85,000	
		618,000	618,000

T, B/S Closing Stock at 31 December 1992 was IR£31,000

1. (a) From the above figures, prepare a Trading and Profit and Loss Account and an Appropriation Account for the year ended 31 December 1992, and a Balance Sheet at that date. **(46)**
1. (b) Explain what 'Bank Overdraft' means. **(7)**
1. (c) What is the main reason why a Profit and Loss Appropriation Account is prepared? **(7)**

Source: Junior Certificate Ordinary Level 1993. **(60 marks)**

Solution to Question 1.

1. (a)

Trading and Profit and Loss Account for Year Ending 31 December 1992

	Sales			480,000
	Deduct Cost of Sales			
	Opening stock 1/1/92		22,000	
	Purchases		312,000	
	Carriage Inwards		4,500	
	Cost of Goods Available for Sale		338,500	
	Less Closing Stock 31/12/92		31,000	
	Cost of Sales			307,500
	Gross Profit			172,500
	Less Expenditure			
	Insurance		13,150	
	Wages and Salaries		49,500	
	Interest on Bank Overdraft		850	
	Light and Heat		15,300	
	Telephone		1,200	80,000
	Net Profit			92,500

Profit and Loss Appropriation A/C for Year Ending 31 December 1992

	Net Profit	92,500
	Less Dividends	25,000
	Reserves/Retained Earnings (Profit and Loss Balance)	67,500

Balance Sheet as on 31 December 1992

		Cost	Depre-ciation	Net Book Value
	Fixed Assets			
	Premises	80,000	—	80,000
	Machinery	85,000	—	85,000
		165,000	—	165,000
	Current Assets			
	Closing stock	31,000		
	Cash	9,500	40,500	
	Less Current Liabilities			
	Bank overdraft		18,000	
	Working capital			22,500
	Total Net Assets			187,500
	FINANCED BY			
	Authorised Share Capital			
	150,000 Ordinary Shares @ IR£1 ea.			150,000
	Issued Share Capital			
	120,000 Ordinary Shares @ IR£1 ea.			120,000
	Reserves			
	Profit and Loss A/C balance			67,500
	Capital employed			187,500

1. (b) Bank Overdraft

A short-term loan whereby a bank gives permission to a current account holder to write cheques and withdraw more money than there is in the account up to a certain limit.

1. (c) A profit and loss appropriation account is prepared in order to show how the net profit was distributed.

PRACTICE QUESTIONS

(i) Question 6, Section B, Ordinary Level, Sample Paper.
(ii) Question 6, Section B, Ordinary Level, 1992.

Higher Level

Chapter 43 — Adjustments to Final Accounts

The aim of final accounts is to give a 'true and fair picture' of the business, i.e. finding true figures for gross profit and net profit. To do this certain adjustments must be made.

- ➢ Accruals (amounts due)
- ➢ Prepayments (amounts paid in advance)
- ➢ Bad debts written off
- ➢ Depreciation — straight line
- ➢ Dividends
- ➢ Closing stocks.

These adjustments not being in the trial balance therefore are not in the books of account and must be included in the accounts twice, once debit/once credit. One entry will be in the **trading or profit and loss account**.

The second entry will be in the **balance sheet**.

A. Accruals (Amounts Due)

(1) ACCRUED EXPENSES (EXPENSES DUE BY A FIRM)

All expenses relating to the trading period must be included in the accounts whether paid or not.

Question

O'Flynn Ltd paid IR£10,000 insurance by cheque on 1 January 1996 but on 31 December there was still IR£1,000 due for the year 1996.

Solution

Bank Account

Date	Details	Fo	Total	Date	Details	Fo	Total
				1 Jan.	*Insurance*		*10,000*

Insurance Account

Date	Details	Fo	Total	Date	Details	Fo	Total
1 Jan.	*Bank*		*10,000*	*31 Dec.*	*Profit and Loss A/C*		*11,000*
31 Dec.	*Balance (Ins. Due)*	*C/d*	*1,000*				
			11,000				*11,000*
				31 Dec.	*Balance (Ins. Due) (Current Liability)*	*B/d*	*1,000*

ENTRIES IN THE PROFIT AND LOSS ACCOUNT AND BALANCE SHEET

RULES
(i) Add amount due on to amount paid in profit and loss account.
(ii) Show amount due as a current liability in balance sheet.

Profit and Loss Account (Extract) for Year Ending 31 December 1996

	Expenses				
	Insurance		10,000		
	Add insurance due		1,000	11,000	

Balance Sheet (Extract) as on 31 December 1996

	Current Liabilities				
	Insurance due		1,000		

(2) ACCRUED INCOME (EXPENSES DUE TO THE FIRM)

This is income for the period in question but not yet received, e.g.

➢ Rent receivable due
➢ Commission receivable due
➢ Insurance receivable due.

RULES
Add amount due to the amount received in the gains section of the profit and loss account. Show amount due as a current asset in balance sheet.

Question

Insurance received IR£15,000 for year ending 31 December 1997.
Insurance received due IR£2,000, at the end of December 1997.

Solution

Profit and Loss Account (Extract) for Year Ending 31 December 1997

	Gains				
	Insurance received			15,000	
	Add insurance received due			2,000	17,000

Balance Sheet (Extract) as on 31 December 1997

	Current Assets				
	Insurance received due		2,000		

B. Prepayments (Amounts Paid in Advance)

(1) PREPAYMENT MADE BY OUR BUSINESS

This occurs when an amount is paid in this trading period but it is for the next trading period (i.e. paid in advance). Since we can put only expenses that belong to a trading period into the profit and loss account, prepayments must be deducted.

RULES
(i) Deduct amount prepaid from expense figure in profit and loss account.
(ii) Show amount prepaid as a current asset in Balance Sheet.

Question
O'Callaghan Ltd rented a warehouse on 1 February 1996 for IR£500 per month. It paid IR£6,000 rent for the year ended 31 January 1997 (twelve months).

NB We can charge only eleven months rent to the profit and loss account for 1996 because one month's rent is paid for January 1997.

Solution

Bank Account

Date	Details	Fo	Total	Date	Details	Fo	Total
				1 Feb.	Rent		6,000

Rent Account

Date	Details	Fo	Total	Date	Details	Fo	Total
1 Feb.	Bank		6,000	31 Dec.	P & L A/C		5,500
				31 Dec.	Balance (Rent P/p)	C/d	500
			6,000				6,000
31 Dec.	Balance (Rent P/p) (Current asset in balance sheet)	B/d	500				

Profit and Loss Account (Extract) for Year Ending 31 December 1996

	Expenses				
	Rent		6,000		
	Less rent prepaid		500	5,500	

Balance Sheet (Extract) as on 31 December 1996

	Current Assets				
	Rent prepaid		500		

(2) PREPAYMENTS MADE TO OUR BUSINESS

If a business has surplus storage space it may (sublet) rent some of it to another business. The rent we get is called rent receivable. Sometimes this rent receivable is prepaid to us (i.e. it is received before it is due).

RULES

(i) Subtract amount prepaid from amount received in the gains in profit and loss account.

(ii) Show amount prepaid as a current liability in balance sheet.

Question

Rent received IR£1,000 for year ending 31 December 1997.
Rent receivable prepaid IR£100 at end of December 1997.

Solution

Profit and Loss Account (Extract) for Year Ending 31 December 1997

	Gains				
	Rent received			1,000	
	Subtract rent receivable prepaid			100	900

Balance Sheet (Extract) as on 31 December 1997

	Current Liabilities				
	Rent receivable prepaid			100	

C. Bad Debts Written Off

A bad debt arises when a debtor is declared bankrupt and cannot pay what is owed. The business must then write the amount off as a bad debt (loss to the business).

Question

Debtors IR£10,000.

Adjustment Bad debts to be written off IR£1,000.

Solution **Debtors Account**

Date	Details	Fo	Total	Date	Details	Fo	Total
	Balance		10,000		*Bad debts*		1,000
					Balance	C/d	9,000
			10,000				10,000
	Balance	B/d	9,000				

Bad Debts Account

Date	Details	Fo	Total	Date	Details	Fo	Total
	Debtors		*1,000*		*Profit and Loss A/C*		*1,000*

WRITING UP PROFIT AND LOSS ACCOUNT AND BALANCE SHEET

> **RULES**
> **(i)** Show bad debts written off as an expense in the profit and loss account.
> **(ii)** Deduct bad debts from debtors in the balance sheet.

Profit and Loss Account (Extract)

	Expenses Bad debts		1,000		

Balance Sheet (Extract)

	Current Assets Debtors Less bad debts written off		10,000 1,000	9,000	

NB Bad debts figure in trial balance — show as expense in P & L A/C. Do not deduct from debtors in balance sheet. (It is already deducted.)

D. Depreciation — Straight Line

Depreciation is the reduction in the value of an asset due to usage, wear and tear, and age.

Depreciation is calculated by getting a percentage of the cost of the asset — the figure will be the same every year. This is called straight line depreciation.

> **RULES**
> **(i)** Show depreciation as an expense in the profit and loss account.
> **(ii)** Deduct depreciation from the cost of the asset in the fixed assets section of the balance sheet.

Question
Machinery 1 January 1997 IR£10,000.
Adjustment Depreciate machinery by 20%.

Solution

Machinery Account

Date	Details	Fo	Total	Date	Details	Fo	Total
1.1.97	Balance		10,000	31/12/97	Depreciation		2,000
				31/12/97	Balance	C/d	8,000
			10,000				10,000
31/12/97	Balance	B/d	8,000				

Depreciation Account

Date	Details	Fo	Total	Date	Details	Fo	Total
31/12/97	Machinery		2,000	31/12/97	Profit and Loss A/C		2,000

Profit and Loss Account (Extract) for Year Ending 31 December 1997

	Expenses				
	Depreciation of machinery			2,000	

Balance Sheet (Extract) as on 31 December 1997

			Cost	Deprec.	Net Bk Val.
	Fixed Assets				
	Machinery		10,000	2,000	8,000

E. Dividends

Dividends can be paid or proposed.

(1) DIVIDENDS PAID

Dividends paid will appear in the debit column of the trial balance. Since they are paid there is no liability in the balance sheet. **Dividends paid are entered in the profit and loss appropriation account only.**

(2) DIVIDENDS PROPOSED

Dividends proposed will appear as an adjustment. Dividends proposed are calculated as a percentage of the issued share capital of the company.

RULES

(i) Calculate the dividend and enter it as a deduction from net profit in the profit and loss appropriation account.

(ii) Show dividend due as a current liability in the balance sheet.

F. Closing Stocks

(1) CLOSING STOCK OF GOODS

Closing stock is entered in the trading account and as a current asset in the balance sheet.

(2) CLOSING STOCKS OF — OIL, STATIONERY, ETC., I.E. NON-TRADING STOCKS.

RULES

(i) Subtract closing stock from appropriate expenses in the profit and loss account.

(ii) Show closing stock as a current asset in the balance sheet.

Chapter 44 — Revision Final Accounts and Balance Sheet (Including Adjustments)

Higher Level

A. Type of Exam Question

This question is given in the form of a trial balance, i.e. figures in the debit column and credit column.

Debit Column Assets/Expenses	Credit Column Liabilities/Gains

B. Adjustments

Adjustments will be given under the totals of the trial balance and items in the trial balance that must be adjusted should be marked with '*'.

C. Summary of Adjustments

Adjustment	How Adjustment Is Treated in Profit and Loss Account	How Adjustment Is Treated in Balance Sheet
(1) Accruals		
(a) Due by firm	Add to amount paid	Current liability
(b) Due to firm	Add to amount received	Current asset
(2) Prepayments		
(a) Made by us	Deduct from expense	Current asset
(b) Made to us	Deduct from amount received	Current liability
(3) Bad debt written off	Show as expense	Deduct from debtors
(4) Depreciation	Show as expense	Deduct from fixed asset
(5) Dividends		
(a) Paid	Enter in profit and loss appropriation account	No entry
(b) Proposed	Enter in profit and loss appropriation account	Current liability
(6) Closing Stock		
(a) Goods	Trading account	Current asset
(b) Non-trading stock	Deduct from expense	Current asset

Examination-Style Question and Solution

Question 1.

Answer (a) and (b). This is a Final Accounts and Balance Sheet Question.

1. (a) The following Trial Balance was extracted from the books of Paintwell Ltd on 31 May 1992. You are required to prepare the company's Trading, Profit and Loss and Appropriation Accounts for the year ended 31/5/92, and a Balance Sheet as at that date. The Authorised Share Capital is 200,000 IR£1 Ordinary Shares.

FB

		DR IR£	CR IR£
T	Purchases and Sales T	189,000	290,000
CA	Debtors and Creditors CL	56,000	45,300
T	Sales Returns and Purchases Returns T	11,000	4,000
E	Bad Debts	2,500	
E	Insurance	8,500	
G	Rent Receivable *		7,800
T	Carriage Inwards	4,600	
FA	Buildings at Cost *	120,000	
T	Opening Stock 1/6/91	14,400	
LTL	15 Year Loan		20,000
CA	Cash	2,500	
FA	Equipment at Cost *	80,000	
CL	Bank Overdraft		3,000
E	Wages and Salaries *	30,000	
E	Bank Interest	1,600	
FB	Issued Share Capital: 150,000 IR£1 shares		150,000
		520,100	520,100

You are given the following additional information as on 31/5/92:

- **(i)** Closing Stock IR£18,000; [T + CA]
- **(ii)** Wages and Salaries due IR£6,000; [E + CL]
- **(iii)** Dividends Declared 10%; (App. A/C + CL)
- **(iv)** Rent receivable prepaid IR£200; [G + CL]
- **(v)** Depreciation: Buildings 5%; Equipment 15%. [E + FA] **(35)**

(b) Write a brief note on how the company might reduce bad debts in the future. **(5)**

Source: Junior Certificate Higher Level 1992. **(40 marks)**

*	=	Adjust figure
T	=	Trading account
E	=	Expense — profit and loss account
G	=	Gain — profit and loss account
App.	=	Appropriation account
FA	=	Fixed assets
CA	=	Current assets
CL	=	Current liabilities
FB	=	Financed By

Solution

PAINTWELL LTD

Trading and Profit and Loss Account for Year Ending 31 May 1992

(A)	**Sales**		290,000	
	Less Sales Returns		11,000	279,000
	Deduct Cost of Sales			
	Stock 1/6/91 (opening)		14,400	
	Purchases	189,000		
	Less Purchases Returns	4,000	185,000	
	Carriage Inwards		4,600	
	Cost of Goods Available for Sale		204,000	
	Less Stock 31/5/92 (closing)		18,000	
	Cost of Sales			186,000
	Gross Profit			93,000
	Add Gains			
	Rent receivable		7,800	
	Less rent receivable prepaid		200	7,600
				100,600
	Less Expenses			
	Bad Debts		2,500	
	Insurance		8,500	
	Wages and Salaries	30,000		
	Add Wages Due	6,000	36,000	
	Bank Interest		1,600	
	Depreciation — Equipment	12,000		
	Depreciation — Buildings	6,000	18,000	66,600
	Net Profit			34,000
	Profit and Loss Appropriation A/C for Year Ending 31 May 1992			
	Net Profit			34,000
	Less 10% Dividend			15,000
	Reserves (Retained Earnings)			19,000

PAINTWELL LTD

Balance Sheet as at 31 May 1992

	Cost	Depre-ciation	NBV
Fixed Assets			
Buildings	120,000	6,000	114,000
Equipment	80,000	12,000	68,000
	200,000	18,000	182,000
Current Assets			
Closing Stock	18,000		
Debtors	56,000		
Cash	2,500	76,500	
Less Current Liabilities			
Creditors	45,300		
Bank Overdraft	3,000		
Dividends due	15,000		
Rent Receivable Prepaid	200		
Wages Due	6,000	69,500	
Working Capital			7,000
Total Net Assets			189,000
FINANCED BY			
Authorised Share Capital			
200,000 Ordinary Shares @ IR£1 each			200,000
Issued Share Capital			
150,000 Ordinary Shares @ IR£1 each			150,000
Reserves			
Retained Earnings			19,000
Long-Term Liabilities			
15-yr loan			20,000
Capital Employed			189,000

1. (b) How Company Might Reduce Bad Debts in the Future

(i) Get a reference from customer's bank.

(ii) Get a reference from another firm that customer deals with.

(iii) Give less credit in future.

PRACTICE QUESTIONS

(i) Question 4, Section A, Paper I, Higher Level, Sample Paper.

(ii) Question 2, Paper II, Higher Level, Sample Paper.

(iii) Question 1, Section A, Paper I, Higher Level, 1992.

(iv) Question 3, Paper II, Higher Level, 1993.

(v) Question 3, Paper II, Higher Level, 1994.

REPORTING ON ACCOUNTS

Chapter 45 — Assessing a Business

Higher Level

A. Introduction

It is important that accounts are interpreted or made clear for the benefit of interested parties.

This is done by the use of **ratios** which show the relationships between figures. These figures are then compared with

(1) Previous year's figures.
(2) Other firms in the same industry.

B. Parties Interested in the Accounts of a Company

(1) **Banker** — Can loans and overdrafts be repaid?
(2) **Creditors** — Can business pay for goods supplied on credit?
(3) **Shareholders** — How much profit does the company make and what will the dividend per share be?
(4) **Employees** — Is employment secure?
(5) **Investors** — Is company a good investment?
(6) **Management** — Is company performing better or worse than last year?
(7) **Revenue Commissioners** — How much profit is company making for tax purposes?

C. Interpretation of Accounts Using Ratios

A company can be assessed by using the following headings or areas:

➢ Profitability
➢ Liquidity
➢ Activity
➢ Solvency
➢ Dividend Policy.

(1) PROFITABILITY

The profitability ratios show how successful the management of the business was in making profit in the company.

The profitability ratios are

Ratio	Formula	Ans.	Information Given by Ratio
(a) Return on share capital	$\frac{\text{Net Profit x 100}}{\text{Issued Share Capital}}$	Percentage %	Shows return shareholders are getting on their own investment and should be compared with return from banks or other firms.
(b) Return on capital employed	$\frac{\text{Net Profit x 100}}{\text{Capital Employed}}$	Percentage %	Shows return on total amount invested in company and should be compared with return from banks or other firms.
(c) Gross profit percentage/ margin	$\frac{\text{Gross Profit x 100}}{\text{Sales}}$	Percentage %	Tells us how much gross profit was made on each IR£1.00 of sales. Compare with last year or other firms.
(d) Net profit percentage/ margin	$\frac{\text{Net Profit x 100}}{\text{Sales}}$	Percentage %	Tells us how much net profit was made on each IR£1.00 of sales. Compare with last year or other firms.

(2) LIQUIDITY

Liquidity is the ability of the company to pay its debts as they fall due. Liquidity is measured by subtracting current liabilities from current assets. This is called working capital.

Working Capital = Current Assets – Current Liabilities

If the working capital is positive the firm is said to be liquid. If the working capital is negative the firm is said to be **overtrading**.

The Liquidity Ratios are

Ratio	Formula	Ans.	Information Given by Ratio
(a) Current ratio or working capital ratio	Current Assets: Current Liabilities	Ratio	Tells us if the company has enough current assets to pay its current liabilities. A company should have a current ratio of 2:1, i.e. current assets should be double current liabilities.
(b) Quick asset ratio or acid test ratio	Current Assets – Closing Stock: Current Liabilities	Ratio	Omits closing stock as stock may not be quickly turned into cash. The recommended ratio is 1:1, i.e. a healthy firm should be able to pay its current liabilities out of liquid assets (i.e. CA – stock).

(3) ACTIVITY

The ratios tell us how active the company was during the year.
The Activity Ratios are

Ratio	Formula	Ans.	Information Given by Ratio
(a) Rate of stock turnover	$\frac{\text{Cost of Sales}}{\text{Average Stock}}$	Times	Tells us how many times the stock is replaced in the business during the year.
(b) Period of credit given to debtors	$\frac{\text{Debtors x 365}}{\text{Credit Sales}}$	Days	Tells us how many days credit we give debtors **OR** how long it takes debtors to pay.
(c) Period of credit received from creditors	$\frac{\text{Creditors x 365}}{\text{Credit Purchases}}$	Days	Tells us how much credit we receive from creditors or how long it takes our firm to pay its creditors.

(4) SOLVENCY

A firm is **solvent** if total assets are greater than outside liabilities, thus it can continue in business.

Total Assets = Fixed Assets + Current Assets
Outside Liabilities = Current Liabilities + Long-Term Liabilities

If outside liabilities are greater than total assets the firm is said to be **insolvent** or **bankrupt.** (Firm cannot continue in business.)

Ratio	Formula	Ans.	Information Given by Ratio
Solvency	Total Assets: Outside Liabilities	Ratio	Tells us whether business is solvent or insolvent.

(5) DIVIDEND POLICY

Dividend is the amount of profit given to shareholders. It is the board of directors who decide how much of a dividend will be paid to shareholders. The rate of dividend ratio tells us how much dividends are paid to shareholders.

Ratio	Formula	Ans.	Information Given by Ratio
Rate of dividend	$\frac{\text{Dividend Paid x 100}}{\text{Issued Share Capital}}$	Percentage %	Rate of dividend paid to shareholders.

Sample Question and Solution

Question

Scott Ltd has an authorised share capital of 400,000 IR£1 ordinary shares. Its accounts for year ended 31 December 1996 are as follows.

Trading and Profit and Loss Account for Year Ending 31 December 1996

	Sales		100,000
	Deduct Cost of Sales		
	Opening stock	6,000	
	Purchases	44,000	
	Cost of goods available	50,000	
	Less closing stock	10,000	
	Cost of Sales		40,000
	Gross Profit		60,000
	Less expenses		10,000
	Net Profit		50,000

Profit and Loss Appropriation Account for Year Ending 31 December 1996

	Net profit		50,000
	Less dividend 10%		20,000
	Retained earnings		30,000

Balance Sheet as on 31 December 1996

	FIXED ASSETS			260,000
	Current Assets			
	Closing stock	10,000		
	Debtors	10,000		
	Bank	60,000	80,000	
	Current Liabilities			
	Creditors	8,000		
	Dividend due	20,000		
	Accruals	12,000	40,000	
	Working capital			40,000
	Total Net Assets			**300,000**
	FINANCED BY			
	Authorised Share Capital			400,000
	Issued share capital			200,000
	Retained Earnings			30,000
	Long-Term Liabilities			
	Long-term loan			70,000
	Capital Employed			**300,000**

Calculate and comment on:

(1) Return on share capital
(2) Return on capital employed
(3) Gross profit margin
(4) Net profit margin
(5) Working capital ratio
(6) Acid test ratio
(7) Rate of stock turnover
(8) Period of credit given to debtors
(9) Period of credit received from creditors
(10) Solvency ratio
(11) Rate of dividend.

Solution

Ratio	Formula	Figures	Answer	Comment
1. Return on share capital	Net Profit x 100 / Issued Share Capital	50,000 x 100 / 200,000	25%	This rate of return is very satisfactory when compared with rate that could be earned by investing the same amount in a bank or building society.
2. Return on capital employed	Net Profit x 100 / Capital Employed	50,000 x 100 / 300,000	16.66%	Satisfactory when compared with rates of return from bank or building society.
3. Gross profit margin	Gross Profit x 100 / Sales	60,000 x 100 / 100,000	60%	This business is making a gross profit of 60p on every IR£1.00 of sales.
4. Net profit margin	Net Profit x 100 / Sales	50,000 x 100 / 100,000	50%	This business is making a net profit of 50p on each IR£1.00 of sales.
5. Working capital ratio	Current Assets : Current Liabilities	80,000:40,000	2:1	This ratio is ideal because the recommended working capital ratio is 2:1. Firm can pay debts so they fall due from current assets. Firm has no liquidity problem.
6. Acid test ratio	CA – Closing Stock:CL	80,000 – 10,000:40,000 70,000:40,000	1.75:1	This ratio is very satisfactory as the recommended acid test ratio is 1:1. Firm can pay current liabilities from liquid assets.
7. Rate of stock turnover	Cost of Sales / Average Stock	40,000 / 8,000	5 times	Stock is being replaced 5 times a year in business. (New stock is purchased every 10.5 weeks.)
8. Period of credit given to debtors	Debtors x 365 / Credit Sales	10,000 x 365 / 100,000	36.5 days	This firm is giving debtors 36.5 days credit or it is taking 36.5 days to get money from debtors.
9. Period of credit received from creditors	Creditors x 365 / Credit Purchases	8,000 x 365 / 44,000	66 days	This firm paid its creditors in 66 days.
10. Solvency ratio	Total Assets : Outside Liabilities	340,000:110,000	3.09:1	This business is solvent as total assets are greater than outside liabilities.
11. Rate of dividend	Dividend Paid x 100 / Issued Share Capital	20,000 x 100 / 200,000	10%	Firm paid a 10% dividend to shareholders.

COMPARISON OF ACCOUNTS AND BALANCE SHEET AND PREPARATION OF A REPORT
To get an accurate picture of any business it is necessary to compare the accounts and balance sheets of a number of trading periods. Once the accounts have been assessed and the ratios prepared, a report on the performance of the company is compiled for interested parties.

Examination-Style Question and Solution

Question 1.
This question is about Reporting on the Performance of a Business.

Assume you are Joe Cronin, Financial Consultant, of 10 Cork Road, Waterford. Study the Final Accounts and Balance Sheets of King Ltd, Waterford, set out below, for the years 1993 and 1994. Prepare a Report, using today's date, for the shareholders of King Ltd comparing the performance of the company in the two years under the following three headings:

(a) Profitability; **(b) Liquidity;** **(c) Dividend Policy.**

1993			1994		
Trading, Profit and Loss and Appropriation Accounts for Year Ending 31/5/1993			**Trading, Profit and Loss and Appropriation Accounts for Year Ending 31/5/1994**		
		IR£			**IR£**
Sales		140,000	Sales		270,000
Less Cost of Sales		84,000	Less Cost of Sales		108,000
Gross Profit		56,000	**Gross Profit**		162,000
Less Expenses		44,600	Less Expenses		133,500
Net Profit		11,400	**Net Profit**		28,500
Less Dividends		1,400	Less Dividends		10,500
Reserves		10,000	Reserves		18,000
Balance Sheet as at 31/5/1993			**Balance Sheet as at 31/5/1994**		
	IR£	**IR£**		**IR£**	**IR£**
Fixed Assets		105,000	Fixed Assets		95,000
Current Assets	20,000		Current Assets	30,000	
Less Current Liabilities	30,000	–10,000	Less Current Liabilities	15,000	15,000
		95,000			110,000
Financed By			**Financed By**		
Ordinary Share Capital		70,000	Ordinary Share Capital		70,000
Reserves		10,000	Reserves		28,000
Long-Term Loan		15,000	Long-Term Loan		12,000
		95,000			110,000

Source: Junior Certificate Higher Level 1994. **(40 marks)**

Solution to Question 1. — Reporting on the Performance of a Business

10 Cork Road
Waterford

15 June 1994

Title: *Report Comparing Performance of King Ltd in the Years 1993 and 1994*

To *Shareholders*
King Ltd
Waterford

INTRODUCTION

I was asked on your behalf to prepare a report comparing the performance of King Ltd in the years 1993 and 1994 under the headings profitability, liquidity and dividend policy. I used all the relevant ratios, which are also attached to my report. My main findings are laid out below.

BODY OF REPORT

1. (a) Profitability

The company is profitable. The profit in 1994 is bigger than in 1993.

	1993	1994
Gross margin	40.00%	60.00%
Net margin	8.14%	10.56%
Return on share capital	16.29%	40.71%
Return on capital employed	12.00%	25.90%

It can be seen from the above figures that King Ltd is profitable and this profitability is on the increase. Return on share capital and return on capital employed compare very well with what is available from banks or building societies.

1. (b) Liquidity

The company has a minus working capital in 1993. Thus it has a liquidity problem. In 1994 the working capital is positive thus it has no liquidity problem.

	1993	1994
Working capital ratio	0.66:1	2:1

The liquidity position of King Ltd is improving and in 1994 it is at the recommended level of 2:1.

1. (c) Dividend Policy

The company paid dividends in both years. The 1994 dividend was greater than the 1993 dividend.

	1993	1994
Rate of dividend	2%	15%

The shareholders received a big increase in dividends in 1994 in line with the increase in profits.

I am available to discuss this report if required.

Signed
Joe Cronin
Financial Consultant

RATIO ANALYSIS

Ratio	Formula	Figures		Answers	
		1993	1994	1993	1994
Gross margin	Gross Profit x 100 / Sales	56,000 x 100 / 140,000	162,000 x 100 / 270,000	40%	60%
Net margin	Net Profit x 100 / Sales	11,400 x 100 / 140,000	28,500 x 100 / 270,000	8.14%	10.56%
Return on share capital	Net Profit x 100 / Issued Share Capital	11,400 x 100 / 70,000	28,500 x 100 / 70,000	16.29%	40.71%
Return on capital employed	Net Profit x 100 / Capital Employed	11,400 x 100 / 95,000	28,500 x 100 / 110,000	12%	25.9%
Working capital ratio	CA:CL	20,000:30,000	30,000:15,000	0.66:1	2:1
Rate of dividend	Dividend Paid x 100 / Issued Share Capital	1,400 x 100 / 70,000	10,500 x 100 / 70,000	2%	15%

LIMITATION OF FINAL ACCOUNTS IN ASSESSING A BUSINESS

The final accounts of a business give us financial information only. The following are not taken into account.

(1) Experienced and efficient staff. Management/staff relationships. Loyal staff and customers.
(2) Balance sheet holds only for a particular day.
(3) Assets may not be shown at their current values — some assets may have appreciated over the years, e.g. premises.
(4) The accounts of a business are a record of past transactions and can be used only as an estimate of future performance.
(5) GOODWILL how good the reputation of the company is.

PRACTICE QUESTIONS

(i) Question 15, Section A, Paper I, Higher Level, 1992.
(ii) Question 6, Paper II, Higher Level, 1992.

APPLIED ACCOUNTS

Chapter 46 — Club Accounts

A. Introduction

A club is an organisation set up for the benefit of its members. Members elect officers at its AGM to run the club.

All clubs must keep a record of their financial activities during the year. They are non-profit-making organisations.

B. Functions of Club Officers

Chairperson	Secretary	Treasurer
1. Runs club.	1. Calls meetings.	1. Collects subscriptions and issues receipts.
2. Chairs meetings.	2. Sends agenda to members.	2. Lodges money received to bank account.
3. Keeps order at meetings.	3. Arranges the meetings.	3. Pays all bills.
4. Follows agenda.	4. Takes notes at meetings and writes up minutes.	4. Keeps records.
5. Puts motions to a vote.		5. Prepares final accounts.
		6. Makes a report on finances at AGM.

C. Annual General Meeting (AGM)

Members attend, speak and vote on various items on the agenda (programme for meeting).

Treasurer presents his report to the members at the AGM.

(1) AGENDA

The agenda is the programme for the meeting sent by the secretary to all members, outlining the items to be discussed at the meeting.

Agenda for AGM of Manchester United FC

The AGM of Man Utd FC will be held on 10 March 1995 at 8 pm at Old Trafford. The agenda is as follows:

(a) Minutes of last AGM
(b) Matters arising from minutes
(c) Chairperson's Report
(d) Secretary's Report
(e) Treasurer's Report
(f) Election of Officers
(g) AOB.

M E Edwards
Secretary

(2) MINUTES OF MEETINGS

Minutes are a written record of discussions and decisions taken at meetings. They are prepared by the secretary of the club.

D. Accounts Kept by a Club

The following accounts are usually kept by the treasurer of a club.

- Analysed cash book/analysed receipts and payments book, usually written up on a monthly basis.
- Receipts and payments account for the year.
- Income and expenditure account for the year.
- Balance sheet on the last day of the year.

(1) ANALYSED CASH BOOK/ANALYSED RECEIPTS AND PAYMENTS BOOK

- It is the same as a cash book for business.
- Receipts on the debit side.
- Payments on the credit side.
- It is analysed into suitable columns to meet the requirements of the club.

Examination-Style Question and Solution

Question 1.

The Hightown Girls Football Club play all their games in the summer. In the winter, they practise in a local indoor sports centre which they use as their clubhouse. They have to pay rent for the use of the sports centre. They sell drinks (minerals) and run a disco every two weeks in order to raise money for playing gear. They also collect the subscriptions (membership fees) for the year.

Here is what happened in January 1992 (all dealings are in cash):

- 1 Jan. Cash on hand since last year IR£300
- 2 " Received subscriptions IR£50
- 3 " Paid for cans of drinks IR£30
- 5 " Disco night: received IR£350 at the door
- 5 " Received IR£45 from sale of drinks
- 6 " Paid disc-jockey (DJ) IR£50 for running the disco
- 8 " Received subscriptions IR£60
- 9 " Bought drinks for IR£70 and paid for them
- 10 " Paid IR£10 for posters for next disco
- 11 " Paid for rent of sports centre IR£25
- 12 " Received subscriptions IR£25
- 14 " Sold drinks IR£30
- 16 " Paid local radio for advertising disco IR£15
- 17 " Bought and paid for more drinks IR£40
- 19 " Disco night: received IR£400 at the door and IR£150 for sale of all drinks
- 20 " Paid disc-jockey IR£50 for running the disco
- 25 " Paid for rent of sports centre IR£25
- 30 " Received more subscriptions IR£55

1. (a) Using your answer book, write up and balance the Receipts and Payments Account of the club for the month of January 1992.
Use the following headings for Receipts and Payments and total each column:
Receipts: Total, Subscriptions, Disco, Drinks.
Payments: Total, Disco, Drinks, Rent. **(50)**
1. (b) What is the title given to the person who keeps the books for the club? **(5)**
1. (c) What profit (surplus) did the club make on discos for the month? **(5)**

Source: Junior Certificate Ordinary Level 1992. **(60 marks)**

Solution to Question 1.

1. (a) Hightown Girls Football Club

Receipts and Payments Account Analysed for Month of January 1992

Receipts | Payments

Date	Details	Total	Subscrip-tions	Disco	Drinks	Date	Details	Total	Disco	Drinks	Rent
1 Jan.	Cash on hand	300				3 Jan.	Drink purchases	30		30	
2 Jan.	Subscriptions	50	50			6 Jan.	Disc-jockey (DJ)	50	50		
5 Jan.	Disco receipts	350		350		9 Jan.	Drink purchases	70		70	
5 Jan.	Drink sales	45			45	10 Jan.	Posters	10	10		
8 Jan.	Subscriptions	60	60			11 Jan.	Rent	25			25
12 Jan.	Subscriptions	25	25			16 Jan.	Advertising	15	15		
14 Jan.	Drink sales	30			30	17 Jan.	Drink purchases	40		40	
19 Jan.	Disco receipts	400		400		20 Jan.	Disc-jockey (DJ)	50	50		
19 Jan.	Drink sales	150			150	25 Jan.	Rent	25			25
30 Jan.	Subscriptions	55	55			31 Jan.	Balance C/d	1,150			
		1,465	190	750	225			1,465	125	140	50
31 Jan.	Balance B/d	1,150									

1. (b) Treasurer.
1. (c) Profit made on discos for month = IR£625 (Receipts 750 – payments 125).

(2) RECEIPTS AND PAYMENTS ACCOUNT (CASH BOOK)

A receipts and payments account is prepared at the end of the year using totals from analysis columns.

It shows

(a) Cash balance at **start** of year.
(b) **Receipts** — on the debit side.
(c) **Payments** — on the credit side.
(d) Cash balance at **end** of year.

Rule for Receipts and Payments Account
Debit — Receipts
Credit — Payments

SAMPLE RECEIPTS AND PAYMENTS ACCOUNT

Receipts and Payments Account of Killeen GAA Club for Year Ending 31/12/93

1/1/93	Balance B/f	13,200	Caretaker's wages	4,200
	Subscriptions	3,300	Travel expenses	2,910
	Bar sales	34,400	Insurance	1,290
	Gate receipts	4,250	Bar purchases	30,150
			Secretary expenses	850
			Purchase of equipment	9,800
			Balance C/d	5,950
		55,150		55,150
31/12/93	Balance B/f	5,950		

Club has IR£5,950 cash on hand on 31 December 1993. This will be shown as a current asset in balance sheet.

(3) INCOME AND EXPENDITURE ACCOUNT

An income and expenditure account for a club is the same as a profit and loss account used in business. It shows all the club's **income** and all the club's **expenditure** for the year.

Expenditure	Income
Cleaning	Subscriptions
Repairs	Bar profit
Insurance	Catering profit
Light and heat	Competition receipts
Depreciation of assets	Dance receipts
Telephone and stationery	Raffle profit
Secretarial expenses	
Wages	

If income is greater than expenditure it is called excess of income over expenditure. If expenditure is greater than income it is called excess of expenditure over income.

HOW TO PREPARE AN INCOME AND EXPENDITURE ACCOUNT

From a given receipts and payments account with adjustments included:

(i) Exclude opening and closing balances.
(ii) Exclude purchase or sale of assets.
(iii) Include adjustments.

(4) BALANCE SHEET

Balance sheet of a club is exactly the same as balance sheet of a business. It shows assets and liabilities as usual.

There are two differences in the 'Financed By' section:

Capital is called **Accumulated Fund**.

Net Profit is called **Excess of Income over Expenditure**, which is added to accumulated fund.

E. Adjustments in Club Accounts — Higher Level

(1) BAR TRADING ACCOUNT

If the club operates a bar it will be necessary to prepare a bar trading account. The profit or loss on the bar is transferred to the income and expenditure account.

Example

Bar sales	10,000
Bar purchases	6,000
Bar stock at start	2,000
Bar stock at end	1,800

	Bar Trading Account		
	Bar sales		10,000
	Deduct Cost of Sales		
	Opening stock	2,000	
	Bar purchases	6,000	
	Cost of goods available for sale	8,000	
	Less closing stock	1,800	
	Cost of Sales		6,200
	Bar profit		3,800

(2) FUNCTIONS

Most clubs run functions such as dances, dinners, concerts, competitions. A profit or loss must be worked out on these functions and entered in the income and expenditure account.

Profit ⇛ Income
Loss ⇛ Expenditure

Example

Dance receipts	2,000	
Dance expenses	1,200	
Profit on dance	800	⇛ Income

(3) SUBSCRIPTIONS

Clubs get their finance mainly from members' subscriptions. We must include in the income and expenditure account only subscriptions for the period of account we are dealing with. Thus subscriptions will need to be adjusted.

Rule for Adjusting Subscriptions

— Start with subscriptions received.
— Add subscriptions due at end.
— Deduct subscriptions prepaid at end.

Balance Sheet

Subscriptions due at end
⇛ **Current Assets**
Subscriptions prepaid at end
⇛ **Current Liability**

Example
Subscriptions received 2,000
Subscriptions due at end 100
Subscriptions prepaid at end 300

Solution

Subscriptions received	2,000
Add subscriptions due end	100
	2,100
Less subscriptions prepaid end	300
Income and expenditure account	1,800
Balance Sheet	
Subscriptions due	100 ⇛ CA
Subscriptions prepaid	300 ⇛ CL

(4) DEPRECIATION OF FIXED ASSETS
(a) Calculate percentage depreciation on the cost figure at end of year. Enter figure in **expenditure** section.
(b) Deduct depreciation from cost of asset in the fixed assets section of balance sheet.

(5) ACCRUALS AT END OF YEAR (AMOUNTS DUE)
(a) Add to expenditure figure in income and expenditure account.
(b) Show amount due as **current liability** in balance sheet.

(6) AMOUNTS PAID IN ADVANCE AT END OF YEAR
(a) Deduct prepaid amount from expenditure in income and expenditure account.
(b) Show prepaid amount as **current asset** in balance sheet.

(7) CALCULATION OF ACCUMULATED FUND IF NOT GIVEN
Add up all assets in club at start of year. Add up all liabilities in club at start of year. Subtract liabilities from assets. Difference is accumulated fund.

Examination-Style Question and Solution

Question 1.
Answer (a) and (b). This is a Club Account Question.
1. (a) The Treasurer of the local Social Club has been taken ill and you have been asked to prepare accounts for the Annual General Meeting next week. You are required to prepare:

- ➢ An Income and Expenditure Account for the year ended 31/5/1992. **(15)**
- ➢ A separate Trading Account for the canteen for the same period. **(6)**
- ➢ A Balance Sheet as at 31/5/1992. **(15)**

The Trial Balance at 31/5/1992 is as shown:

Trial Balance	**Dr**	**Cr**
Clubhouse	15,000	
Equipment	4,200	
Canteen Sales		8,500
Members' Subscriptions		4,600
Canteen Purchases	6,850	
Light and Heat	800	
Telephone	350	
Postage and Stationery	70	
Wages	3,200	
Repairs to Equipment	530	
Furniture	2,500	
Profit on Raffle		900
Canteen Stock (1/6/91)	440	
Accumulated Fund (1/6/91)		19,940
	33,940	33,940

The following matters must also be taken into consideration:
(i) Subscriptions due IR£310;
(ii) Canteen Stock (31/5/1992) IR£490;
(iii) Telephone due IR£40;
(iv) Depreciate equipment by 10% and furniture by 5%.

1. (b) Calculate the gross profit percentage on the canteen sales and make a comment on it. **(4)**

Source: Junior Certificate Higher Level 1992. **(40 marks)**

Solution to Question 1.

1. (a)

Income and Expenditure Account for Year Ending 31 May 1992

	Income			
	Members' Subscriptions	4,600		
	Add Subscriptions Due	310	4,910	
	Profit on Raffle		900	
	Profit on Canteen		1,700	7,510
	Less Expenditure			
	Light and Heat		800	
	Telephone	350		
	Add Telephone Due	40	390	
	Postage and Stationery		70	
	Wages		3,200	
	Repairs		530	
	Depreciation			
	Equipment 10%	420		
	Furniture 5%	125	545	5,535
	Excess Income over Expenditure			1,975

Trading Account Canteen for Year Ending 31 May 1992

Canteen Sales		8,500
Deduct Cost of Sales		
Stock 1/6/91	440	
Canteen Purchases	6,850	
Cost of Goods Available for Sale	7,290	
Less Closing Stock 31/5/92	490	
Cost of Sales		6,800
Canteen Profit		1,700

Balance Sheet as at 31 May 1992

	Cost	Deprec.	NBV
Fixed Assets			
Clubhouse	15,000		15,000
Equipment	4,200	420	3,780
Furniture	2,500	125	2,375
	21,700	545	21,155
Current Assets			
Stock (Canteen)	490		
Subscriptions Due	310	800	
Less Current Liabilities			
Telephone Due		40	
Working Capital			760
Total Net Assets			21,915
Financed By			
Accumulated Fund 1/6/91		19,940	
Add Excess Income over Expenditure		1,975	
			21,915

1. (b)

$$\frac{\text{Gross Profit} \times 100}{\text{Sales}} \qquad \frac{1{,}700 \times 100}{8{,}500} = 20\%$$

Comment: Satisfactory margin before expenses but lower than a business percentage.

F. Treasurer's Report

The treasurer will present the treasurer's report at the AGM. It informs the members of the financial situation of the club.

Treasurer's Report on Local Social Club Refer to Accounts and Solution above (1992 Higher Level Question)

LOCAL SOCIAL CLUB
Treasurer's Report

To All Club Members 3 June 1992
From Ryan Giggs Treasurer

Please find attached with this report final accounts and balance sheet of club.

Body of Report

1. Canteen profit was IR£1,700 as shown in canteen trading account.
2. The income and expenditure shows that the club had a surplus of IR£1,975 for the year.
3. There is IR£310 owing in subscriptions at end of year.
4. To improve facilities for members for the future I recommend that members' subscriptions be increased from IR£5 to IR£10 per year.

I am available to discuss this report if required.

Signed

Ryan Giggs
Treasurer

G. Business Terms

Accumulated Fund = Capital (assets – liabilities).
Agenda Programme for meeting.
AGM Annual General Meeting.
Deficit Loss made by a club.
Excess/Surplus Profit made by a club.
Income and Expenditure Account Profit and loss account
Minutes of Meeting Record of meeting.
Receipts and Payments Account Cash account for a club.
Subscriptions Amount of money paid each year to a club in order to remain a member.

PRACTICE QUESTIONS

(i) Question 20, Section A, Paper I, Higher Level, 1992.
(ii) Question 2, Section A, Paper I, Higher Level, 1994.
(iii) Question 6, Section A, Paper I, Higher Level, 1993.
(iv) Question 13, Section A, Paper I, Higher Level, 1992.
(v) Question 4, Section B, Ordinary Level, Sample Paper.
(vi) Question 4, Section B, Paper I, Higher Level, Sample Paper.
(vii) Question 6, Section B, Paper I, Higher Level, 1994.

Chapter 47 — Farm Accounts

A. Introduction

Farming in Ireland is a big and important business. Farmers, like any other business, must keep proper accounts.

B. Purpose of Farm Accounts

(1) To find out whether the farm made a **profit** or **loss**.
(2) To find out **which sections** of farming are most profitable.
(3) For submission to **Revenue Commissioners** for tax liability.
(4) To provide information to **bank manager** when making a loan application.
(5) To provide information if applying for **government** or **EC grants**.

C. Farm Accounts

(1) Most farmers will keep an **analysed cash book** to record daily receipts and payments.
(2) At the end of the year an **income and expenditure account** is prepared to find profit or loss made.
(3) A **balance sheet** is also prepared to show the farmer's assets, liabilities and capital.

ANALYSED CASH BOOK

This book is used to record the daily receipts and payments of the farmer.

Receipts — Debit side. **Payments — Credit side.**

Sample Question and Solution on Analysed Cash Book

Question

John and Mary Keane run a farm in Co. Meath. The following is a list of their receipts and payments for the month of October 1995.

1 Oct.	Balance at bank	IR£1,500
5 Oct.	Contractors for beet Ch. No. 1	IR£700
7 Oct.	Tractor insurance Ch. No. 2	IR£560
10 Oct.	Sales of potatoes	IR£1,600
12 Oct.	Sales of vegetables	IR£1,200
14 Oct.	Wages, potato picking Ch. No. 3	IR£200
15 Oct.	Purchase of vegetable bags Ch. No. 4	IR£260
19 Oct.	Sales of sugar beet	IR£6,000
20 Oct.	Sales of vegetables	IR£1,400
20 Oct.	Wages, vegetable packing Ch. No. 5	IR£180
21 Oct.	Contractors for beet Ch. No. 6	IR£600
22 Oct.	Haulage of beet to factory Ch. No. 7	IR£300
23 Oct.	Diesel and oil for tractor Ch. No. 8	IR£400

24 Oct.	Wages, potato picking Ch. No. 9	IR£290	27 Oct.	Repairs to potato digger Ch. No. 10	IR£170
25 Oct.	Sales of potatoes	IR£2,000	29 Oct.	Purchase of potato bags Ch. No. 11	IR£700
26 Oct.	Sales of sugar beet	IR£2,600	30 Oct.	Telephone bill Ch. No. 12	IR£180
27 Oct.	Receipt of EC grant	IR£1,500			

Prepare an analysed cash book for the Keanes using the following headings.

Receipts: Total, Potatoes, Vegetables, Sugar Beet, Other.
Payments: Total, Potatoes, Vegetables, Sugar Beet, Other.

Solution

ANALYSED CASH BOOK

Date	Details	Total	Potatoes	Veg.	Sugar Beet	Other	Date	Details	Chq. No.	Total	Potatoes	Veg.	Sugar Beet	Other
1 Oct.	Balance	1,500					5 Oct.	Contractors — beet	1	700			700	
10 Oct.	Sales — potatoes	1,600	1,600				7 Oct.	Tractor — insurance	2	560				560
12 Oct.	Sales — vegetables	1,200		1,200			14 Oct.	Wages — potato picking	3	200	200			
19 Oct.	Sales — sugar beet	6,000			6,000		15 Oct.	Purchases — veg. bags	4	260		260		
20 Oct.	Sales — vegetables	1,400		1,400			20 Oct.	Wages — veg. packing	5	180		180		
25 Oct.	Sales — potatoes	2,000	2,000				21 Oct.	Contractors — beet	6	600			600	
26 Oct.	Sales — sugar beet	2,600			2,600		22 Oct.	Haulage — beet to factory	7	300			300	
27 Oct.	EC — grant	1,500				1,500	23 Oct.	Diesel, oil — tractor	8	400				400
							24 Oct.	Wages — potato picking	9	290	290			
							27 Oct.	Repairs — potato digger	10	170	170			
							29 Oct.	Purchases — potato bags	11	700	700			
							30 Oct.	Telephone bill	12	180				180
		17,800	3,600	2,600	8,600	1,500				4,540	1,360	440	1,600	1,140
							31 Oct.	Balance C/d		13,260				
		17,800								17,800				
31 Oct.	Balance B/d	13,260												

Sample Question and Solution on Income and Expenditure Account and Balance Sheet

Denis and Mary O'Leary run a farm. The following figures are taken from their books.

Gross Income	
Potatoes	7,000
Vegetables	9,000
Sugar beet	6,000
Fruit	8,000

Expenditure	
Interest on loan	1,500
Wages	4,500
Light and heat	700
Hire of equipment	600
Rent	550
Seeds	1,200
Plants	2,500
Telephone	1,300
Insurance — tractor	650
Diesel and oil	700
Fertiliser	1,500
Repairs to machinery	120
Contractors — beet	700

Assets and Liabilities	
Land	100,000
Buildings	50,000
Stock	3,000
Debtors	5,000
Creditors	2,650
ACC loan	28,000
Tractors	20,000
Equipment	10,000
Cash	700
Bank	2,900
Capital	150,000
Drawings	2,530

The following information is also available on 31 December 1996.

- Light and heat due IR£50
- Rent prepaid IR£100
- Depreciate tractors by 5% of cost.

Prepare:

(1) Income and expenditure account for the year ending 31 December 1996.
(2) Balance sheet as at 31 December 1996.

Solution

(1) Income and Expenditure Account for Year Ending 31 December 1996

	Income			
	Potatoes		7,000	
	Vegetables		9,000	
	Sugar beet		6,000	
	Fruit		8,000	30,000
	Less Expenditure			
	Interest on loan		1,500	
	Wages		4,500	
	Light and heat	700		
	Add light and heat due	50	750	
	Hire of equipment		600	
	Rent	550		
	Less rent prepaid	100	450	
	Seeds		1,200	
	Plants		2,500	
	Telephone		1,300	
	Insurance — tractor		650	
	Diesel and oil		700	
	Fertiliser		1,500	
	Repairs to machinery		120	
	Contractors — beet		700	
	Depreciation of tractors		1,000	17,470
	Farm net profit/excess income over expenditure			12,530

(2) **Balance Sheet as at 31 December 1996**

	Cost	Deprec.	NBV
Fixed Assets			
Land	100,000	–	100,000
Buildings	50,000	–	50,000
Tractors	20,000	1,000	19,000
Equipment	10,000	–	10,000
	180,000	1,000	179,000
Current Assets			
Stock	3,000		
Debtors	5,000		
Cash	700		
Bank	2,900		
Rent prepaid	100	11,700	
Less Current Liabilities			
Creditors	2,650		
Light and heat due	50	2,700	
Working capital			9,000
Total net assets			188,000
Financed By			
Capital	150,000		
Add farm profit	12,530	162,530	
Less drawings		2,530	160,000
Long-Term Liabilities			
ACC loan			28,000
Capital employed			188,000

D. Farm Report

To Denis and Mary O'Leary
From J.P. Kiely Teagasc Farm Advisor

High Street
Kerry

10 January 1997

Introduction
I was asked by you to assess the performance of your farm.

Having visited your farm and examined your account the following are my findings.

Body of Report:

1. Farm profit was IR£12,530 for year ending 31 December 1996.

2. Return on capital invested was 8.3%

i.e. $\frac{\text{Net Profit x 100}}{\text{Capital Invested}}$ $\frac{12{,}530 \times 100}{150{,}000}$ = 8.3%

a reasonably satisfactory return comparable to bank interest rates.

3. The net profit margin was 42.76%

$\frac{\text{Net Profit x 100}}{\text{Sales}} = \frac{12{,}530 \times 100}{30{,}000}$ = 41.76%

4. The working capital ratio was 4.3:1

CA:CL
11,700:2,700
4.3:1

Very satisfactory and well above the recommended ratio of 2:1.

5. There is IR£2,900 in the bank deposit account and IR£700 in cash.

I am available to discuss this report if required.

Signed

J.P. Kiely
Teagasc Advisor

Chapter 48 — Service Firms

A. Introduction

Service firms supply and sell a service rather than a product.

Examples: Travel agencies, hairdressing, accounting, banking, insurance, cleaning, secretarial, horse training.

B. Accounts Prepared by Service Firms

➢ **Analysed cash book** to record daily receipts and payments.
➢ **Operating statement** (profit and loss account) for year.
➢ **Balance sheet** as at last day of the year.

(1) ANALYSED CASH BOOK

Most service firms will keep an analysed cash book as their main financial record.

Sample Question and Solution

Question

Jim Coppell Ltd trains horses. The following is a list of his receipts and payments for the month of July 1993.

1 July	Cash on hand	IR£800
1 July	Training fees received	IR£2,900
2 July	Vet's fees paid Ch. No. 1	IR£740
4 July	Rates Ch. No. 2	IR£2,100
7 July	Race winnings	IR£2,400
10 July	Hay sales	IR£3,800
11 July	Insurance Ch. No. 3	IR£1,890
13 July	Postage and telephone Ch. No. 4	IR£700
16 July	Wages Ch. No. 5	IR£4,000
17 July	Hay sales	IR£2,600
18 July	Training fees received	IR£1,800
19 July	Light and heat Ch. No. 6	IR£1,780
20 July	Race winnings	IR£1,900
21 July	Vet's fees Ch. No. 7	IR£900
22 July	Wages Ch. No. 8	IR£2,540
24 July	Race winnings	IR£2,400
25 July	Light and heat Ch. No. 9	IR£2,600
28 July	Hay sales	IR£2,900
29 July	Vet's fees Ch. No. 10	IR£900
30 July	Training fees received	IR£750
31 July	Wages Ch. No. 11	IR£640

Prepare an analysed cash book for Jim Coppell Ltd using the following headings.
Receipts: Total, Training Fees, Race Winnings, Hay Sales.
Payments: Total, Rates and Insurance, Wages, Postage and Telephone, Light and Heat, Vet's Fees.

Solution

ANALYSED CASH BOOK

Date	Details	Total	Trg Fees	Race Wngs	Hay Sales	Date	Details	Chq. No.	Total	Rates & Insur.	Wages	Postage & Phone	Light & Heat	Vet's Fees
1 July	Balance	800				2 July	Vet's fees	1	740					740
1 July	Training fees	2,900	2,900			4 July	Rates	2	2,100	2,100				
7 July	Race winnings	2,400		2,400		11 July	Insurance	3	1,890	1,890				
10 July	Hay sales	3,800			3,800	13 July	Post and telephone	4	700			700		
17 July	Hay sales	2,600			2,600	16 July	Wages	5	4,000		4,000			
18 July	Training fees	1,800	1,800			19 July	Light and heat	6	1,780				1,780	
20 July	Race winnings	1,900		1,900		21 July	Vet's fees	7	900					900
24 July	Race winnings	2,400		2,400		22 July	Wages	8	2,540		2,540			
28 July	Hay sales	2,900			2,900	25 July	Light and heat	9	2,600				2,600	
30 July	Training fees	750	750			29 July	Vet's fees	10	900					900
						31 July	Wages	11	640		640			
		22,250	5,450	6,700	9,300				18,790	3,990	7,180	700	4,380	2,540
						31 July	Balance	C/d	3,460					
		22,250							22,250					
31 July	Balance B/d	3,460												

(2) FINAL ACCOUNTS OF SERVICE FIRMS

(a) Service firms will prepare an **operating statement** (profit and loss account) to find out whether the firm made a profit or a loss.

(b) Service firms will also prepare a **balance sheet** and it is the same as any other balance sheet.

Examination-Style Question and Solution

Question 1.

Answer (a) and (b). This is a question on Final Accounts and Balance Sheet of a Service Firm.

(To be completed in your Answer Book.)

Jim Coppell Ltd trains horses. He prepares an Operating Statement (Profit and Loss A/C) and Balance Sheet at the end of each year.

The following Trial Balance was taken from the books on 31 December 1993.

Trial Balance as at 31 December 1993

	Dr IR£	Cr IR£
Sales income from:		
– Training Fees		116,405
– Race Winnings		44,600
– Sale of Hay		5,000
Rates	4,630	
Insurance	12,310	
Wages	37,950	
Postage and Telephone	2,540	
Light and Heat	4,635	
Vet's Fees	2,775	
Bank Overdraft		14,720
Cash on Hand	6,385	
Ordinary Share Capital (50,000 IR£1 shares)		50,000
Land	80,000	
Stables	59,500	
Motor Vehicles	20,000	
	230,725	230,725

1. (a) Prepare an Operating Statement for Jim Coppell Ltd for the year ended 31 December 1993 and a Balance Sheet as on that date. **(50)**

1. (b) State **one** reason why Jim Coppell Ltd should keep accounts. **(10)**

Source: Junior Certificate Ordinary Level 1994. **(60 marks)**

Solution to Question 1.

JIM COPPELL LTD

Operating Statement for Year Ending 31 December 1993

	Sales Income		
	Training Fees	116,405	
	Race Winnings	44,600	
	Sale of Hay	5,000	
	Total Income		166,005
	Less Expenditure		
	Rates	4,630	
	Insurance	12,310	
	Wages	37,950	
	Postage and Telephone	2,540	
	Light and Heat	4,635	
	Vet's Fees	2,775	
	Total Expenditure		64,840
	Net Profit		101,165

Balance Sheet as on 31 December 1993

		Cost	Deprec.	NBV
	Fixed Assets			
	Land	80,000	–	80,000
	Stables	59,500	–	59,500
	Motor Vehicles	20,000	–	20,000
		159,500		159,500
	Current Assets			
	Cash		6,385	
	Less Current Liabilities			
	Bank Overdraft		14,720	
	Working Capital			- 8,335
	Total Net Assets			151,165
	Financed By			
	50,000 Ordinary Shares @ IR£1 each			50,000
	Reserves			
	Net Profit			101,165
	Capital Employed			151,165

1. (b) Reasons Why Jim Coppell Should Keep Accounts

➢ To find out whether he is making a profit or loss.
➢ To see how much tax he has to pay.
➢ To help him plan for the future.
➢ To provide information for bank if making a loan application.

PRACTICE QUESTIONS

(i) (Higher Level only)
Redo the Jim Coppell Ltd question — operating statement and balance sheet — taking the following adjustments into account on 31 December 1993.

➢ Wages due IR£1,300.
➢ Insurance prepaid IR£770.
➢ Depreciate motor vehicles by 10%.
➢ Stock of postage stamps on hand IR£100.
➢ Vet's fees due IR£250.

(ii) Question 18, Section A, Ordinary Level, 1993.

SECTION FOUR — INFORMATION TECHNOLOGY

Chapter 49 — Modern Information Technology

A. Introduction

Information Technology (IT) is a modern term applied to the processing of knowledge and data using computers and other electronic advances.

Data Processing (DP) is the operation of collecting, storing, processing and transmitting data.

B. A Computer

A computer is a device capable of solving problems by accepting data, performing mathematical operations on the data, and giving out results.

C. Types of Computer System

(1) MAIN FRAME COMPUTERS

Large powerful and expensive computers that are used for processing information in large businesses and organisations, e.g. Telecom, ESB.

(2) MINI COMPUTERS

Smaller and more compact systems. Found in medium-sized businesses or in government departments.

(3) MICRO COMPUTERS

The smallest and cheapest class of computer. They are used in many homes as personal computers; operated by one person, they fit on a desk. They are widely used in schools and businesses for word processing, data base and spreadsheets.

D. Hardware and Software

HARDWARE

Physical part of a computer system, e.g. monitor, keyboard, disk drive, printer.

SOFTWARE

Programs or instructions that tell a computer what to do. Software may be built into the computer's ROM or can be stored on disk and loaded into the computer when required.

E. Hardware/Computer Equipment

A computer is made up of many parts called hardware, and includes monitor, keyboard and system unit. The system unit holds the computer's processor (CPU), memory and disk drives.

F. Parts of a Computer

The **Keyboard** is used to get the information into the computer.

The **CPU** is used to process the information, i.e. do calculations.

The **Monitor** displays the result.

The **Printer** produces a hard copy of this display.

The **Disk Drive** makes it possible for the information to be stored on disk for use in the future.

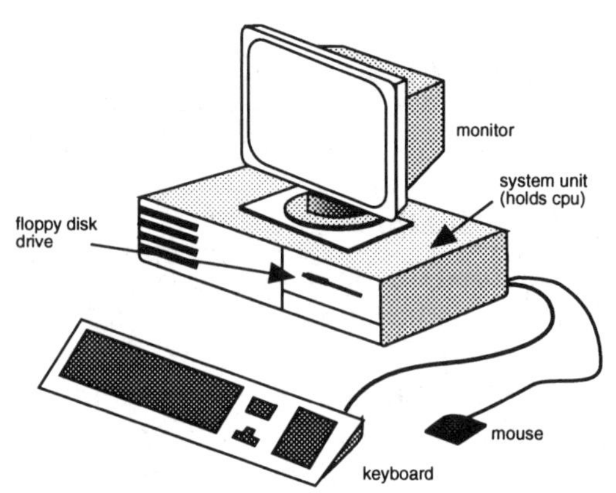

G. Main Components of a Computer

(1) **Input devices** — hardware used to enter data.
(2) **Processor** — hardware that produces results.
(3) **Output devices** — hardware that displays results.
(4) **Storage** — hardware used to store information.

H. Input Devices

(1) KEYBOARD

A device for entering data and programs into the computer. It is a display of keys which produce characters on display when pressed.

(2) MOUSE

A small device with a ball underneath, when moved it guides a pointer across the screen. Used in many programs, especially graphics.

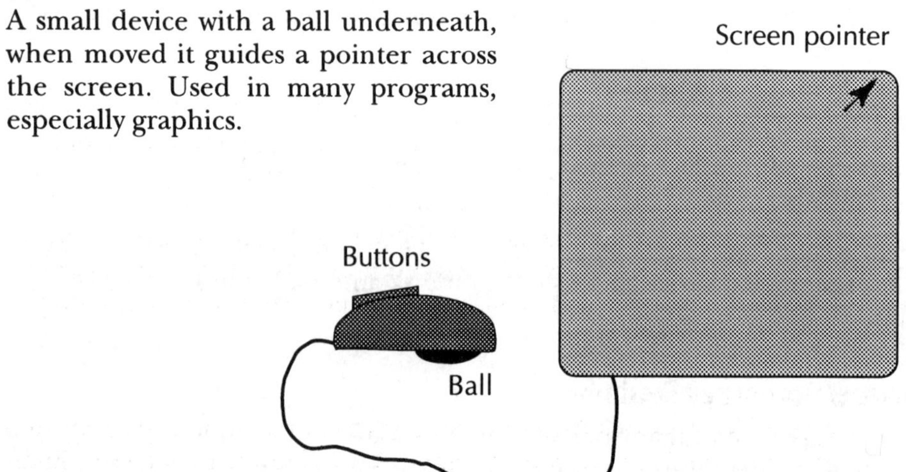

(3) SCANNER
A scanner can read bar codes by scanning the pattern of lines.

(4) LIGHT PEN
A device resembling a pen connected to the computer by cable, it can be used to write or draw on the screen. Used mainly in graphics.

(5) MAGNETIC CARD READER
This machine reads data from the magnetic strip on a plastic card, e.g. cash dispensing machines reading ATM plastic card.

(6) TOUCH SCREEN
The screen displays choices and the user touches the desired choice, used mainly in banks.

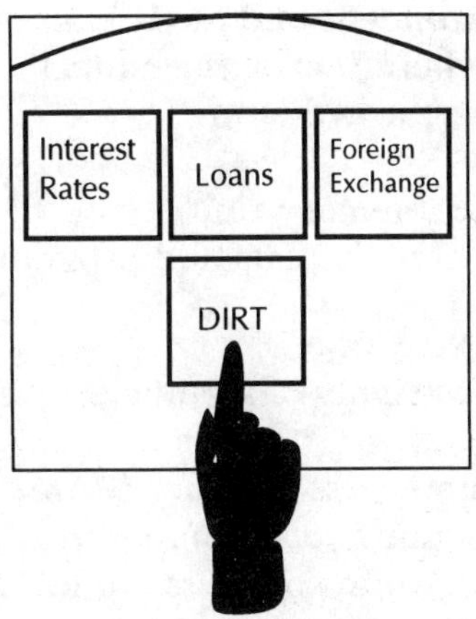

(7) MICROPHONE/VOICE ENTRY DATA (VDE)
A microphone is connected to the computer. The information put into the computer is interpreted by a special program. Can be used for the physically handicapped.

(8) MODEM (**MO**DULATOR/**DEM**ODULATOR)
This is a device for connecting two computers by a telephone line. It is used to transfer information from one computer to another.

(9) JOYSTICK
This is a device attached to the computer by a cable. It is a hand-held lever and when moved it sends signals to the CPU. It is used for playing computer games.

(10) MAGNETIC INK CHARACTER RECOGNITION (MICR)
This is used in banking. The numbers along the bottom of each cheque are printed in magnetic ink. The bank staff write the amount of the cheque in magnetic ink and with the use of a magnetic ink character reader linked to a computer, the customer's bank account is updated.

(11) OPTICAL MARK READER (OMR)
The device is connected to a computer and detects the presence or absence of a mark in a given position, each position having a value known to the computer. Used in Lotto, and multiple choice exam questions.

I. Processing Hardware

CENTRAL PROCESSING UNIT (CPU)

This is the brain of the computer, where all calculations on the data are carried out. It is the place where the computer interprets and processes information.

There are three main areas in the CPU.

(1) The Control Unit

The part which makes the computer carry out each instruction of a program in sequence.

(2) The Arithmetic and Logic Unit (ALU)

The part where the mathematical calculations are carried out and logic operations are performed.

(3) Storage/Memory Unit

The part where the data and programs are stored. It is like our own memory.

MEMORY AND STORAGE

There are two types of memory.

(1) Random Access Memory (RAM)

The instructions your computer gets and information it processes are kept in RAM during your work session. RAM is not a permanent storage place for information as it is active only while your computer is on. When you turn off your computer, information is deleted from RAM so always save it on a disk before switching off your computer.

(2) Read Only Memory (ROM)

This memory holds the data and instructions permanently needed by the computer, e.g. the instructions needed for the operation of the computer. This information is entered at the time of manufacture and cannot be altered by the user. When the computer is turned off, this information is not lost.

MEASURING COMPUTER MEMORY

(1) Byte is the amount of storage needed to hold one character (character is any keyboard symbol, e.g. digit 0 1 2; letter A B C; punctuation mark , : ?; sign + – =.
(2) Kilobyte (KB) one kilobyte = 1,024 bytes.
(3) Megabyte (MB) one megabyte = 1,048,576 bytes.

Memory capacity is the number of bytes that a computer can hold in RAM at one time, e.g. a computer with 4MB RAM will hold 4 x 1,048,576 bytes.

The more RAM available in a computer, the more data it can handle and the bigger the programs it can accommodate.

SECONDARY STORAGE

This storage supplements the main storage of a computer: for instance, floppy disks and hard disks.

(1) Diskette or floppy disk — a thin flexible disk inside a protective plastic cover, it is removed from the disk drive when not in use. Floppy disks vary in size —130 mm (5 1/4") or 90 mm (3 1/2") — and vary in the amount of information that they hold.

(2) Fixed disk — hard disk — permanently installed inside the case of the computer. It can store very large amounts of information, which can be accessed much more quickly.

J. Output Hardware

Output devices allow you to see the information entered and processed.

(1) MONITOR/VDU

A monitor (Visuals Display Unit) is the most common method of displaying information. There are many types of monitor. Monochrome screens display only one colour, i.e. black on white or green on black. Colour screens can display many colours.

(2) PRINTER

A printer is a device that allows you to put the information on paper. This is a permanent copy, sometimes called a 'printout' or 'hard copy'.

TYPES OF PRINTER

(1) Dot matrix printers

These form characters on paper by printing a pattern of dots. They are cheap but slow and do not produce high-quality copies.

(2) Daisy wheel printers

The hammer strikes the character, which in turn strikes the paper through the ribbon. The output of these printers is 'letter quality', i.e. the characters are fully formed and continuous lines are produced similar to a typewriter.

(3) Laser printers

Similar to photocopying. Capable of very high speeds, top-quality copies, good graphics, good colour but the printers are expensive.

(4) Ink jet printers

A fine jet of quick-drying ink is fired at the paper and forms characters as it lands. They are very quiet and produce high-quality copies. They can achieve speeds of up to 200 characters per second.

(5) Plotters

Devices for drawing lines on paper. Mainly used for diagrams and drawing plans, etc.

K. Computer Software/Packages

Software is the set of instructions that enables the computer to perform its functions. There are two types of software.

(1) OPERATING SYSTEM

The operating system gets your computer running and controls the operation of its activities. It looks after the internal running of the computer, i.e. reading disks, listing contents of disks, saving and loading programs, etc. A common operating system used with IBM is Microsoft Disk Operating System — MS DOS.

(2) PROGRAMS

A program is a coded set of instructions that interprets the information you give the computer. There is a wide variety of programs, including word processing, e.g. Microsoft Word, Word Perfect; spreadsheets, e.g. Lotus 1-2-3; database management, e.g. dBASEIII; accounting, e.g. SAGE, graphics.

INTEGRATED SOFTWARE

Programs that can exchange data with each other, e.g. a software package that has a word processor, database, spreadsheet and communications program — like Microsoft Works.

L. Software Programs Used in Business

(1) WORD PROCESSING

A software system that allows you to write sentences and paragraphs. You can produce letters, documents and reports. Text can be moved, copied, replaced and checked for spelling, print sizes can be changed, and when finished it can all be printed on paper.

(2) DATABASE

A database is a filing system on computer. It can be used in business for names and addresses of customers, in schools for students and class lists, in hospitals for patients, etc.

(3) SPREADSHEET

A spreadsheet is used for doing mathematical and financial calculations, e.g. budgets, accounts, stock records, payroll and business planning. The screen is divided into rows and columns and each intersection contains a cell. The big advantage of using a spreadsheet is that if you change one figure all other figures involved will be automatically adjusted.

(4) MAIL MERGE

This program allows you to produce personalised letters, i.e. they look as if they were written specially for a particular person. To do this you type out a letter on the word processor and merge with name and address from the database. The same letter can be addressed to a number of people.

(5) GRAPHICS
This program allows the user to produce and print out pie charts and bar charts. Very useful in business when trying to illustrate figures or accounting information.

(6) DESK TOP PUBLISHING (DTP)
This program is used to produce professional-quality reports, booklets, magazines, brochures and other publications on computer. A high-quality printer is essential.

(7) SPELL CHECKER
Most word processing programs include a dictionary. It compares typed words with words in its dictionary and will highlight any words with incorrect spelling.

M. Use of Computers

(1) IN BUSINESS
(a) For **typing** letters, documents and reports using word processor.
(b) For **filing**, e.g. names and addresses of customers using database.
(c) For **doing accounts, payroll and wages slip, stock records** using spreadsheet.
(d) For **illustrating information** graphically.
(e) For **sending personalised letters** to people using mail merge.
(f) For **reading bar codes** in shops and controlling stock.
(g) Some firms use computers for **designing products** (CAD), and in **manufacturing** (CAM).
(h) For **communicating** with other firms and customers.

(2) IN COMMUNICATIONS
(a) Through **satellite TV** we can get immediate coverage of all major events throughout the world, e.g. World Cup soccer.
(b) Cellular phones, e.g. Eircell, can be used by reporters to send information back to radio or TV headquarters.
(c) A modem can be used to transfer information from one computer to another over a telephone line, e.g. foreign journalists can send information back to headquarters using a PC and modem.
(d) Telecom call card, where a computer in the phone can read the card.
(e) Fax machine can be used to transmit information; this is made up of a scanner, modem and printer.
(f) Telecom Éireann provides a wide range of services which are computer-based, e.g. video conferencing.

(3) IN HOME
There are many computer-based items of equipment in the home.
(a) Automatic **washing machines** with different wash programmes, dishwashers and microwaves with different facilities.
(b) Central heating systems are usually computer-controlled.
(c) Fridges and freezers are usually temperature-controlled by computer.
(d) Fire alarms, burglar alarms and smoke detectors are computer-controlled.
(e) Remote control **TV** and digital-controlled **hi-fi systems**.

(f) **Personal computers** are used for playing games, word processing, accounts, budgeting and other educational purposes.
(g) **Digital watches** and pocket **calculators**.
(h) **Compact disc players** and **Sega and Nintendo systems**.

(4) IN BANKING
(a) All **deposit** accounts, **current** accounts, **loan accounts** and **overdrafts** are recorded on computer.
(b) **All information processed** through banks is done on computer — direct debits, standing orders, credit transfers and paypath.
(c) **Bank statements** are prepared through computer.
(d) The **numbers** along the bottom of each **cheque** are printed in magnetic ink. The cheque is read by MICR linked to computer and cheque is cleared.
(e) All **bank information** is kept on computer, e.g. interest rates on mortgages and term loans, deposit account rates of interest, rates of exchange of foreign currency.
(f) All **ATMs** are linked to computer and allow customers to withdraw, lodge, check balance, order a cheque book, order a statement twenty-four hours a day.
(g) **Electronic Funds Transfer at Point of Sale (EFTPOS):** the customer is given a plastic card and when he comes to a shop checkout the card is inserted into an electronic device, the PIN is keyed in and the amount of the bill is deducted from the customer's bank account and put into the shop's bank account.

N. Computerised Accounts

Computers have many uses in accounting.
(1) Day books, debtors, creditors and nominal ledger, cash book, and preparing trial balance.
(2) Business documents — invoicing, credit notes, etc. and printing statements for customers.
(3) VAT analysis.
(4) Trading and profit and loss account and balance sheet.
(5) Wages/pay roll/wages slips.
(6) Stock control/stock records.

Most accounting packages are 'integrated' — this means that when data is entered all the records are updated at once. For example, sold goods for IR£1,000 VAT @ 21% to O'Flynn Ltd. When this is entered in computer
➢ Sales day book updated
➢ O'Flynn Ltd updated
➢ Debtors control account updated
➢ Sales account updated
➢ VAT account updated.

O. Keyboarding

The keyboard is used to type instructions for your computer and to type information you want your computer to process. Efficient keyboarding involves being able to type properly, i.e. resting fingers on home keys ASDF JKL; and moving around the keyboard without looking at keyboard. Here are some of the keys on a computer keyboard and their use.

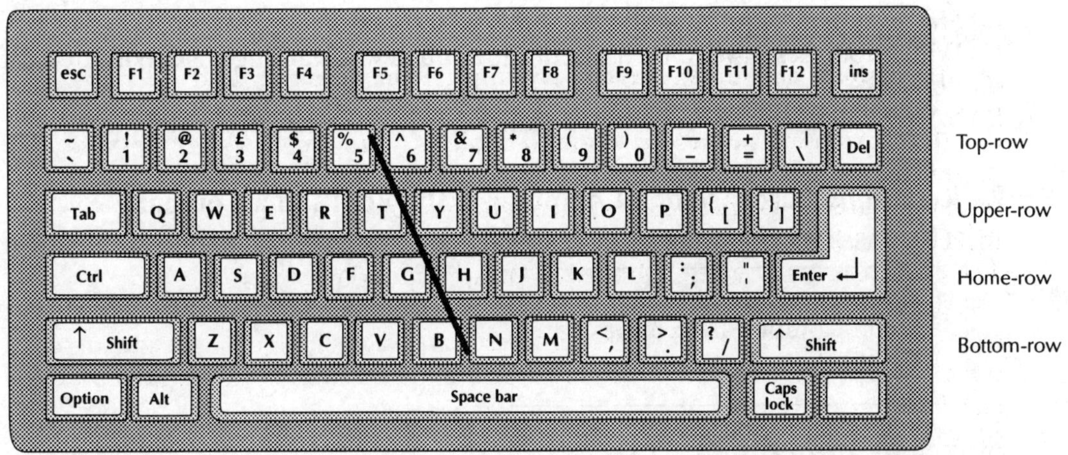

(1) QWERTY — First six letters on the second row.
(2) Home Keys — ASDF JKL;.
(3) Space Bar — To move on one space, i.e. between words.
(4) Shift Key — To make capital letters.
(5) Caps Lock Key — To make a line of capital letters.
(6) Enter/Return Key — Moves cursor to next line or when using a program tells the computer to carry out instruction.
(7) Function Keys — To perform special functions within a program, e.g. F1 — Help.
(8) Del (Delete) — To eliminate data from screen.
(9) Ins (Insert) — To insert a character omitted.
(10) Tab Key — To set margins.
(11) Esc (Escape) — To cancel an operation.

P. Proofreading

Proofreading is checking your work for errors and making the necessary corrections before making a printout.

Q. Factors to Be Considered Before Purchasing a Computer System

(1) How much will system cost and how will it be financed?
(2) Is a computer system required and how will firm benefit from owning a computer?
(3) Size of system required and availability of software.
(4) Will employees have to be trained? How much will training cost? Will there be staff lay-offs?
(5) Where will computer system be located and is the location suitable?

R. Recording Purchase of a Computer in the Books of a Company

(1) PURCHASE OF COMPUTER BY CHEQUE

Rule
Debit Computer Account
Credit Bank Account

(2) PURCHASE OF COMPUTER ON CREDIT

The purchase of an asset on credit is recorded in the **general journal** then posted to **ledger**.

Rule
Debit Computer Account
Credit Supplier's Account

Example

1 January 1996 Purchased computer system on credit from Lotus Ltd for IR£5,000.

General Journal — **Page 1**

Date	Particulars	Fo	Debit	Credit
1/1/96	Computer A/C	GL1	5,000	
	Lotus Ltd			5,000
	Purchase of computer system on credit			

Ledger

Computer A/C

Date	Particulars	Fo	Total	Date	Particulars	Fo	Total
1/1/96	Lotus Ltd	GJ	5,000				

Lotus Ltd

Date	Particulars	Fo	Total	Date	Particulars	Fo	Total
				1/1/96	Computer	GJ1	5,000

S. Dictionary of Information Technology Terms

Apple Brand name for a family of microcomputers manufactured by Apple.
Back-Up Copy Copy of the file kept for reference in case original data is lost or destroyed.
Backspace A keyboard operation that moves cursor one space to the left.
Basic Computer programming language.
Business Graphics Pie chart, bar charts, graphs, etc.
Byte Amount of storage needed to hold one character.
Bug Mistake in a computer program or an error in the working of the computer.
Central Processing Unit (CPU) Part of computer system which interprets and carries out instructions.
COBOL Language developed for business data processing applications.
CD ROM (Compact Disk Read Only Memory) An optical disk five-inch diameter on which data is recorded.
Computer-Aided Design (CAD) A program that converts rough sketches into a finished form.
Computer-Aided Manufacture (CAM) Using computers in manufacturing.
Cursor A symbol on the screen that indicates where the next character will appear.
Disk A magnetic device for storing information and programs.
Disk Operating System (DOS) Gets your computer running and controls the operation of computer.
Editing Correcting or changing programs or data.
Facsimile/Fax Scanning of a document and transmission of it via wires. Copy is produced at destination.
File A collection of data on a particular topic.
Formatting Preparing a disk for holding information.
Kilobyte abbreviated K. = 1,024 bytes.
Lotus 123 An electronic spreadsheet.
Megabyte 1,048,576 bytes or 1,024 kilobytes.
Microsoft An American company producing software systems.
MS DOS Microsoft Disk Operating System.
Network Where many computers are linked together.
Programmer A person who designs and writes programs.
Programming Translating information into a language that the computer can understand.
Scrolling Continuous movement of data on the screen, i.e. one line appears on bottom and all lines move upwards, line on top disappears from view.
Software Package A prewritten program that can be purchased for specific use, e.g. word processing package.
Spell Checker A program that informs user of spelling mistakes.
Virus A program that damages files.

Examination-Style Questions and Solutions

Question 1.

Answer (a) and (b). This is a Question on Information Technology.

Philip Ryan is a final year university student of architecture. He lives with his parents who own and run a bar and disco. He is trying to convince his parents to buy a new computer which could be used by all the family.

1. (a) State **two** uses to which the new computer could be put by **each** of the following:

- **(i)** The Ryans in their business.
- **(ii)** Philip in his studies.
- **(iii)** The Ryans in running their home. **(24)**

1. (b) Philip shopped around for a computer and saw the following advertisement:

A P.C. with VGA colour monitor Dot Matrix Printer, 2 Megabytes RAM 40 MB H.D. storage fast running speed, keyboard and mouse including packages work for word processing, spread sheets, database. All for the amazing price of

£689
incl. VAT

WINDOWS SYSTEM
WITH COLOUR MONITOR AND HARD DISK

Explain any four of the words underlined in the above advertisement. **(16)**

Source: Junior Certificate Higher Level 1994. **(40 marks)**

Solution to Question 1.

1. (a) *(i) Stock control, accounting, word processing, databases, communications, payroll.*

(ii) Mathematical calculation, writing reports, language learning, database.

(iii) Household budgets, household accounts, word processing, database.

1. (b) *Monitor*

A visual display unit or screen which shows information being inputted into the computer. It is also used for viewing output before printing a hard copy.

Megabyte

The measure of the RAM of the computer. It is 1,048,576 bytes. The bigger the RAM capacity, the larger the program the machine can operate.

Keyboard

The main input device for communicating information and instructions to the computer. It is similar to the keyboard of a typewriter but has additional special function keys and number pads.

Mouse

A hand-operated device which moves the cursor on the VDU.

Word Processing

This is a program used for typing letters, reports and documents. It is possible to insert, delete and rearrange the text until it is satisfactory before printing out a hard copy. Some programs have a spell checker built in.

Database

An electronic filing cabinet in which information can be inputted, stored and later retrieved when required.

Question 2.

Answer all sections. This is an Information Technology question.

The directors of P.J. Ltd, manufacturers and suppliers of household furniture, were very impressed with the quotation from Hiteck Computers. Hiteck Ltd were offering an 'all in' package, which included the computer system and a selection of business software, at a special price of IR£10,000.

2. (a) What are the three main hardware parts of a computer system? **(6)**
2. (b) Give three types of computer software suitable for the business. **(6)**
2. (c) State three ways in which P.J. Ltd may benefit from purchasing a computer system. **(9)**
2. (d) P.J. Ltd purchased the computer system from Hiteck Ltd on credit, on 25/5/92. Record this purchase in the appropriate book of first entry of P.J. Ltd and post the relevant figures to the ledger. **(12)**
2. (e) State two suitable outside sources of finance that P.J. Ltd could use to finance the computer system.

Give a brief explanation of any **one** of these **two** sources. **(7)**

Source: Junior Certificate Higher Level 1992. **(40 marks)**

Solution to Question 2.

2. (a) *Visual display unit, keyboard, disk drive, printer, mouse.*
2. (b) *Since P.J. Limited manufacture and supply household furniture, the main type of software would be Computer-Aided Design (CAD), Computer-Aided Manufacture (CAM) plus any of the following: word processing, spreadsheet, database, payroll, accounts, stock control.*

2. (c) *(i) Reduction in number of staff required.*
(ii) Speed in production.
(iii) Letter designs.
(iv) More accurate work.

2. (d)

General Journal

25/5/92	Computer A/C Hiteck Ltd A/C Purchase of computer system on credit	GL1 GL1	10,000	 10,000

LEDGER

Computer A/C

25/5/92	Hiteck Ltd	GJ1	10,000				

Hiteck Ltd A/C

				25/5/92	Computer	GJ1	10,000

2. (e) Leasing, Term Loan, Hire Purchase.

Leasing — *This is a form of renting, where you obtain the use but never the ownership.*

Term Loan — *P.J. Ltd could get a loan from the bank of IR£10,000 and repay it over three to five years.*

Hire Purchase — *This is a system where you pay a deposit and the balance over an agreed number of instalments. P.J. Ltd would get immediate possession of the computer system but become the legal owner only when the last instalment was paid.*

PRACTICE QUESTIONS

(i) Question 20, Section A, Ordinary Level, Sample Paper.
(ii) Question 20, Section A, Ordinary Level, 1992.
(iii) Question 19, Section A, Ordinary Level, 1994.
(iv) Question 8, Section B, Ordinary Level, Sample Paper.
(v) Question 8, Section B, Ordinary Level, 1992.
(vi) Question 20, Section A, Paper I, Higher Level, Sample Paper.
(vii) Question 10, Section A, Paper I, Higher Level, 1992.
(viii) Question 18, Section A, Paper I, Higher Level, 1993.
(ix) Question 6, Paper II, Higher Level, Sample Paper.

Chapter 50 — Examination Format

Ordinary Level **1 Paper** **400 Marks** **2 1/2 Hours**

Section	Time Allocated	Description of Questions	Marks per Question	Total Marks
A	25 mins	20 short questions ranging over entire syllabus. Answer all 20 questions. Calculators may be used. Remember to include all of Section 'A' in your answer book.	5	100
B	25 mins per question	8 long questions given. Answer any 5 questions. These questions range over entire syllabus. Calculators may be used. Marks will be given for layout and presentation.	60	300

Higher Level **2 Papers** **400 Marks**

Paper I **240 Marks** **2 1/2 Hours**

Section	Time Allocated	Description of Questions	Marks per Question	Total Marks
A	30 mins	20 short questions ranging over the entire syllabus. Answer all questions. Calculators may be used. Remember to include all of Section 'A' in your answer book.	4	80
B	30 mins per question	6 long questions given. Answer any 4 questions. Questions in this section will deal mainly with the **personal** and **social** development to include **economics**, **club accounts** and practical **personal business** knowledge and skills. Calculators may be used. Marks will be given for layout and presentation.	40	160

Paper II **160 Marks** **2 Hours**

Section	Time Allocated	Description of Questions	Marks per Question	Total Marks
No sections	30 mins per question	6 long questions given. Answer any 4 questions. Questions will focus on the syllabus from perspective of operating a business. Calculators may be used.	40	160

Chapter 51 — Examination Structure and Advice

Section A — Ordinary and Higher Level

All twenty short questions must be answered on the question paper.

Allow approx. twenty-five minutes for Section A.

These short questions can be chosen from any part of the syllabus.

Remember to return completed Section A with your answer book.

Remember (a) Short correct answers are required.

(b) Where one tick (✓) is required tick only **once**, otherwise no marks allowed.

(c) If more than one tick (✓) is required tick **required** number only.

(d) Rough work and calculations must be shown.

(e) Calculators are allowed — but show workings clearly.

SECTION A-TYPE QUESTIONS

Ordinary Level 20 Qs x 5 marks	Higher Level 20 Qs x 4 marks
1. Writing out in full initials used in business. 2. Writing most correct word in space provided. 3. Filling missing words in a sentence. 4. Tick (✓) appropriate box. 5. Multiple choice. 6. ESB meter reading calculation. 7. Currencies and countries of EC. 8. Currency exchange calculations. 9. True/False questions. 10. Definitions of business terms. 11. Putting names in alphabetical order. 12. Entering book-keeping transactions in accounts. 13. Balancing an account. 14. Questions on distance table — delivery systems. 15. Questions on business documents.	1. Writing out in full initials used in business. 2. Matching terms with explanations. 3. Mark-up and margin. 4. Tick (✓) appropriate box. 5. Multiple choice. 6. Converting 'T' A/Cs to continuous balance and vice versa. 7. Currencies and countries of EC. 8. Currency exchange calculations. 9. Source documents of day books. 10. Definitions of business terms. 11. Control accounts. 12. Double entry book-keeping questions. 13. Completing A/Cs, e.g. insurance.

Section B — Ordinary Level

Attempt any five out of eight questions given. There will be three or four parts to each question.

The first four questions usually deal with household budgets, household accounts, consumer/letter of complaint, money and banking. The remaining questions may deal with business documents, final A/Cs, information technology, economic issues, delivery systems, insurance, communications, marketing, etc.

Allow about twenty-two minutes for each long question. This will ensure that you have time to read the paper carefully at the beginning of the exam and time to read back on your answer at the end of the exam.

ANALYSIS OF PAST EXAM PAPERS
Section B — Ordinary Level

	Sample 1992	1992	1993	1994	1995	1996
Household budget	Q1	Q1	Q1	Q1	Q1	Q1
Household a/cs/analysed cash book	Q2(b)	Q2(b)		Q2		
Consumer/letter of complaint	Q3	Q3			Q3	
Money and banking						
(i) cheque, lodgment, withdrawal	Q2(a)	Q2(a)			Q2(b)(c)(d)(e)	
(ii) bank statement/bank rec.			Q7			Q4
Credit and borrowing/HP and letter writing			Q3			
Insurance			Q8			
Economic framework/inflation	Q7					Q7(a)
National budgeting/foreign trade				Q7		
Forms of business		Q7(a)			Q7	
Communications/bar chart/sales		Q7(b)				
Chain of production and channels of distribution						Q8
People at work		Q7(e)		Q4	Q2(a)	Q7
Bar chart/pie chart/advertising			Q4			
Delivery systems				Q8		
Letter writing				Q3		Q3
Business documents	Q5	Q5	Q5	Q5	Q5	Q5
Petty cash			Q2			Q2
Final A/Cs — business	Q6	Q6	Q6		Q6	
Club A/Cs	Q4	Q4			Q4	
Final A/Cs — service firm				Q6		Q6
Information technology	Q8	Q8			Q8	

Paper I Section B — Higher Level

Attempt any four out of six questions given.

Paper I Section B will examine business of living and economic awareness sections of the course.

Questions may deal with household budgeting/household accounts, consumer, money and banking, credit and borrowing, personal insurance, economic framework/inflation, national budgeting, foreign trade, club A/Cs, people at work and information technology.

Allow about twenty-eight minutes for each question.

ANALYSIS OF PAST EXAM PAPERS
Paper I Section B — Higher Level

	Sample 1992	1992	1993	1994	1995	1996
Household budget	Q1	Q1	Q1	Q1	Q1(b)(c)	Q1
Household A/Cs/analysed cash book			Q2		Q1(a)	
Consumer		Q2	Q3		Q3	
Money and banking						
(i) Bank A/C/bank st/bank rec	Q2	Q4				
(ii) Saving, investing, interest calculations			Q5			Q6
(iii) Methods of payment				Q2		
(iv) Cheques					Q2	
Credit and borrowing						
(i) Hire purchase				Q3		
(ii) Cost of borrowing	Q3					
Insurance		Q3	Q6			Q5
Economic framework/inflation				Q4(a)		
National budgeting	Q6		Q4			Q4
Foreign trade				Q4(b)(c)		
People at work	Q5	Q5			Q5	
Being an employer						Q2
Petty cash/club account						Q3
Club accounts	Q4	Q6		Q6	Q4	
Information technology				Q5	Q6	

Paper II — Higher Level

Attempt any four out of six questions given.

Paper II will examine enterprise and information technology. However, there may be some overlap between Paper I and Paper II at Higher Level.

Questions may deal with forms of business, financial planning and cash flow statements, insurance for business, being an employer, marketing, delivery systems/ cost of transport, business documents, books of first entry and ledger, final accounts including adjustments, reporting on financial accounts, information technology.

Allow about twenty-eight minutes for each question.

ANALYSIS OF PAST EXAMINATION PAPERS

Paper II — Higher Level

	Sample 1992	1992	1993	1994	1995	1996
Bank statement/bank account/ bank rec.						Q6
Forms of business		Q5(a)(b)	Q2	Q4		
Finance for business						Q5(c)
Financial planning/ cash flow statements				Q6		
Insurance for business	Q5		Q5		Q6	
Being an employer					Q5	
Industrial relations						Q4
Marketing	Q4	Q5(c)(d)		Q2(a)(b)		
Delivery systems/cost of transport			Q6			Q5(a)(b)
Business documents	Q3	Q3	Q4	Q2(c) (d)(e)	Q2(c)	Q2
Selling on credit and bad debts					Q4	
Books of first entry and ledger	Q1	Q1	Q1	Q1	Q1	Q1
Trading A/C and stocktaking					Q2 (a) (b)(d)	
Depreciation						Q5(d)
Final A/C incl. adjustments	Q2	Q2	Q3	Q3	Q3	Q3
Reporting on accounts		Q6		Q5		
Information technology	Q6	Q4				

General Advice

(i) Read paper carefully before you start.

(ii) Begin with Section A, these questions are easier and will build up your confidence for the remainder of the paper.

(iii) When dealing with long questions

➔ do the questions you know best first

➔ look at the breakdown of marks for each part of the question

➔ attempt all parts of questions chosen and divide your time according to the marks available for each part.

(iv) Write the number of each question clearly alongside the answer and label each part (a) (b) (c), etc.

(v) Use blank documents supplied with the questions and return with your answer book.

(vi) Marks are given for layout and presentation so accuracy and neatness are vitally important, especially when answering book-keeping and business document questions.

(vii) Calculators may be used, but you must show your workings. Make sure your calculator is in good working order and be familiar with it. Be careful of the decimal point. Department of Education will not supply calculators on day of exam.

(viii) A specially designed and suitably ruled answer book is available to all candidates. The main benefit in using this stationery is that it saves considerable time during the examination in ruling various columns for answering questions. It is clearly stated on the front cover of the answer book what each page is suitable for (see sample cover on p. 310).

(ix) Allow a few minutes at end of exam for reading back over your answers.

(x) Good luck in the exam.

WARNING

You must return this paper with your answerbook, otherwise marks will be lost.

Write your Examination Number here. ____________________

AN ROINN OIDEACHAIS

JUNIOR CERTIFICATE EXAMINATION, 1997

BUSINESS STUDIES – HIGHER LEVEL – PAPER I
SECTION A
(80 Marks)

WEDNESDAY, 18 JUNE – MORNING 9.30 to 12.00

Answer all 20 questions. Each question carries 4 marks. Calculators may be used.
Please enclose this section in your answerbook.

1. A firm's final accounts showed that it had made a net profit IR£45,700. It later realised it had omitted its purchase returns of IR£1,300 from its final accounts. Calculate the correct net profit after the error is taken into account and corrected.

Workings

45,700
− 1,300
44,400

Answer 44,400

2.

Allied Irish Bank Ltd
Carlow *20/5/96*

Pay: *Mary O'Neill* or order
Thirty punts

IR £ *30.00*

Tom Nolan

168 225763 4963120

In the cheque above name the following parties:

(a) Drawee: ....
(b) Payee: ....

3. Indicate, by means of a tick (✓), the correct answer to the following.

To which of the following would you complain about a misleading advertisement?

(a) Ombudsman ☐
(b) Director of Public Prosecutions ☐
(c) Director of Consumer Affairs ☐
(d) Consumer Association of Ireland ☐

4. The following account appeared in the ledger of Hidro Ltd.

Wages Account

24/12/96	Bank	C. B9	300	31/12/96	Profit & Loss	GL	400
31/12/96	Balance	c/d	100				
			400				400
				31/12/96	Balance	b/d	100

Indicate, by means of a tick (✓), the correct answer to the following.

(a) Does the above account have a debit or credit balance?

Debit Balance ☐
Credit Balance ☐

(b) What does the balance in this account mean? ....
....

5. An IR£50 investment matured to IR£52 after 6 months.
Calculate the annual percentage rate of return.

Answer %

Workings

6. Select the correct word from the following list and write it in the space provided to complete the statements below.

Debit,	No,	Credit

(*a*) Assets have .... balance in their accounts.
(*b*) Liabilities have .... balances in their accounts.

7. Indicate by means of a tick (✓) whether or not the following statement is true or false.

The National Debt is the total money owed by the Irish Government to other countries.

☐ True
☐ False

8. Show how the following transaction would be recorded in the ledger of Abbey Motors, a garage.

Abbey Motors bought cars for re-sale on credit from Car Importers Ltd.

Debit .... Account

Credit .... Account

9. Place a tick (✓) in the appropriate box to indicate the price at which *closing stock* is normally valued.

Cost Price ☐
Selling Price ☐
Replacement Price ☐
The lowest of the above prices (i.e. cost, selling or replacement) ☐

10. Give two advantages of Bar Codes.

1. Quick reference to price

2. no need to stamp everything

11. In the space provided, write the names of the currencies used in the following countries.

Country	Currency
Portugal	
England	Sterling
Greece	
Netherlands	

12. The following sign was displayed in a shop.

No cheques accepted
under any circumstances.

(a) Is this sign legal (Yes or No)

(b) Give a reason for your answer.

13. Column 1 is a list of day books.
Column 2 is a list of source documents.

Match the two lists by placing the letter of the correct document under the number of the relevant day book.
(One source document does not apply.)

Column 1. Day Books	Column 2. Source Documents
1 Sales Book	**A** Copy of Credit Notes issued to customers
2 Purchases Returns Book	**B** Copy of receipts issued to customers
3 Sales Returns Book	**C** Credit Notes received from suppliers
4 Cheque Payments Book	**D** Counterfoil of cheque book
	E Copy of Invoices issued to customers

1	2	3	4
A	C	E	D

14. Name four Commercial Banks operating in Ireland.

1. AIB
2. Bank Of Ireland
3. Ulster Bank
4. TBS

15. Name two costs other than price involved in buying a house.

1. Mortage
2. Insurance

16.

Balance Sheet as at 31/12/96

	IR£	IR£
Fixed Assets		220,000
Current Assets	80,000	
Current Liabilities	75,000	
		5,000
		225,000
Financed by:		
Ordinary Shares	150,000	
Revenue Reserves	50,000	
Term Loan		200,000
		25,000
		225,000

(a) What is the figure for Retained Profits?

Answer 225,000

(b) If the net profit for the year was IR£45,000 calculate the percentage return on Capital Employed on 31/12/96.

Workings

Answer

17. Indicate, by means of a tick (✓), whether or not the following statements are true or false.

	True	False
(a) In deferred payments the purchaser does not become the owner until the last instalment is paid.	☐	☐
(b) A firm's credit customers (buyers) are called its debtors.	☐	☐

18. Indicate, by means of a tick (✓), the correct answer to the following.
The surrender value of a life assurance policy is:

(*a*) the capital sum received when the policy matures ☐
(*b*) the amount the insured received if he/she has an accident ☐
(*c*) the money value of the policy if cashed in before maturity ☐
(*d*) the profit earned by the policy over the life of the policy. ☐

19. Trading A/C for year ending 31/12/93.

	IR£	IR£
Sales		60,000
Opening Stock	5,000	
+ Purchases	—	
	54,000	
less Closing Stock	6,000	
Cost of Sales		48,000
Gross Profit		12,000

Calculate:

(*a*) Purchases figure omitted above.

Answer ☐

(*b*) Mark up (percentage).

Answer ☐

Workings

20. You are anxious to telephone a friend who lives in St. Moritz in Switzerland. Your friend's local number is 77793.

With the help of the following information taken from the telephone directory, write out in full the numbers to be dialled by you.

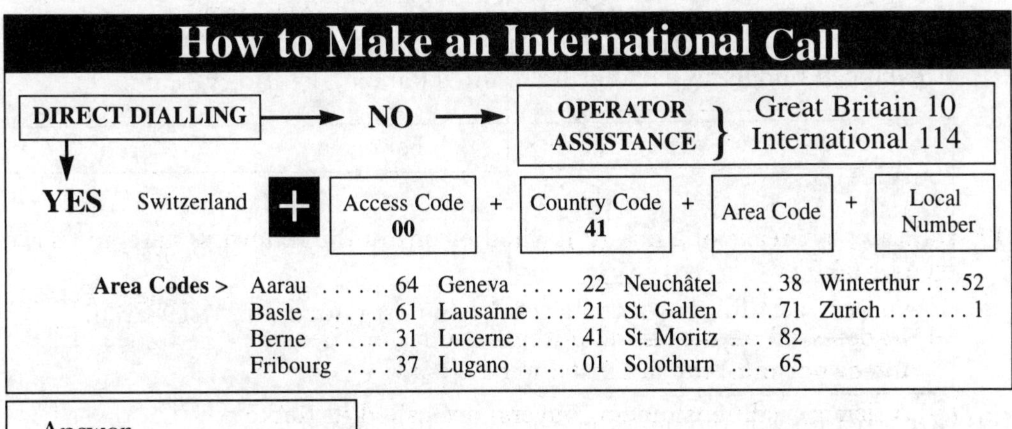

Answer

For use with Question 1. Section B.

1. Personal Budget for the O'Malley household

	Jan	Feb	Mar	Total Jan-Mar	Estimate Apr-Dec	Total for year Jan-Dec
PLANNED INCOME	IR£	IR£	IR£	IR£	IR£	IR£
Enda O'Malley – Salary	560	560	560	1,680		
Grainne O'Malley – Salary	580	580	580	1,740		
Child Benefit	40	40	40	120		
TOTAL INCOME	**1,180**	**1,180**	**1,180**	**3,540**		
PLANNED EXPENDITURE						
Fixed						
House Mortgage	320	320	320	960		
Car Insurance	270	-	-	270		
Annual Car Tax	180	-	-	180		
House Insurance	15	15	15	45		
Subtotal	**785**	**335**	**335**	**1,455**		
Irregular						
Household Expenses	480	480	480	1,440		
Car Running Costs	60	60	60	180		
Light and Heat Costs	-	75	-	75		
Telephone	90	-	90	180		
Subtotal	**630**	**615**	**630**	**1,875**		
Discretionary						
Presents	-	-	40	40		
Entertainment	40	55	35	130		
Holidays						
Subtotal	**40**	**55**	**75**	**170**		
TOTAL EXPENDITURE	**1,455**	**1,005**	**1,040**	**3,500**		
Net Cash	-275	175	140	40		
Opening Cash	100	-175	-	100		
Closing Cash	-175	-	140	140		

For use with Question 1 (B) in Section B.

(i) Indicate by means of a tick (✓) if the O'Malley family had a surplus, deficit, or balanced budget in each of the months January, February, March.

	January	February	March
Surplus	....	....	....
Deficit	....	....	....
Balanced	....	....	....

(ii) How much cash did they save, in total, from 1st January to 31st March?

Answer

(iii) Give a reason why the house mortgage costs declined. ....
....

AN ROINN OIDEACHAIS

JUNIOR CERTIFICATE EXAMINATION, 1997

BUSINESS STUDIES – HIGHER LEVEL – PAPER I
SECTION B
(160 Marks)

WEDNESDAY, 18 JUNE – MORNING 9.30 to 12.00

All questions carry equal marks. Attempt any **FOUR** questions.
Marks will be awarded for layout and presentation. Calculators may be used.

1. Answer (A) and (B). This is a Household Budget Question.

(A) At the end of Section A is a partially completed Personal Budget form for the O'Malley family for 1997.

You are required to complete this form by filling in the figures for the "**Estimate April to December**" column, and the "**Total for year**" column. The following information should be taken into account.

- Edna O'Malley is due a salary increase of 5% from July 1st 1997.
- Grainne O'Malley expects to earn an extra IR£100 per month in November and December 1997.
- Child benefit will increase by IR£10 per month from October 1st 1997.
- House mortgage is expected to decrease by IR£50 per month from November 1st 1997.
- House insurance, payable monthly, will continue as for the first 3 months of the year.
- Household costs, per month, are expected to remain the same for each month until September and to increase by IR£40 a month beginning in October 1997.
- Car running costs are expected to remain at IR£60 a month with an additional car service cost of IR£70 each in June and December 1997.
- ESB for the 12 months (Jan-Dec '97) is estimated at IR£460.
- The telephone bill is paid every second month and it is estimated that the cost will remain the same as at the beginning of the year.
- Christmas presents are expected to cost IR£230 in December 1997.
- Entertainment is estimated at IR£750 for the twelve months (Jan.–Dec. 1997).
- The family holiday in August 1997 is expected to cost IR£1,000. **(30)**

(B) Answer the following questions in the space provided at the end of Section A (page 10).

(i) Did the O'Malley family have a surplus, deficit or balanced budget in each of the months January, February, March?
(ii) How much cash did they save, in total, from 1st January to 31st March?
(iii) Give a reason why the house mortgage costs declined. **(10)**

(40 marks)

2. Answer all sections. This is a Banking Question.

Bríd O'Mara has a current account with the Ulster Bank. She received this bank statement on 31st March 1997.

Statement of Account with

ULSTER BANK LIMITED
Celbridge Branch, Co. Kildare

Account Holder
Bríd O'Mara
Oak Lawn
Celbridge.

Branch Code: 91–63–24
Account No.: 473815
Type of Account: Current
Statement No.: 73

Date	Particulars		Debit	Credit	Balance
1997					
1 Mar.	Balance forward				157 DR
9 Mar.	Cheque	454	84		241 DR
10 Mar.	Lodgement			879	638
11 Mar.	A.T.M.		59		579
13 Mar.	Cheque	452	124		455
16 Mar.	S.O. E.B.S.		118		337
18 Mar.	Credit Transfer			93	430
22 Mar.	D./D. Telecom		57		373
25 Mar	Cheque	455	88		285
30 Mar.	Current A/C fees		8		277
31 Mar.	Interest		6		271

Study this statement and answer the following questions.

(A) Explain what is meant by DR on 1st March. **(3)**

(B) Explain the appearance of interest on the Bank Statement on the 31st March. **(3)**

(C) Name one use for each of the following:
(i) A.T.M. Card.
(ii) Cheque Card. **(6)**

(D) Bríd O'Mara's employment has offered to pay her salary using Paypath. Explain what his means and give one advantage of it to her. **(6)**

(E) The following is Bríd's own account of her bank transactions. Compare this Bank Account/Cash Book with the Bank Statement she received from the bank and answer (i) and (ii) below.

Bank Account/Cash Book

	F	£			Chq. No.	F	£
Mar 7 Salary		879	Mar 1	Balance			157
Mar 31 Sale of Bicycle		45	Mar 5	T Nolan Plumber	452		124
			Mar 6	Foley's Hardware	453		87
			Mar 8	Car Repairs	454		84
			Mar 11	ATM Groceries			59
			Mar 16	S.O. E.B.S.			118
			Mar 21	Insurance	455		88
			Mar 31	Balance		c/d	207
		924					924
Mar 31 Balance	b/d	207					

(i) Make whatever adjustments are necessary to Bríd's own records in your answer book to update her Bank account/Cash Book.
(ii) Prepare a Bank Reconciliation Statement at the 31st March 1997. **(22)**

(40 marks)

3. **Answer (A) and (B). This is a Club Account Question.**

Killinane Drama Society gives two public performances each year at Easter and November.

On the 1st January 1996 it had an overdraft of IR£379 in the Bank. The following extracts show the **totals** of the Cash Received and Lodgement Book and the Cheque Payments Book for the year ending 31/12/96.

Analysed Cash Receipts and Lodgement Book

Date	Particulars	Total Bank	Raffle	Concert	Refreshments	Subscriptions
31/12/96	Total	3,637	933	2,057	247	400

Analysed Cheque Payments Book

Date	Particulars	Total Bank	Advertising	Refreshments	Rent	Travel	Equipment
31/12/96	Total	2,641	193	152	340	156	1,800

The following additional information is available at the end of the financial year:

(i) Subscriptions due IR£45
(ii) Rent due IR£160
(iii) Advertising prepaid IR£69

Assume you are the treasurer finalising the accounts for the A.G.M.

(A) Prepare
(i) a Receipts and Payments Account **(13)**
and
(ii) an Income and Expenditure Account for the year ending 31/12/96 from the information above. **(15)**

(B) (i) Name **one type** of insurance which the society should take out before organising a public performance. **(3)**
(ii) Name **three items** which would normally be listed on the agenda for the Annual General Meeting of a club/society. **(9)**
(40 marks)

4. This a Cost of Borrowing and Report Writing Question.

Na Fianna Sports Club, Clonkeen, Co. Kerry, has one hundred members. It is considering the purchase of a new grass mower which has a retail price of IR£7,000. The club has got very little money to invest in it.

David Donnelly, the club's treasurer, approached Money Matters Ltd, Ballyvourney, Co. Cork, to investigate the sources and costs of a IR£7,000 load to purchase the mower.

Ciara O'Mahony, Financial Consultant, working at Money Matters Ltd, investigated and came up with the following alternatives:

Option 1. Bank loan. Borrow IR£7,000 for 3 years on which interest is charged at a flat rate of 11% per annum. The loan and interest would be repaid in six equal half yearly instalments.

Option 2. Hire Purchase. Pay a deposit of IR£500 plus 36 monthly instalments of IR£270 each.

Option 3. Rental Purchase. Pay a monthly rental of IR£190 each month for 4 years plus a final payment of IR£99 at the end of the lease to acquire ownership of the item.

(A) Calculate the total cost of each option. Show workings. **(12)**

On the 20th May 1997 the consultant wrote a report to the treasurer of the club, showing the total cost of each option and recommended the cheapest one. The consultant also suggested in the report that the club should organise some fund raising activity. The money raised could be used to finance future capital expenditure.

(B) Write the report which the consultant sent to the club's treasurer. **(20)**

(C) (i) Name two ways by which the club could raise IR£2,000 per annum, to be set aside for the future.
(ii) If the club managed to raise IR£5,000 from its fund raising activity and wished to invest it for 5 years, name a suitable investment for the club and give a reason for your choice. **(8)**
(40 Marks)

5. Answer all sections. This is a Question on Factors of Production, Local Government and Balance of Payments.

(A) (i) Name three factors of production other than land. **(3)**
(ii) Explain briefly what is meant in economic terms by the term **land** and give two examples. **(9)**
(iii) Name two services provided by local councils/corporations. **(6)**
(iv) Name two sources of income for local councils/corporations. **(6)**

(B) The following data relates to the international trade of a country called Somore for the year 1996.

Consumer goods sold abroad by Somore firms	£800 Million
Income from foreign tourists visiting Somore	£502 Million
Prize money earned by horses from Somore racing abroad	£2 million
Capital goods bought from foreign countries by Somore firms	£1,100 Million
Payments to foreign pop stars for performing in Somore	£4 Million

From the above information calculate the following trade figures in relation to Somore and state whether they are a surplus or a deficit. Show your workings.
(i) Balance of Trade. **(4)**
(ii) Net earnings from invisible trade. **(5)**
(iii) Balance of Payments on current account. **(4)**
(iv) Explain what is meant by Capital goods and give an example. **(3)**

(40 Marks)

6. This is an Information Technology and Leasing Question.

Sharon Burke is the owner of a small business. She has little knowledge of computers but has recently done some **desk research** on them and their workings. She is confused with some of the terminology/terms used and requests your help and advice.

(A) (i) Explain what is meant by the underlined words above.
(ii) Explain the difference between **hardware** and **software**. **(10)**

(B) What is the function of computer **input devices**? Give two examples of them. **(9)**

(C) Name two important technical factors (excluding price) which a computer owner should take into consideration when selecting a program for a computer. **(6)**

(D) What type of computer programs are required to undertake the following tasks?
(i) Information storing.
(ii) Budgets and accounts. **(6)**

(E) Sharon was offered a new computer by her local supplier of office equipment at a cash price of IR£9,500 or a leasing arrangement at a cost of IR£1,200 per annum.
(i) Name two advantages to Sharon of leasing rather than purchasing the computer.
(ii) If Sharon leased it, would this expense be considered a revenue or a capital expense? **(9)**

(40 Marks)

AN ROINN OIDEACHAIS

JUNIOR CERTIFICATE EXAMINATION, 1997

BUSINESS STUDIES – HIGHER LEVEL – PAPER II

(160 Marks)

WEDNESDAY, 18 JUNE – AFTERNOON, 2.00 to 4.00

All questions carry equal marks. Attempt any **FOUR** questions.
Marks will be awarded for layout and presentation including where appropriate Folios and Dates showing the day, month and year.
Calculators may be used.

1. **Answer ALL sections. This is a Book of First Entry and Ledger Question.**
The books of REPAP Ltd. showed the following balances on 1st May, 1997:

	IR£
Buildings	120,000
Creditor: Cover Ltd.	12,400

(A) Enter these balances in the GENERAL JOURNAL, find the ORDINARY SHARE CAPITAL balance and post these balances to the ledgers. **(8)**

(B) Post the relevant figures from the Purchases Book and Sales Book below to the ledgers.

PURCHASES BOOK (Page 1)

DATE	DETAILS	INVOICE No.	F	NET	VAT	TOTAL
7/5/1997	Cover Ltd.	56	CL2	24,000	5,040	29,040

SALES DAY BOOK

DATE	DETAILS	INVOICE No.	F	NET	VAT	TOTAL
2/5/1997	Copy Ltd.	34	DL4	17,000	3,570	20,570

(8)

(C) Record the following Bank Transactions for the month of May. Post relevant figures to the ledger.
Note: Analyse the transactions using the following money column headings:
Debit (Receipts) side: Bank; Sales; VAT; Debtors.
Credit (Payments) side: Bank; Purchases; VAT; Creditors; Advertising

3/5/1997 Cash Sales lodged IR£43,660 (IR£36,000 + IR£7,660 VAT)
6/5/1997 Paid advertising (cheque No. 1) IR£2,300
9/5/1997 Paid Cover Ltd (cheque No. 2) IR£20,400
23/5/1997 Purchases for resale (cheque No. 3) IR£16,000 + VAT 21%
29/5/1997 Copy Ltd. paid its account in full and it was lodged (receipt No. 35) **(17)**

(D) Balance the accounts on the 31st May, 1997 and extract a Trial Balance as on that date. **(7)**

(40 Marks)

2. Answer ALL sections. This is an Integrated Business Documents Question.

(A) What is the purpose of a Delivery Docket? **(5)**

(B) Sam Electric Ltd. sold the following goods on credit to Tap Ltd., 9 High St., Cavan.
15 Ever Brown Toasters;
22 Deep Fat Friers;
50 Sony Walkmans;

Sam Electric Ltd. prepared a Delivery Docket for these goods on the 21st May, 1997, and this was signed on behalf of Tap Ltd. by Phil Tap.

Complete this Delivery Docket, including the signature, on the blank delivery document, on the separate sheet, supplied with this paper. **(6)**

(C) On checking the goods a day later, Phil Tap found that ten of the Deep Fat Friers, costing IR£40 **each**, were leaking. Sam Electric Ltd., on being informed, agreed to issue a Credit Note No. 45 for the damaged goods on the 24th May, 1997. Trade Discount was 25% and VAT was 21%. Complete the Credit Note No. 23 sent by Sam Electric Ltd. on the 24th May, 1997, on the blank credit note document, supplied with this paper. **(10)**

(D) Record the credit note sent by Sam Electric Ltd. in the Sales Return Book and in the Sales Returns, VAT, and Tap Ltd. accounts, on the blank bookkeeping sheet, supplied with this paper. **(19)**

(40 marks)

3. Answer (A) and (B). This is a Final Accounts and Balance Sheet Question.

The following Trial Balance was extracted from the books of EURO Ltd. on the 31st May, 1997. The Authorised Share Capital is 250,000 IR£1 ordinary shares.

(A) You are required to prepare the company's Trading, Profit and Loss and Appropriation Accounts for the year ended 31 May, 1997 and a Balance Sheet as at that date.

	DR. IR£	**CR IR£**
Purchases and Sales	99,000	167,400
Sales returns and Purchases returns	6,500	4,100
Issued Share Capital 195,000 IR£1 shares		195,000
Repairs	3,400	
Carriage Inwards	1,800	
Advertising	7,000	
Machinery	190,000	
Debtors and Creditors	16,000	19,000
Rent Receivable		18,000
Motor Vans	120,000	
Cash	800	
Bank Overdraft		2,100
Opening Stock 1/6/1996	17,000	
Long Term Loan		60,000
Reserves (Profit and Loss Balance)		17,400
Wages	21,500	
	483,000	483,000

You are given the following information as at 31st May, 1997.

(i) Closing Stock IR£14,000;
(ii) Dividends declared 8%
(iii) Rent receivable prepaid IR£1,000;
(iv) Advertising prepaid IR£2,600;
(v) Depreciation: Machinery 6%; Motor Vans 10%. **(35)**

(B) EURO Ltd. is a sports equipment company. List two types of advertising it could use to advertise its products, and in each case give your reason. **(5)**

(40 marks)

4. Answer (A) and (B). This is a Question about Assessing the Performance of a business.

(A) Explain **two** limitations of Final Accounts and Balance Sheets in assessing a business. **(8)**

(B) Examine the Final Accounts and Balance Sheets of Buz Ltd., set out below, for the years 1995 and 1996. **Compare** and comment on the performance of the company for the two years using the following ratios:

(i) Gross Profit Margin; (ii) Return on Capital Employed;
(iii) Acid Test (quick) ratio; (iv) Rate of Dividend paid.

Show workings.

1995 Trading, Profit and Loss and Appropriation Account for the year ended 31/5/1995		**1996** Trading, Profit and Loss and Appropriation Account for the year ended 31/5/1996	
	IR£		**IR£**
Sales	190,000	Sales	230,000
Gross Profit	75,000	Gross Profit	82,000
Net Profit	43,000	Net Profit	55,000
Dividends Paid	14,300	Dividends Paid	16,900
Reserves	28,700	Reserves	38,100

Balance Sheet as at 31/5/1995			**Balance Sheet as at 31/5/1996**		
	IR£	IR£		IR£	IR£
Fixed Assets		180,000	Fixed Assets		198,000
Current Assets (including Closing Stock IR£7,000)	25,700		Current Assets (including Closing Stock IR£5,300)	36,800	
Less Current Liabilities	17,000	8,700	Less Current Liabilities	18,000	18,800
		188,700			216,800
Financed By			Financed By		
130,000 IR£1 Ordinary Shares		130,000	130,000 IR£1 Ordinary Shares		130,000
Reserves		28,700	Reserves		66,800
Long Term Liabilities		30,000	Long Term Liabilities		20,000
		188,700			216,800

(32)

(40 marks)

5. Answer ALL sections. This is a Distribution of Goods/Cost of Transport Question.

(A) (i) What is meant by the term Channels of Distribution?
(ii) Describe (illustrate) **three** channels of distribution and give an example of a good distributed by each channel. **(16)**

(B) Transport is very important in the distribution of goods.
Explain **three** factors that should be taken into account when deciding on the type of delivery system to be used by a business. **(9)**

(C) What is the name given to the Cost of Delivering goods in the accounts of a business? **(3)**

(D) Champ Ltd., Sligo, asks you to calculate the total cost of a journey (round trip) from Sligo to Dublin and back again to Sligo on the 29th May, 1997 from the following data:

The distance from Sligo to Dublin is 217KM;
The diesel van can do 14KM per litre of diesel;
The cost of diesel is 50p per litre;
The van driver's wages are IR£75 per day;
The Annual Motor Tax is IR£450;
The Annual Motor Insurance is IR£1,200;
The Annual Repairs are IR£600. **(12)**

Champ Ltd., **operates 300 working days in the year.** **(40 marks)**

6. Answer ALL sections. This is an Integrated Question on Farm Accounts/Co-operatives.

(A) List **four** reasons why farmers should keep accounts. **(8)**

(B) Dinny and Teasie own a farm in Wicklow and have a balance of IR£3,500 in the bank on 1 May, 1997. They ask you to help them write up their Analysed Cash Book (Analysed Receipts and Payments Book) for the month of May, 1997 from the data below:

Use the following money column headings:

Debit (Receipts) side: Bank; Sheep; Cattle; Grants; Other.
Credit (Payments) side: Bank; Feed; Fertiliser; Cattle; Vet; Expenses.

2/5/1997	Paid the vet	(cheque No. 11)	IR£130
5/5/1997	Sale of sheep	(cheque No. 2)	IR£1,600
8/5/1997	Purchased calves	(cheque No. 12)	IR£1,500
12/5/1997	Received EU Grant		IR£2,000
13/5/1997	Purchased fertiliser	(cheque No. 13)	IR£400
16/5/1997	Purchased feed	(cheque No. 14)	IR£200
19/5/1997	Paid ESB	(cheque No. 15)	IR£165
21/5/1997	Sold cattle	(receipt No. 3)	IR£3,000
24/5/1997	Paid insurance	(cheque No. 16)	IR£460
27/5/1997	Received a loan		IR£12,000
28/5/1997	Paid contractor	(cheque No. 17)	IR£18,500
30/5/1997	Purchased tractor	(cheque No. 18)	IR£5,700
31/5/1997	Sold cattle	(receipt No. 4)	IR£6,900
31/5/1997	Sale of vegetables	(receipt No. 5)	IR£145 **(23)**

(C) Dinny and Teasie were advised that they should join a local co-operative.
(i) Explain briefly what a co-operative is, and give an example of one.
(ii) State **three** advantages of joining a co-operative. **(9)**

(40 marks)

BUSINESS STUDIES – PAPER II, 1997

EXAMINATION NUMBER . . . .

For use with Question 2(B)

DELIVERY DOCKET **No: 34**
SAM ELECTRIC Ltd.
TRALEE
CO. KERRY

Tel: (066) 434317
VAT Reg. IE 343457

ORDER No. 200 **Date** . . . .

To: . . . .
. . . .
. . . .

Quantity	**Description**

Received the above goods in good condition.

Signed . . . .

For Purchaser

REMEMBER TO RETURN THIS SHEET WITH YOUR ANSWER BOOK.

BUSINESS STUDIES – PAPER II, 1997
EXAMINATION NUMBER . . . .

For use with Question 2(C)

CREDIT NOTE No: 23

SAM ELECTRIC Ltd.
TRALEE
CO. KERRY

Tel: (066) 434317
VAT Reg. IE 343457

To: . . . .
. . . .
. . . .

Date . . . .

ORDER No. 200

Quantity	Description	Unit Price IR£	Total (Ex. VAT) IR£
		Total (Ex. VAT)	
		Less: Trade Discount	
		Add VAT:	
E & O E		TOTAL	

For use with Question 2(D)

SALES RETURNS DAY BOOK (page 9)

Date	Details	Credit Note No.	F	Net	VAT	Total

SALES RETURNS A/C (page 2)

Date	Details	F	IR£	Date	Details	F	IR£

VAT A/C (page) 3

Date	Details	F	IR£	Date	Details	F	IR£

TAP Ltd. A/C (page 4)

Date	Details	F	IR£	Date	Details	F	IR£

WARNING

You must return this paper with your answerbook, otherwise marks will be lost.

Write your Examination Number here

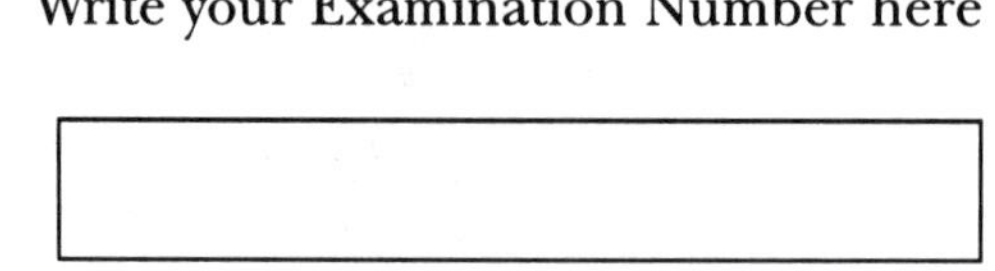

AN ROINN OIDEACHAIS
JUNIOR CERTIFICATE EXAMINATION, 1996

BUSINESS STUDIES — HIGHER LEVEL — PAPER I
SECTION A
(80 MARKS)

WEDNESDAY, 12 June — MORNING, 9.30 to 12.00

Answer all 20 questions. Each question carries 4 marks. Calculators may be used.
Please enclose this section in your Answer Book.

1. Complete the organisational chart below by writing in the appropriate terms in the blank spaces marked A and B.

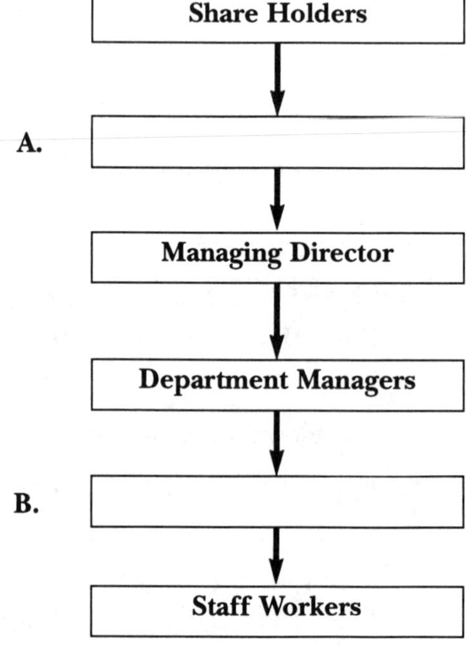

2. Tick (√) the correct answer.

Which of the business firms listed below would have the highest stock turnover?

Jeweller ☐ Newsagent ☐

Draper ☐ Pharmacy ☐

3. The following is an extract from Bus Éireann's timetable.

Table No. 115

GALWAY — LIMERICK — KERRY

EXPRESSWAY SERVICE

	MONDAYS TO SATURDAYS											SUNDAYS							
								FO											
Galway (Railway Stn.) .... dep.	09.00	11.15	11.15	15.15	15.15	....	18.00	18.00	....	....	....	....	11.15	16.15	16.45	16.45	18.00	20.30	....
Limerick (Railway Stn.) .... arr.	10.55	13.10	13.10	17.10	17.10	..	20.00	20.00	..	..	..	..	13.10	17.10	18.40	18.40	20.05	..	..
Limerick (Railway Stn.)............... dep.	11.25	13.30	13.30	17.35	17.35	....	....	....	....	....	....	....	13.30	....	19.00	19.00	....	....	....
Limerick (Todds)........................ dep.	..	..	..	..	..	..	21.00	21.00	..	..	..	..	..	..	..	..	21.30	22.25	..
Tralee (Railway Stn.).................... arr.	13.40	....	15.45	19.50	....	....	23.00	....	....	....	....	....	15.30	....	21.00	....	23.30	00.25	....
Tralee (Railway Stn.).................. dep.	..	..	..	..	..	..	..	..	..	..	..	..	15.30	..	..	..	..	..	..
Castleisland (Main St.) .... dep.	....	15.15	....	....	19.25	....	....	22.35	....	....	....	....	....	....	....	20.35	....	....	....
Killarney (Bus Stn.) .... arr.	..	15.40	..	..	19.50	..	..	23.00	..	..	..	..	16.05	..	..	21.00	..	..	..
Killorglin (Library) .... arr.	....	16.15	....	....	20.20	....	....	....	....	....	....	....	....	....	....	21.30	....	....	....
	MO							☐1	FO		☐								
Killorglin (Library) .... dep.	....	..	..	08.15	..	12.00	..	..	..	..	..	..	..	..	14.45	..	..	17.30	..
Killarney (Bus Stn.)..................... dep.	06.30	....	....	08.55	....	12.40	....	14.45	14.45	17.10	17.50	08.15	....	11.45	15.25	....	....	18.00	....
Castleisland (Main St.) .... dep.	06.55	..	..	09.20	..	13.05	..	15.10	15.10	..	18.15	..	..	12.10	15.50	..	..	18.25	..
Tralee (Railway Stn.).................... arr.	....	....	.....	....	....	....	....	....	....	17.45	....	08.50	....	....	....	....	....	....	....
Tralee (Railway Stn.).................. dep.	..	06.30	08.55	..	12.40	..	14.45	..	..	17.50	..	08.55	11.45	..	..	15.30	..	..	18.00
Limerick (Railway Stn.) .... arr.	08.50	08.50	11.10	11.10	14.55	14.55	16.50	16.50	16.50	20.00	20.00	11.10	14.00	14.00	17.30	17.30	....	20.00	20.00
Limerick (Railway Stn.)............... dep.	09.00	09.00	11.35	11.35	15.05	15.05	17.35	17.35	17.35	20.15	20.15	11.35	14.05	14.05	17.30	17.30	19.05	20.20	20.20
Galway (Railway Stn.)................. arr.	11.15	11.15	13.40	13.40	17.00	17.00	19.30	19.30	19.30	22.10	22.10	13.40	16.00	16.00	19.30	19.30	21.00	22.15	22.15

☐ :– Summer only service; operates 27th June to 27th August 1994. ☐1 :– Summer only service; operates 30th May to 24th September 1994.

FO:– Fridays only. MO :– Mondays only.

PASSENGERS CHANGE COACHES AT LIMERICK.

SEE TABLE 110 FOR DETAILS OF SEASONAL SERVICES BETWEEN GALWAY AND KERRY VIA KILLIMER/TARBERT FERRY.

With the help of the timetable above, answer the following:

(a) At what time does the first bus, destined for Killarney, leave Galway on Wednesday?

Answer ....

(b) At what time is the first bus from Galway expected to arrive in Killarney?

Answer ....

4. Name two forms of business ownership in which the owners have limited liability.

Answer 1. ....

Answer 2. ....

5. The following is an extract from a Profit and Loss account of a firm for the year ending 31/12/1995.

Dr.	Profit & Loss Account		Cr.
Insurance	560		
Less insurance pre-paid	160		
		400	

(a) What is the figure for insurance used during the year?
Answer. . . . .

(b) What is the figure for insurance paid during the year?
Answer . . . .

6. **Column 1** is a list of business terms. **Column 2** is a list of possible explanations for these terms.

Match the two lists by placing the letter of the correct explanation under the relevant number below (one explanation does not refer to any of the terms).

Column 1 Terms
1. Fastrack
2. FAX
3. Eircell
4. Aertel

Column 2 Terms
A. A service for the instant transmission of an exact copy of a document
B. Information service provided by RTE.
C. Mobile phone service provided by Telecom.
D. Fast delivery service provided by An Post.
E. Delivery service provided by Irish Rail.

1	2	3	4

7. Áine had 30p pocket money and was undecided whether to spend it on an orange or a bar of chocolate. She eventually bought the orange.

(a) What was the opportunity cost involved? . . . .
. . . .

(b) What was the financial cost involved? . . . .
. . . .

8. The following account appeared in your creditors ledger.

D. Nolan's Account

Dr.							Cr.
May 6	Bank	C.B.	580	May 1	Balance	b/d	460
				May 4	Purchase	P/B	370

Rewrite D. Nolan's account in continuous balance form below.

D. Nolan's Account

Date	Particulars		Dr.	Cr.	Balance
May 1	Balance				460
May 4	Purchases	P.B.			
May 6	Bank	C.B.			

9. Name two laws or Acts which protect consumers' rights.

1. ....
2. ....

10. The following figures appeared in a firm's final accounts for the year ending 31/12/95.

Sales	300,000
Total expenses	60,000
Net Profit	40,000

(a) Calculate the gross profit for the year. Answer ....

(b) Calculate the percentage Net Margin. Answer ....

Workings

11. For each item listed below, tick (√) the appropriate box to show whether it would be classified as revenue or capital expenditure for a grocery business.

	Revenue Expenditure	**Capital Expenditure**
Purchase of Stock	....	....
Paid Wages	....	....
Shop Extension	....	....
Repaid Bank Loan	....	....

12. Write a brief note on:

(a) Mail-merge ....
....
....

(b) RAM ....
....
....

13. In the space provided, name the two accounts affected by the following transaction in the ledger of Mary Kelly, a retail grocer.

Mary Kelly sold equipment on credit to Gromore Ltd for £3,000.

Debit .... account

Credit .... account

14. Explain the purpose of each of the following in book-keeping?

Trial Balance: ....
....

Folio: ....
....

15. Tick (√) the correct answer below.

The payment of creditors by cash effects the Balance Sheet in one of the following ways:

(i) Current Assets increases and Current Liabilities increases ☐
(ii) Current Assets decreases and Current Liabilities decreases ☐
(iii) Current Assets increases and Current Liabilities decreases ☐

16. The following initials appeared on your bank statement. What do they stand for?

OD ....
S O ....
D D ....
C/T ....

17. The following is a summary of the Balance Sheet of CBA Ltd.

Balance Sheet as at 31/3/96

Fixed Assets		40,000
Current Assets	15,000	
Current Liabilities	18,000	
		– 3,000
		37,000
Financed by	Authorised	Issued
Ordinary Share	40,000	30,000
Reserve		(– 9,000)
		21,000
Long Term Liabilities		16,000
		37,000

Tick (√) the correct answer.

(a) Is the firm solvent? Yes ☐ No ☐
(b) Is the firm liquid? Yes ☐ No ☐

18. Tick (√) the correct answer below.

The capital of a club is called

Excess of Income ☐
Net Assets ☐
Accumulated Fund ☐
Liquid Capital ☐

19. Place a tick (√) opposite each statement to indicate whether it is true or false.

	True	False
(a) The PAYE tax year starts on 6 April	☐	☐
(b) The Government's financial year begins on 1 January	☐	☐

20. A sales agent for a product had total sales for the year £240,000.

The pie chart shows the breakdown of sales for the seasons.

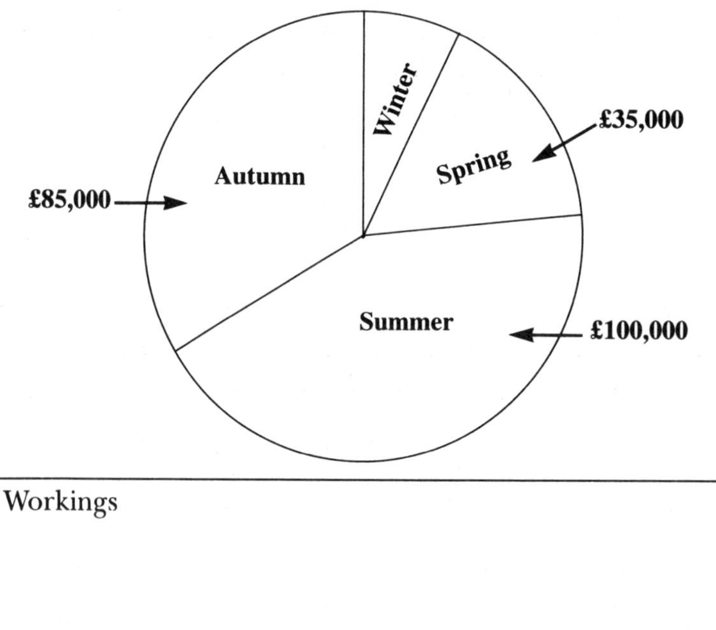

Workings

(a) What percentage of total sales were in winter?

Answer . . . .

(b) Name a product which might have a similar yearly sales cycle as the product sold by this agent.

Answer . . . .

REMEMBER TO RETURN THIS SECTION A WITH YOUR ANSWER BOOK.

Document for use in Question 1 — Section B

	BUDGET				REVISED BUDGET			
	APRIL	MAY	JUNE	TOTAL	APRIL	MAY	JUNE	TOTAL
INCOME								
Mr O'Mara Wage	900	900	900	2,700				
Mrs O'Mara Wage	595	595	595	1,785				
Child Benefit	25	25	25	75				
Total Income	1,520	1,520	1,520	4,560				
EXPENDITURE								
Fixed								
Car Loan	240	240	240	720				
Car Insurance			205	205				
Car Tax	220			220				
House Insurance		75		75				
Video/TV								
Sub Total	**460**	**315**	**445**	**1,220**				
Irregular								
House Keeping	600	600	600	1,800				
Car Running Costs	125	125	125	375				
ESB	105		85	190				
Telephone		130		130				
Sub Total	**830**	**855**	**810**	**2,495**				
Discretionary								
Holidays	75	75	75	225				
Entertainment	60	60	60	180				
Birthdays/Presents		60		60				
Sub Total	**135**	**195**	**135**	**465**				
Savings	120	120	120	360				
Total Expenditure Including Savings	**1,545**	**1,485**	**1,510**	**4,540**				
Net Cash	**–25**	**35**	**10**	**20**				
Opening Cash	**180**	**155**	**190**	**180**				
Closing Cash	**155**	**190**	**200**	**200**				

Document for use in answering Question 2 — Section B

Week 5 NAME	GROSS PAY Basic	O/Time	Total	Tax Free Allow.	PAYE	PRSI	UNION	VHI	Total Deductions	NET PAY

(iii) **Document for use in answering Question 3 — Section B**

Petty Cash Voucher

No. 23 . . Date: . . . .

Details	Amount	

Signature: Of Claimant . . . .
Passed by: . . . .

Ledgers for use in answering Question 3 — Section B

Dr. **Postage Account 6** **Cr.**

Date	Details		IR£	Date	Details		IR£

Stationery Account 7

Date	Details		IR£	Date	Details		IR£

Cleanings Account 8

Date	Details		IR£	Date	Details		IR£

Other Expenses Account 9

Date	Details		IR£	Date	Details		IR£

(iv) Where would the Petty Cash balance be shown in the final accounts?
Answer . . . .

REMEMBER TO RETURN THIS SECTION A WITH YOUR ANSWER BOOK.

AN ROINN OIDEACHAIS
JUNIOR CERTIFICATE EXAMINATION, 1996

BUSINESS STUDIES — HIGHER LEVEL — PAPER I
SECTION B
(160 MARKS)

WEDNESDAY, 12 June — MORNING, 9.30 to 12.00

All questions carry equal marks. Attempt any **FOUR** questions.
Marks will be awarded for layout and presentation. Calculators may be used.

1. **Answer (A) and (B). This is a Household Budget Question.**

(A) At the end of Section A of this paper is a completed Budget and a revised Budget form for the O'Mara family from April to June.

After preparing the Budget for April–June the O'Mara family were informed that Mr O'Mara was to go on a three-day week in his employment. This would result in a substantial drop in the family's income. The O'Maras decided to revise their budget in view of the changed circumstances.

(i) You are required to complete the revised budget form taking the following into account.
- Mr O'Mara's wages to be reduced by 40%.
- They decided to install Cablelink TV and rent a video at a monthly cost of £30 to occupy his spare time.
- Car running costs to be reduced by £20 per month.
- Telephone expenses to be reduced to £100 per bill.
- It is decided to omit holiday expenses.
- Savings plan to be abandoned.
- All other income and expenses are to remain the same. **(24)**

(B) (i) If Mr O'Mara had not suffered a drop in income, would you consider the original budget a good one? Give two reasons for your answer. **(7)**

(ii) Is their revised budget a good one to overcome their problem? Give two reasons for your answer. **(6)**

(iii) What alternative action would you suggest? **(3)**

(40 marks)

2. Answer all sections. This is an Employer and Wages Question.

Róisín Maguire's basic pay is IR£195 gross for a 39-hour week. Overtime is paid at time and a half. Her tax free allowances are £90 per week. Her tax rate is 27%, and employee PRSI contribution is 6% of gross. Trade Union subscription of £3 per week and VHI contribution of £6 per week are deducted at source. In week number 5 Róisín worked 45 hours.

(A) (i) Calculate her net pay for the week and complete the pay slip at the end of Section A page 336. **(16)**

(ii) Who decided that Róisín's tax free allowance was £90 per week? **(3)**

(iii) State two benefits she may receive from her PRSI contribution. **(6)**

(B) Róisín has worked with her present employer for the past eight years and is regarded as a very reliable employee. She is now considering setting up her own business.

(i) Name three responsibilities of an employer to an employee. **(9)**

(ii) List two advantages of becoming self-employed. **(6)**

(40 marks)

---

3. This is a Club Account Question.

The Ahalana Golf Club, in addition to using a cheque book, also makes cash payments for small amounts. These cash payments are authorised by the office manageress Orla O'Sullivan and recorded in a Petty Cash Book.

The following cash transactions occurred in the month of April.

April	1	Received imprest for the month £200 cheque		
April	4	Bought typing paper	Voucher No. 21	IR£27
April	6	Bought postage stamps	" No. 22	IR£10
April	7	Refunded the office assistant Aisling Fitzgerald the price of office groceries	" No. 23	IR£3
April	9	Gave donation to charity	" No. 24	IR£5
April	12	Bought cleaning materials	" No. 25	IR£6
April	14	Paid for registered letter	" No. 26	IR£3
April	18	Paid cleaner's wages	" No. 27	IR£25
April	23	Purchased computer paper	" No. 28	IR£15
April	26	Paid for parcel post	" No. 29	IR£3

(i) Complete and balance the Petty Cash Book for the month of April, using the following analysis columns; Postage, Stationery, Cleaning, Other Expenses. **(20)**

(ii) Show the posting of the totals of the analysis columns to their accounts in the ledger. Use the accounts supplied at the end of Section A page 336. **(8)**

(iii) Complete the petty cash voucher used by Aisling Fitzgerald to recoup her expenses of 7 April. Use the blank voucher supplied at the end of Section A page 336. **(10)**

(iv) Answer the following question in the space provided at the end of Section A page 336. (2)
Where would the petty cash balance be shown in the final accounts? **(2)**

(40 marks)

---

4. **Answer (A) and (B). This is a Government Finances Question.**

The following figures were produced by a Minister for Finance on Budget Day as projections for the year.

Main items of expenditure and Revenue	Estimated figures in millions
Debt Servicing	2410
Social Welfare	4290
Corporation Tax	1300
Health Services	2167
VAT	2837
Educational Services	1980
Income Tax	3939
Customs and Excise Duty	2325

(A) (i) From the above information, draft the National Budget current account, showing clearly total income and total expenditure and balance it. Give the correct economic term to the balance in this budget. You may present your answer in vertical or T-shaped form. **(13)**

(ii) Suggest two courses of action which a government could take to rectify a budget deficit. **(6)**

(iii) What effect, if any, has a budget deficit on the National Debt of a country? **(3)**

(iv) Give one example of Government Capital Income. **(3)**

(B) (i) State whether the current budget in Ireland for this year is a:
(a) Balanced budget.
(b) Surplus budget.
(c) Deficit budget. **(3)**

(ii) Name one advantage and one disadvantage which the Irish economy is experiencing at present. **(6)**

(iii) Name two effects which an increase in employment would have on the Irish Government finances/budget. **(6)**

(40 marks)

5. **Answer all sections. This is an Insurance Question.**

Shane O'Neill had his house valued at £50,000 by an engineer. He insured the house and contents against fire only, with his local insurance agent, at an annual cost of £150.

The building was insured for £40,000 and the contents for £12,000. The policy had an excess clause of £100. Fire damaged the house to the value of £10,000.

A. (i) What document should Shane complete when seeking compensation?
(ii) How much compensation would Shane receive assuming the house was worth £50,000? **(9)**

B. Before the next renewal date. Shane was approached by an insurance broker with a proposal form seeking Shane's insurance business. The broker offered Shane comprehensive all-risks cover on the house and its contents at the following rates: Building £2 per £1,000 cover
Contents 30p per £100 cover

Because the house would be unoccupied during the day, there was a loading on the premium for contents of £10 yearly.

(i) Calculate the annual cost of the insurance quoted by the broker if Shane insured the house and its contents for their full value. **(5)**
(ii) Explain the underlined words. **(12)**
(iii) Would you advise Shane to change his insurance business from the agent to the broker? Give two reasons for your answer. **(8)**
(iv) State the difference between an insurance agent and an insurance broker. **(6)**

(40 marks)

---

6. **Answer all parts. This is a Savings and Investments Question.**

A. (i) What is meant by the term *investment*? Give two reasons why people invest. **(7)**
(ii) Name four factors which one would consider when choosing a suitable place to invest one's savings. **(12)**
(iii) Interest earned by money on deposit accounts is subject to tax. What is this tax called? **(3)**

B. (i) John had IR£5,000 invested at 8% simple interest for 2 $^{1}/_{2}$ years in a special savings account which was subject to tax at 10%. Calculate the net interest earned. Show your workings. **(7)**
(ii) Sharon wishes to invest IR£2,000 but needs it six months later for a deposit on a new car. Choose a suitable place for Sharon to invest her IR£2,000 and give two reasons for your answer. **(8)**
(iii) All investment advertisements by financial institutions show the letters C.A.R. What do these letters mean? **(3)**

(40 marks)

AN ROINN OIDEACHAIS
JUNIOR CERTIFICATE EXAMINATION, 1996

BUSINESS STUDIES — HIGHER LEVEL — PAPER II

(160 MARKS)

WEDNESDAY, 12 June — AFTERNOON, 2.00 to 4.00

All questions carry equal marks. Attempt any **FOUR** questions.
Marks will be awarded for layout and presentation including where appropriate Folios and Dates showing the day, month and year. Calculators may be used.

1. **Answer ALL sections. This is a Book of First Entry and Ledger Question.**

BIA Ltd had the following balances in its General Journal on 1 May 1996:

General Journal (Page 1)

Date	Details	F	Dr. IR£	Cr. IR£
May 1	Bank	GL 1	18,000	
	Debtor — ARK Ltd	DL 1	6,000	
	Ordinary Share Capital	GL 2		24,000
	Assets, Liabilities and Share Capital of BIA Ltd on 1/5/1996		24,000	24,000

(A) Post the balances given in the General Accounts to the relevant accounts. **(5)**
(B) Post the relevant figures from the Sales Book and Sales Returns Book below to the ledgers. **(9)**

SALES DAY BOOK (Page 1)

Date	Details	Invoice No.	F	Net	VAT	Total
				IR£	IR£	IR£
5/5/1996	ARK Ltd	100	DL 1	6,400	800	7,200
7/5/1996	NOAH Ltd	101	DL 2	32,000	4,000	36,000
				38,400	4,800	43,200
				GL 3	GL 4	

SALES RETURNS BOOK (Page 2)

Date	Details	Credit Note No.	F	Net	VAT	Total
20/5/1996	NOAH Ltd	7	DL 2	IR£ 9,000	IR£ 1,125	IR£ 10,125
				GL 5	GL 4	

(C) Record the following Bank transactions for the month of May. Post relevant figures to the ledger.

Note: Analyse the bank transactions using the following money column headings:
Debit (Receipts) Side: Bank; Sales; VAT; Debtor; Ordinary Share Capital.
Credit (Payments) Side: Bank; Purchases; VAT; Insurance.

BANK TRANSACTIONS

4/5/1996	Paid Insurance	(Cheque No. 7)	IR£ 3,500
6/5/1996	Cash sales lodged		IR£47,250 (IR£42,000 + IR£5,250 VAT)
12/5/1996	Purchases for resale	(Cheque No. 8)	IR£21,000 + VAT 12 ½%
21/5/1996	ARK Ltd paid its account in full		(receipt No. 73)
30/5/1996	BIA shareholders invested IR£50,000 and this was lodged.		**(19)**

(D) Balance the accounts on 31 May 1996 and extract a Trial Balance as at that date. **(7)**

(40 marks)

---

2. **Answer ALL sections. This is an Integrated Documents and Bookkeeping Question.**

On 15 March 1996 ADAMS Electrical Ltd, Baggot St, Dublin 2, sent an order No. 5 to STONE Ltd, Electrical Suppliers, Limerick, for the following goods:

12	S.M. Walkmans	@ IR£ 15 each excluding VAT
4	True Colour TVs	@ IR£455 each excluding VAT
8	VJ Video Recorders	@ IR£250 each including VAT

STONE Ltd sent an invoice No. 18 on 22 March 1996.

This invoice, which ADAMS Electrical Ltd received on 23 March 1996, stated that the trade discount would be 25% of the retail price and that the goods would be delivered on 28 March 1996. Electrical goods are subject to VAT at 21%.

Tom Adams sent a cheque No. 39 for the amount due on 25 April 1996.

(A) Outline how STONE Ltd should treat outgoing invoices. **(8)**

(B) Complete the invoice of 22 March 1996 and the cheque and counterfoil of 25 April 1996 on the blank document sheets supplied with this paper. **(19)**

(C) Record the invoice received and the cheque paid in the Purchases Book and Analysed Cash Book of ADAMS Ltd, provided on the separate sheet supplied with this paper. **(13)**

(40 marks)

---

3. **Answer (A) and (B). This is a Final Accounts and Balance Sheet Question.**

The following Trial Balance was extracted from the books of Daly Ltd on 31 May 1996. The Authorised Share Capital is 300,000 IR£1 ordinary shares.

(A) You are required to prepare the company's Trading, Profit and Loss and Appropriation Accounts for the year ended 31 May 1996 and a Balance Sheet as at that date.

	DR. IR£	CR. IR£
Purchases and Sales	86,000	194,000
Wages	24,000	
Debtors and Creditors	26,300	11,600
Equipment	84,000	
Import Duty	7,350	
Sales Returns and Purchases Returns	3,500	4,200
Rent	16,400	
Insurance	6,200	
Interest Receivable		5,600
Cash	1,700	
Bank	7,950	
Motor Vehicles	75,000	
Premises	130,000	
Reserves (Profit and Loss Balance)		16,000
Ordinary Stock 1/6/1995	13,000	
Ordinary Share Capital: 250,000 IR£1 shares		250,000
	481,400	481,400

You are given the following information as at 31 May 1996.

(i) Closing Stock IR£15,500

(ii) Import Duty due IR£450

(iii) Rent prepaid IR£800

(iv) Dividends declared 12%

(v) Depreciation: Equipment 15%; Motor Vehicles 20%. **(35)**

(B) Why is it important for a company to have reserves? **(5)**

(40 marks)

4. Answer ALL sections. This is a Question on Industrial Relations.

(A) The following table shows the number of strikes in Ireland for the period 1990–1994.

YEAR	1990	1991	1992	1993	1994
NUMBER OF STRIKES	49	54	38	48	32

(i) Illustrate the above information on a suitable chart or graph, using the graph supplied with this paper.
(ii) Calculate the average number of strikes for the period 1990–1994.
(iii) In what years were the number of strikes below the average for the period? **(16)**

(B) Give *three* reasons why strikes take place. **(12)**

(C) Study the newspaper report on the right and answer the questions that follow.

(i) What was the dispute about?
(ii) Name the two parties in the dispute.
(iii) What forms of action did the union vote to take?
(iv) How might the dispute be settled? **(12)**

(40 marks)

Agriculture staff vote for action

Members of the Civil and Public Service Union in the offices of the Department of Agriculture have voted by four to one to implement industrial action because of what it calls the Department's breach of an agreement on the employment of temporary staff.

The action includes a ban on overtime, refusal to perform duties appropriate to higher grades and a ban on telephone and public office queries.

---

5. Answer ALL sections. This is an Integrated Delivery Systems/Record-keeping (including Depreciation) Question.

(A) Give two reasons why a business might use its own fleet of delivery vans. **(6)**
(B) List three costs which a business incurs in having its own fleet of delivery vans. **(6)**
(C) Explain briefly three sources of finance which a business could use to purchase delivery vans. **(9)**
(D) On 1 January 1995 JUMBO Ltd purchased a delivery van by cheque for IR£26,000. JUMBO Ltd estimated that the delivery van would have a life of four years and an estimated scrap value of IR£2,000. JUMBO Ltd's trading year ends on 31 December 1995.

(i) Record the purchase of the delivery van on 1/1/1995 and the annual depreciation written off for the year ended 31/12/1995 in the relevant accounts.

(ii) Show the relevant entries in the Profit and Loss Account for the year ended 31/12/1995 and in the Balance Sheet as on 31/12/1995/ **(19)**

(40 marks)

---

6. **Answer ALL sections. This is an Integrated Banking/Recordkeeping Question.**

(A) Explain three services that banks provide for businesses. **(11)**

(B) Private limited companies must supply specific information to a bank when opening a current account. List three of these pieces of information, naming relevant documents. **(6)**

(C) Duffy Ltd opened a current account in the Ulster Bank on 1 May 1996 and lodged IR£700.

The following transactions took place in the month of May.

			IR£
May 2	Paid suppliers by cheque	No. 1	550
6	Purchased stock by cheque	No. 2	360
9	Paid ESB by cheque	No. 3	140
11	Paid insurance by cheque	No. 4	120
16	Cash sales lodged		1,600
19	Paid Jones Ltd by cheque	No. 5	1,900
28	Lodged to account		1,700
30	Paid Telecom by cheque	No. 6	320
31	Cash sales lodged		1,450

Duffy Ltd received the following bank statement on 31/5/1996.

Current Account Bank Statement

Date	Details	DEBIT IR£	CREDIT IR£	BALANCE IR£
1996				
1 May	Lodgment		700	700
5 May	Cheque No. 1	550		150
10 May	Cheque No. 3	140		10
14 May	Cheque No. 4	120		110 O.D.
16 May	Lodgment		1,600	1,490
18 May	Cheque No. 2	360		1,130
24 May	Standing Order	400		730
26 May	Credit Transfer		550	1,280
28 May	Lodgment		1,700	2,980
30 May	Current Account Fees	25		2,955

O.D. = Overdrawn

(i) Prepare Duffy Ltd's Bank Account for the month of May.

(ii) Compare the balance in Duffy Ltd's bank account with that in the bank statement and make whatever adjustments that are necessary to Duffy Ltd's bank account.

(iii) Prepare a Bank Reconciliation Statement as on 31 May 1996. **(23)**

(40 marks)

BUSINESS STUDIES — PAPER II, 1996

Candidate's Examination No.

For use with Question 2(B)

INVOICE
STONE LTD
ELECTRICAL SUPPLIERS
LIMERICK

No. 18

Tel. (061) 47231
VAT Reg. I E 112345

Date: ....

To: ....
....
....
....

Order No.: ....

Quantity	Description	Unit Price IR£	Total (Ex. VAT) IR£

Total (Ex VAT)	
Less: Trade Discount	
Add: VAT	
Total	

E&OE

RETURN THIS SHEET WITH YOUR ANSWER BOOK.

For use with Question 2(B)

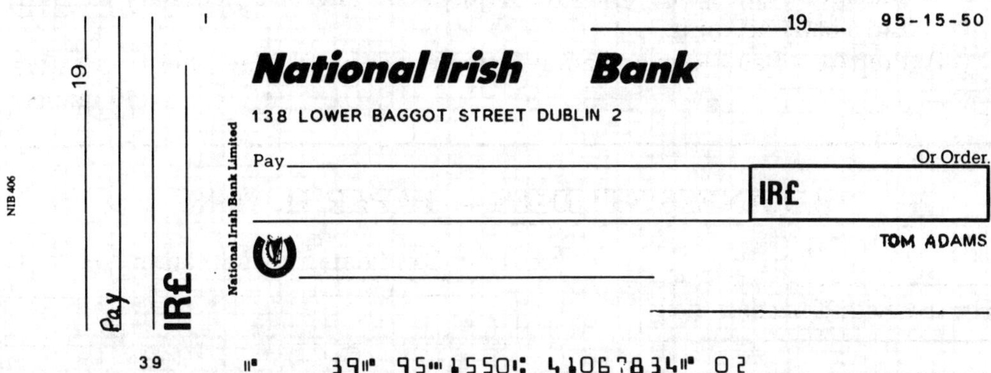

NIB 406

19

Pay

IR£

National Irish Bank Limited

19 95-15-50

National Irish Bank

138 LOWER BAGGOT STREET DUBLIN 2

Pay ______ Or Order.

IR£

TOM ADAMS

39

39 95 1550 41067834 02

For use with Question 2(C)

PURCHASES BOOK Page 1

Date	Details	Invoice No.	F	Net IR£	VAT IR£	Total IR£

ANALYSED CASH BOOK (Credit Side) Page 12

Date	Details	Cheque No.	F	Bank IR£	Creditors IR£

RETURN THIS SHEET WITH YOUR ANSWER BOOK.

For use with Question 4 (A) (i)

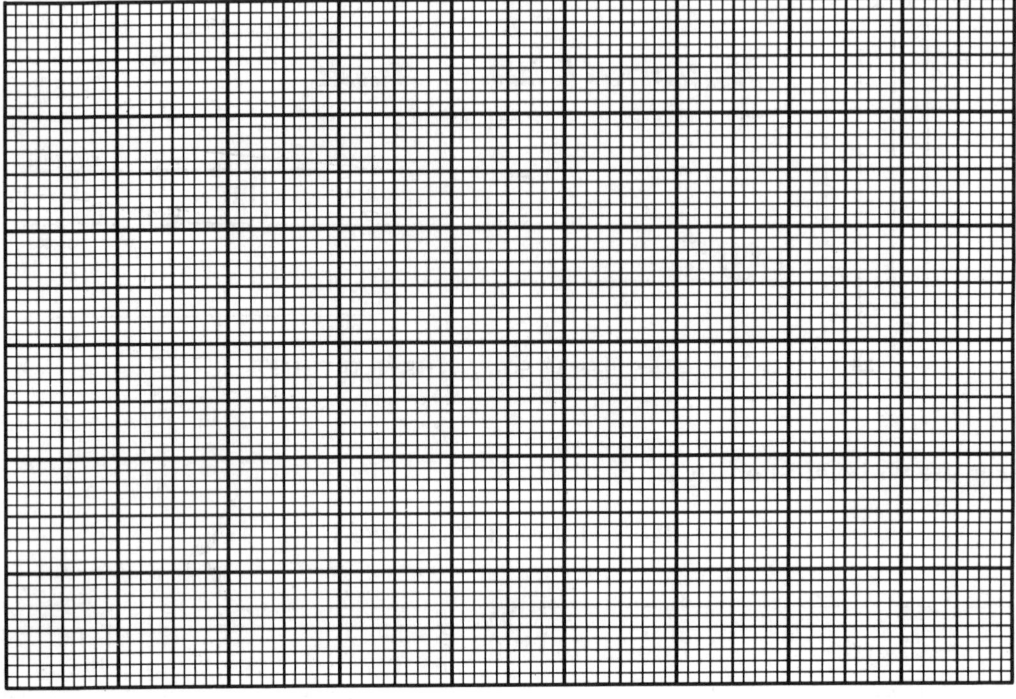

RETURN THIS SHEET WITH YOUR ANSWER BOOK.